PUNKS AND SKINS UNITED

ANTHROPOLOGY OF EUROPE

Europe, a region characterized by its diversity and speed of change, is the latest area to attract current anthropological research and scholarship that challenges the prevailing views of classical anthropology. Situated at the frontier of the social sciences and humanities, the anthropology of Europe is born out of traditional ethnology, anthropology, folklore and cultural studies, but engages in innovative interdisciplinary approaches.

Anthropology of Europe publishes fieldwork monographs by young and established scholars, as well as edited volumes on particular regions or aspects of European society. The series pays special attention to studies with a strong comparative component, addressing theoretical questions of interest to both anthropologists and other scholars working in related fields.

Volume 5
Punks and Skins United
Identity, Class and the Economics of an Eastern German Subculture
Aimar Ventsel

Volume 4
In Pursuit of Belonging
Forging an Ethical Life in European-Turkish Spaces
Susan Beth Rottmann

Volume 3
All or None
Cooperation and Sustainability in Italy's Red Belt
Alison Sánchez Hall

Volume 2
European Anthropologies
The Intertwinement of Intellectual Traditions
Edited by Andrés Barrera-González, Monica Heintz and Anna Horolets

Volume 1
The France of the Little-Middles
A Suburban Housing Development in Greater Paris
Marie Cartier, Isabelle Coutant, Olivier Masclet and Yasmine Siblot

PUNKS AND SKINS UNITED

Identity, Class and the Economics of an Eastern German Subculture

Aimar Ventsel

berghahn
NEW YORK • OXFORD
www.berghahnbooks.com

First published in 2020 by

Berghahn Books

www.berghahnbooks.com

First paperback edition published in 2026

Library of Congress Cataloging-in-Publication Data

Names: Ventsel, Aimar, author.
Title: Punks and Skins United: Identity, Class and the Economics of an Eastern German Subculture / Aimar Ventsel.
Description: New York: Berghahn Books, [2020] | Series: Anthropology of Europe; vol 5 | Includes bibliographical references and index.
Identifiers: LCCN 2020017516 (print) | LCCN 2020017517 (ebook) | ISBN 9781789208603 (hardback) | ISBN 9781789208610 (ebook)
Subjects: LCSH: Punk culture—Germany (East) | Post-communism—Germany (East) | Social classes—Germany (East)
Classification: LCC HM646 .V45 2020 (print) | LCC HM646 (ebook) | DDC 306/.109431—dc23
LC record available at https://lccn.loc.gov/2020017516
LC ebook record available at https://lccn.loc.gov/2020017517

British Library Cataloguing in Publication Data

A catalogue record for this book is available from the British Library

EU GPSR Authorized Representative

LOGOS EUROPE, 9 rue Nicolas Poussin, 17000, LA ROCHELLE, France
Email: Contact@logoseurope.eu

ISBN 978-1-78920-860-3 hardback
ISBN 978-1-80758-082-7 paperback
ISBN 978-1-80758-447-4 epub
ISBN 978-1-78920-861-0 web pdf

https://doi.org/10.3167/9781789208603

To my mother, Georg and Oskar

CONTENTS

ILLUSTRATIONS

PREFACE

In 1986, Roddy Moreno, leader of a Welsh anti-fascist skinhead band The Oppressed from Cardiff, released a record on his label Oi! Records. This was called Skins 'N'Punks Vol. 1 and the record was a split album of two British skinhead-punk bands – Last Rough Cause and Societys Rejects. This series of split albums symbolized a spiritual and musical bond between two subcultures: punks and skinheads. I am not sure whether it was the first time that the slogan 'Punks and skinheads!' was used or when it transformed into 'Punks (or Punx) and Skins United!', but in the 1990s the slogan was widely used, featured on T-shirts and formed the title of numerous songs and albums.

No subculture exists in a vacuum. There are always musical, stylistic or ideological overlaps, and everyone who has had a glimpse into the world of 'spectacular' subcultures has come across these. One often encounters a variety of subcultures at concerts, and it is common to buy and listen to each other's music. Such relationships exist between punks, skinheads, hardcore and psychobilly fans who attend the same concerts. Ska is a music style claimed to be 'their' music by skinheads, mods, rude boys and sometimes by punks. Some hardcore fans tend to go to roots reggae shows, while others like hip-hop. Some dance music subcultures are also closely connected. For instance, dancehall reggae, hip-hop and drum'n'bass are very interlinked scenes, and there is a rich variety of such subcultural conglomerates. Therefore, studying one scene and ignoring such alliances is counterproductive and might even be more complicated than studying the mixed local or national scene. This book does not focus on one single subculture, but depicts a scene where people from different styles intermingle. Drawing borders between subcultural practices is especially complicated in the case of a traditionally mixed small town scene, as in a case study of city of Halle presented in this book. However, the common factor for all these scenes is that they are somehow related to punk, whether musically, ideologically or both.

The picture created by the research would not be complete if I did not examine my personal ties to punk rock music and its various substyles. I was fifteen when I first started listening to punk music, mainly bands from the Estonian second punk wave that were active in the early and mid-1980s (Generaator M, ABS and JMKE). In the Soviet Union, the main source for acquiring new music was copying it from cassettes or reel-to-reel tapes that circulated among those in the know. I probably thought that I had a pretty good idea of punk until I visited my classmate who had better access to punk music (he had more friends who listened to it). During our discussion, he suddenly said 'You should listen to the real punk!' and played the tape of a band I had never heard of. It was an album by the Scottish band The Exploited, The Troops of Tomorrow. I can still remember the feeling when the raw uptempo guitars and brutal voice blasted out from the loudspeakers. I had never heard anything like it! I more or less froze, enjoying the energy and roughness of the music. When I graduated from university, I had an extensive cassette collection, having copied nearly every punk and punkish rock record and cassette in Estonia. My keen interest in this music also meant that I was constantly widening my horizons, discovering other styles of music like metal, experimental jazz, blues, reggae and what is known today as world music. In 1994, I had the good fortune to receive a one-year scholarship from the German DAAD foundation to study in Berlin. I was indeed very fortunate because Berlin was the capital of the underground in those days, a very exciting and dynamic city. When I moved to Berlin, I spent nearly all my disposable income on vinyl records and CDs, but also borrowed them from friends and copied them to tape. Of course, I also attended concerts. In around 1995, I was fondest of the harder kind of punk and became increasingly involved in Berlin's left-wing skinhead scene. However, my career as a musician was limited to a few rehearsals as bass player for a mediocre long-forgotten skinhead band and singing backing vocals on the first album of Berlin's local Oi! hero, Trinkerkohorte. I regularly bought different German punk and skinhead fanzines, and was also the proud owner of some punk-related books. Although my DAAD scholarship was not extended in 1995, I still remained in Berlin doing any kind of odd jobs I was able to find. In 2000, I received a Ph.D. student position in Halle (an der Saale), in the recently established Max Planck Institute for Social Anthropology in its Siberian Studies Group. After my one year of fieldwork in the Russian far north, I returned to the city and discovered a punk hangout close to the Institute. This is the same GiG that acts as a centrepiece in this study. By the time I became heavily involved in the punk life in Halle, I owned a large record collection and possessed – at least to my mind – extensive knowledge of current and past punk music, and also reggae, country, ska and soul. Because going to concerts in Halle is a collective activity, my musical world expanded. I went to concerts and recorded more hardcore bands, and also different styles of German punk, something in which my friends in Berlin were not very much interested. Looking at my expanding music collection, at a certain point I began to understand how much one's taste and record collection is down to one's environment – one gets introduced to new music while spending time with friends, either at home or at festivals; one's surroundings usher one into the world of sounds and affect which groups one goes to see perform live.

I was not only participating in the subculture but also had an academic interest in the field. Therefore, whenever I had the chance, I consumed academic books or articles on punk, reggae and hardcore. Nevertheless, I had no intention of conducting any academic research on the topic. Things changed abruptly during one conference reception at the Max Planck Institute for Social Anthropology. I had almost finished at the Institute and was writing up my dissertation. After my return from fieldwork, I had developed an interest in legal anthropology, as the Department for Legal Anthropology had recently opened in the Institute. In the aforementioned reception I was talking to Keebet von Benda-Beckman, one of the directors of the Department for Legal Anthropology, and I recall telling her: 'Look, you study the coexistence of different laws somewhere in Indonesia or Morocco but not very far away from the institute is a punk club and these punks live according to their own laws. It is not so different from Indonesia.' Keebet thought for a few seconds and said to my great surprise: 'Make a research plan and calculate how much would it cost and we are going to fund this research.' Later, after the research, I was contacted by Hilary Pilkington from the University of Warwick and I joined another research project on punk.

As an anthropologist you usually go through a certain process when doing fieldwork. First, you establish yourself in the field, letting people get to know and trust you. When the fieldwork is carried out for a long duration, you very often become friends with some of your informants and establish another kind of relationship that goes beyond the research. In this research, things were the other way round. I have known most of the people I will quote in this book for years; some of them were my friends and then became my informants. In retrospect, this transition went smoothly. I was quite worried that my friends and acquaintances would not take me seriously or would refuse to talk to me at all. I think that one reason why they opened up to me is related to a topic covered in this book. Most of my informants were ordinary working-class people who were at the very bottom of the German social hierarchy. For them, the fact that someone wanted to write a book about them was an important acknowledgement, proof that they also had a culture that was interesting and that their way of life was worth documenting. This is an appreciation that is often denied to working-class people in Germany, especially when they are unemployed.

This book provides an analysis of the postsocialist transformation in the former German Democratic Republic (GDR) through the lens of a subculture. Punk helps to explain why an East–West divide still exists in Germany. It demonstrates how punk subculture is embedded in the surrounding society; the contradictions of reunification, the lack of social mobility, increasing unemployment and the erosion of the working-class status play a substantial role in forming punk identity. It appears that the subculture offers a social and cultural platform for the creation of a 'substitute society' of working-class youth and young adults. In this book, I not only use material collected during the fieldwork but also draw on my own biography as a participant in the German underground in the 1990s. My own autobiographical approach helps me to contextualize field material and to place it within the bigger picture.

ACKNOWLEDGEMENTS

First of all, I would like to extend my immense gratitude to Keebet and Franz von Benda-Beckman, who believed in my research and gave me the opportunity to start it. I am very much in debt to Keebet and Franz because they helped me to understand that what I was studying had a much larger dimension than merely subcultural identity and practice – that I was studying issues related to class, economy and political change. The staff at the Max Planck Institute for Social Anthropology gave me their assistance when I had to process my pictures and interviews; every time I needed technical help, they were there for me. I owe a lot to members of our 'Post-socialist Punk' research project at the University of Warwick, especially to Hilary Pilkington, but also to Ivan Gololobov, Kirsty Lohman, Yngvar Steinholt, Ivana Mijić and Ben Perasović. I am grateful to Arts and Humanities Research Council, which funded my year of research in the former GDR. My colleagues from the Department of Ethnology of the University of Tartu have supported me enormously, especially Art Leete, Ene Kõresaar and Reet Ruusmann. Lii Araste supported me and always found time to discuss new chapters with me. Toomas Erikson and his lovely wife never let me down and encouraged me to continue with the book. I am also thankful to Patrick Heady and Monica Heinz for offering me the chance to publish in their series, as well as for their comments and advice with the book proposal.

There are several people who helped me indirectly, giving me leads when I searched for music and style examples to be included in the text. As such, I would like to thank Ago Gaskov, Anton Shekovtsov, Raico Rummel, Nadine Paschkowski, Ingo Petz, Matt Worley and Luk Haas. I would also like to thank people from the Subcultures Network (who are too numerous to list here), who helped me when I posted questions on the group's Facebook group when seeking academic and nonacademic literature. Karmo Tüür and

Kate Flynn provided useful comments on my book proposal and helped to improve it.

I would also like to thank the people at Berghahn Books who patiently waited for the manuscript to be finished. Paul Emmet and Mara Woods proofread my text and also made very useful comments. I owe a lot to my children and their mother, who have morally supported me throughout the years. And last but not least, this book only became possible thanks to all the punks, skinheads, hardcore fans, football hooligans and psychobillies who allowed me into their lives. Great respect goes to Ian, Myrko, Olli, Loofie, Nadine, Sandra, Raico, Pyro, Pieps and Pyh.

This research and writing-up process was supported by the institutional research funding IUT34-32 ('Cultural Heritage as a Socio-cultural Resource and Contested Field') of the Estonian Ministry of Education and Research.

INTRODUCTION

Me: What is so punk about you?
Berndt: I say what I think!

The concert was in one of the three main punk clubs in Halle; it was a DIY (Do-It-Yourself; see below) event organized by people living in the same building in which the club is located. During the evening, two skinhead bands performed, drawing a big audience of punks and skins. The concert itself was a celebration of masculinity, typical of the tough street punk music style. The mosh pit mostly consisted of men, heavily tattooed and half-naked. The wild pogo also included hugging each other, a loud singalong chorus and, at some point, even a fight. The musicians of the main band were older than the first band and were in their forties. They were dressed in typical skinhead style, with facial tattoos and heavy piercings. Most of their songs were narratives about their tough street life, being independent or 'staying skinhead forever'. When the concert ended, the promoter of the club moved to the DJ booth and started to play 'punk rock disco'. Most of the songs he played were of the *Neue Deutsche Welle*, German new wave music from the 1980s. The DJ chose mainly dark and existential tunes, experimental electronic songs about alienation and unhappiness. The people danced with passion and I took my time to observe the crowd. Most of the people were in their twenties or thirties, representing the low-paid or unemployed 'lower class'. In front of me stood a rather drunk young girl who was not able – despite all her efforts – to dance. She wore a T-shirt which announced 'Faulheit ist kein Verbrechen' (Laziness is not a crime!). Other badges, buttons or T-shirts of the people signalled their East German origin, musical preferences or leftist anti-state position. I recall that I was so impressed by the dark atmosphere of the event that immediately after returning from the club, I wrote an emotional review in my field diary:

> By 3 o'clock in the night it became very grim. A dark empty room with a wet floor from spilled beer and covered with broken bottles. People dancing and singing resolutely along to very dark music. I had a flash: street punk is about being subversive, demonstratively questioning social norms. (Field diary, 25 September 2010)

Being part of a subculture is an emotional thing. In fact, being part of a subcultural group that radically manifests its identity and is radically different from what is considered to be normal could be considered irrational. Punk and especially skinheads are controversial, misunderstood and, more often than not, disliked subcultures. I remember that years ago, I was in Oxford in a restaurant for a conference dinner and next to me sat a law historian. When we were introduced, I told him briefly about my research in Halle and he looked at me with confusion. After a short silence, he asked me: 'But why do people do things like that?' The only suitable answer I had to mind was: 'But why do you not do such things?' Indeed, it is a difficult question to answer. I recall I put this question to Gavin Watson, a photographer renowned for his photos of the 1980s British skinheads and late 1980s ravers, scenes of which he was part. My question was why does one become a skinhead just to be disliked by everyone? His response was: 'There is no explanation, it's a mystery!'

This book is an attempt to offer one explanatory view to the question of why people adopt subversive subcultures. As there is no single reason as to why the youth join the ranks of ravers, hip-hoppers, punks or something else, there can also be no single clear explanation. One simplistic answer is, of course, identity. People need identity and the subculture gives them a satisfying identity, which the mainstream culture does not. The next question then is what is so special about the identity of an alternative underground group whose borders and content are guarded enviously by its members. In the late 1990s, when I lived in Berlin and was involved in the local skinhead scene, I discussed the meaning of subcultures, especially the more radical and unfavourable ones in the public eye, with my friend, who suddenly said: 'The minority derives its strength from being a minority!' (Die Minderheit bezieht seine Kraft daraus das sie eine Minderheit ist!). I strongly believe that there is a certain truth in the statement that one attraction to joining a subculture is belonging to a close-knit minority group. Broadly, this is a book about how such microcosms function and through which methods its boundaries are maintained.

As an anthropologist, I always felt an uneasiness with the major academic (and mainly sociologist) writing on youth and subcultures. I had the feeling that something was missing in many of these various analyses, but somehow could not understand what. A certain shift came when I read the book *Russia's Skinheads,* where the authors promised to turn the concept of skinhead 'inside out' (Pilkington et al., 2010) and they did. In this book, the researchers demonstrated how Russian skinhead culture is rooted in the Russian proletarian worldview, combining an imported style with a peer group understanding of masculinity, race, nation and gender. Since I discovered the academic writing on youth cultures in my early twenties, I have had an interest in global subcultures in non-Western and non-European countries. There exists a wide range of brilliant publications that discuss these topics from the perspective of 'glocalization' or how subcultures are adapted into a non-Western environment. Take punk in Indonesia. There are some very good studies on how punk struggles to resist the conservative Muslim society. As it happens, Indonesian punks use the US-American and British template of punk culture, introduce it in their environment and lean on international global DIY but also commercial networks to maintain their subcultural identity and local national scene (for the Indonesian punk scene, see Baulch (2002); Dunn (2016); Hannerz (2015)). These struggles are depicted in a documentary about the Indonesian punk scene.[1] In the same documentary, some of the protagonists describe themselves as faithful Muslims who do not seek confrontation with the main spiritual values of their peer society. It is this aspect that disturbed me about many sociological studies of the phenomenon, as they tend to see a complete break or disconnect from the norms and values of the parent society. Studies on subcultures in non-Western societies tend to focus on problems and conflicts the youth have when they discover Anglo-American youth styles and adopt these. However, there is very little research on what young people take with them from their parent culture when they begin to follow punk, metal, hip-hop or other styles. Sometimes the academic literature makes it seem like subcultures subsist outside of the society in a continuous confrontation with it, or, as Gavin Watson said to me in his interview: 'People think that skinheads live in a skinhead town, wear skinhead clothes, listen only to skinhead music and do their skinhead thing.' The book *Russia's Skinheads* was how I viewed the Russian heavy rock scene I came to know when doing research in the Russian Far East from 2000 (I have published on indigenous pop music, but during the research I also became acquainted with the local Russian rock scene; see Ventsel (2004, 2006, 2009)) – these guys were ordinary Russian proletarian thugs, in many respects not dissimilar to those Russian truck drivers, mine and shift workers, builders or even small town policemen I have met in more than two decades of carrying out research there. This was the reason I was able to understand their views on people of colour, factory work, local pride or the opposite sex. These skinheads were Russian proletarians as I knew them.

I moved to Germany as an MA student in 1994 and became affiliated with Berlin's blossoming punk life. In my personal journey through the DIY and squatter scene, I somehow became part of the East Berlin left-wing skinhead scene. Later on, I moved to Halle and discovered a completely different local punk – stylistically more mixed and diverse, centred around three or four clubs and bars. By moving back and forth between Estonia and Germany, and later also Russia, I understood how different the national scenes of the same subculture can be. This was not only because global styles were adopted differently, but also because local histories differed and the understandings of politics, rebellion, gender order and the economy – in short, everything 'good' and 'bad' – were dissimilar.

Punk (and subcultural life in general) is much more than keeping the DIY music scene alive and well, and this is unfortunately often omitted by research that focuses on subculturalists (cf. Dunn, 2016; Thompson, 2004; O'Connor, 2008). As I will show in this book, subculturalists remain subculturalist even when it comes to work, family life or territorial aspects of their being. Simultaneously, the way in which these people see the world and life is rooted in East German working-class culture. This is one of the main arguments of the book. It is a complicated and demanding task to show how class in East Germany is related to a subculture that in its own rhetoric positions itself outside of society and its hierarchies. The task is even more complicated due the long-lasting theoretical debate on the sociology of subcultures, where one dividing line is the discussion of whether the notion of class is important in analysing subcultures (Muggleton and Weinzierl, 2003; Bennett, 1999; Thornton, 1996; Hesmondhalgh, 2005; Gelder, 1997, 2007; Sabin, 1999; Hall and Jefferson, 1986). Another argument advanced here is that subcultures offer a platform for self-expression to people who already have similar attitudes and views that they can combine with the subcultural ideology. The reason why someone chooses a particular style in the 'supermarket of styles' (Polhemus, 1997: 130–32; see also Muggleton, 2000: 198) is because the ethos of that concrete subculture overlaps with his or her personal views. In this way, subculture accommodates people who are attracted by the forms and values of identity (and rebellion) that they understand, accept and wish to follow. I will demonstrate throughout this book that subcultures centred around tough and robust behaviour linked to a fast and loud guitar music style like street punk, hardcore and skinheads are attractive to a certain segment of the working-class youth because they hold values they understand – not least the idealization of pride, loyalty, toughness, masculinity and many other attributes. The third and last but not least argument of this book is that in a wider context, a subculture can be transformed into a substitute society for alienated lower-class people. This is not a problem specific to German society. However, German punk is a space to build up an alternative group culture with structures that offer the individual a path to gain recognition and status, a validation he or she is deprived of in the dominant society. In Germany, this relates to the 'lower class' or 'precariat' as it was defined publicly in around 2010 (see Chapter 3). This process is interesting to observe because a subculture can take the value hierarchy of the dominant society, invert it and make it into its own identification system. As will be shown in this book, qualities that are generally condemned in German society – for example, heavy alcohol consumption, being unemployed and on social benefits, being heavily tattooed – are turned into a virtue because this is what provokes negative reactions in the mainstream society. Moreover, all this includes a healthy portion of irony, something that finds very scarce recognition in academic punk research.

METHODOLOGY AND FIELD SITE

The fieldwork for this research was carried out in two time periods. My acquaintance with Halle starts in 2000, when I became a Ph.D. student at the Max Planck Institute for Social Anthropology. In 2001, I discovered the local punk scene and became part of the group of people around the club GiG. The idea to do research on punk in Halle was suggested by one of the directors of the Legal Anthropology Department of the institute – Keebet von Benda-Beckman – in around 2004 and took the form of a project a few years later. In 2006 and 2007, I spent six months doing field research in Halle and Potsdam, mainly participant observation. This part of the research was supported and financed by the above-mentioned legal department. The research included interviewing people I knew already, but also getting to know people I only knew from seeing them around. I constantly commuted between Halle and Potsdam, toured with a hardcore band – The 4 Shivits – and visited several concerts and festivals. During the research, I discovered how little I knew the people who I had been in close contact for several previous years. The participant observation included going to work with my informants, attending garden parties, hanging out in pubs and participating in several public events like visiting an anti-fascist football match. Most of the results of this fieldwork were documented in my field diary, amassing an extensive collection of fanzines and taking hundreds of photographs. Most of the interviews I conducted during those six months were discussions in a café, pub or while driving to a concert. I often did not use a voice recorder, but noted our discussions down later when I had the time to do so.

It must be admitted that in the beginning I encountered an unexpected wall of mistrust from my informants. I made clear that I wanted to study the punk economy or economic practices, legal and illegal. That did not go down well. The main problem was the illegal work (*Schwarzarbeit*) that all the informants wanted to keep hidden from state officials. I had to explain many times that no identities would be made public and very sensitive information would not be published. In retrospect, I must say that it took a considerable effort to convince some of my research partners, to my surprise even people I had shared an apartment with and many beers in my pre-research years. On the other hand, some people took it all relatively well. As one of the informants said, 'Kein Name muss fallen!' (You should mention no names!) and agreed to tell and show me everything. When I had established a trusting relationship and people opened up to me, the scholars from the local university asked me to include their students as research assistants. I encountered a total block when I mentioned it to the punks. 'Sie wollen alles ausspioniern!' (They want to spy on everything!) was one remark that demonstrated a deep mistrust of any state institution and people of the educated middle class. In order not to make things more complicated, I dropped the whole idea.

From 2009, I was a research associate in the Department of Sociology at the University of Warwick, on a project called 'Post-socialist Punk: The Double Irony of Self-Abasement', funded by the Arts and Humanities Research Council. Within this project, I continued my field research in 2010, which, including some breaks, lasted until the end of 2011. During this time, I conducted 22 semi-organized interviews with people of both sexes and from various age groups. The interviews were analysed in the software NVivo and were made available – alongside fieldnotes – for other participants in the project. In order to exchange and evaluate the fieldnotes of other project members, I – for the first time – wrote them down on the computer and in English. I admit that this effected a certain spontaneity and mobility. When I usually write fieldnotes, it is simultaneously in different languages. Now I had to consider and rephrase my thoughts to make them understandable to my colleagues. Taking notes on a computer also made me miss the spontaneity of writing with pen and paper. Now, I had to go home or to my office in order to formulate a full text from my thoughts. I also had to add clarifications on persons, words, bands or clubs for others, which I usually would not have done in my diary. In this phase of the research, I also made videos of concerts and private parties where I was able to attend with my camera. Several hundred photographs were, of course, a product of this research.

The second period of my research was more in-depth. In interviews I asked about music, style, subcultural careers, family life, attitudes, politics and so forth. I also included people I did not know personally, using the ordinary snowball method. Whereas in the first research period my informants were a relatively coherent age group, mostly between thirty-five and forty, in the second period I also interviewed people who were in their early twenties or late forties. Whereas in 2006–7 male construction workers dominated among my research sample, in the second part of the research the occupational status varied significantly – from students and the unemployed to tattoo artists, a social worker and the odd professional musician.

Halle, the main location of the fieldwork, is a city in the southern part of the German state of Saxony-Anhalt with a population of slightly less than 240,000. Halle is located approximately 200 km south of Berlin and can be reached from Berlin via train in two hours. Halle proudly sports the name Händelstadt (the city of Händel) because the great German composer lived there for eighteen years. The city has the biggest Beatles museum outside of England and is the location of a university and several academic institutions. This is also the reason why the club and bar culture of Halle is very lively. The city attempts to market itself as an innovative location for culture, science and new economies. The city's old town is not very big, but picturesque and old nineteenth-century (or older) apartment buildings take up a large part of the inner city. In between older buildings are occasional socialist-era five-storey concrete apartment houses. There are several suburbs – such as Südstadt and Neustadt – that were built in the German Democratic Republic (GDR) era and are typical socialist concrete housing projects.

In the GDR, Halle was the capital of a district of the same name and was one of the centres for the national chemical industry, being home to the biggest chemistry enterprise of the country – VEB Leuna-Werke Walter Ulbricht. After the German reunification, the big plant was divided into smaller units and sold into private hands. Notwithstanding the fact that the chemical industry is still functioning at the former site, the process meant a loss of approximately 20,000 jobs. The unemployment rate – typical of a former East German industrial city – is high in Halle, being over 10,000 people in March 2019, with nearly 16,000 people in what is called *Unterbeschäftigung* (underemployment). The city of Halle today, according to its official website, attempts to attract start-ups, innovative industry sectors and research institutions to establish in the area[2] and reports relatively good success in this respect. Such a process, as is widely known, does not create employment for the city's working class and is unlikely to decrease the devastating unemployment. The cultural life of Halle is impressively vivid – it is a location for several theatres, clubs, concert venues and an opera house.

Very important for the musical life and subcultural activities is Halle's proximity to Leipzig, which is only a 30-minute train ride away. Leipzig, a big cultural centre of Germany, has a vivid alternative culture scene, including punk. Therefore, going to Leipzig to shop for records and clothes, and to attend concerts is very typical for the punks and skinheads of Halle. Leipzig houses one of the most important alternative music venues, Connie Island, and has always been famous for its active music life.

PUNKS, SKINHEADS, HARDCORE KIDS

Punk as a subculture is mainly associated with loud and fast music, leather jackets and coloured spiky hair. This is the stereotypical picture and the reality is, as usual, more complex. Punk has a double origin, starting in the mid-1970s simultaneously in the United Kingdom and the United States. It is still an unsolved debate as to 'who was the first' to start punk, but the culture spread rapidly and took different forms. As Kirsty Lohman (2017: 7) notes in her book, '"Punk" is notoriously difficult to pin down.' And that is true. Currently we have dozens of different punk styles where musical output, ways of dressing and politics are, at first glance, extremely remote from each other. In contrast to easily recognizable punks in leather jackets, combat boots and coloured hair, today substyles exist where the dress code is not what Hebdige (1979) calls 'spectacular'. Very often, modern punks are recognizable only by someone who has insider knowledge and can read the semiotics of band T-shirts, buttons and brands. All these different styles exist next to each other, often in peaceful coexistence, but sometimes in a competing race for the claim to be the embodiment of 'real punk'. However, the cultural meaning and legacy of punk is difficult to underestimate. Punk invented very little, but by combining the existing elements of alternative culture, it created a symbiosis that has affected Western pop culture, giving a platform to a strong political protest culture (Marcus, 1989; Frith, 1983; Furness, 2012a; Ammann, 1987; Bennett, 2006: 219–35). The most important phenomenon that is associated with punk is Do-It-Yourself culture or DIY. In short, DIY means rejecting existing commercial structures and creating independent institutions of producing, spreading and consuming punk (Clark, 2003: 223–36; Dunn, 2016). DIY has a wide meaning for different activities and is in constant flux. In the 1970s and 1980s it meant recording at independent record labels, amateur music magazines or fanzines, but also independent poetry, theatre and cinema, and today it includes internet activism or releasing and making music available for free in the internet (Savage, 1991; O'Connor, 2004; Williams, 2006: 173–200). The politics of and in punk is another extremely complicated topic. Globally one can encounter right- and left-wing sympathies in punk, but the uniting element seems to be a certain 'anti-' stance to dominant institutions, structures and ideas. Traditionally, UK and US punk has aligned itself with left-wing ideas, but nevertheless has often rejected institutionalized party politics (Worley, 2012, 2013: 606–36, 2017; Bottà, 2014: 155–69). As I will show in this book, some punk practices can be ideologically justified as anti-politics, but by nature can be controversial and even opportunistic when looking at the rhetoric. Moreover, sometimes it is difficult to draw a sharp line between the two; in this way squatting, which is widespread in global punk, can be simultaneously an attempt to be 'outside the system' and a strategy to avoid paying rent. Notwithstanding all the controversy, punk has a history of being involved in left-wing political activism, for example, by participating in the British Rock Against Racism movement or more grassroots initiatives like Food Not Bombs (see, for example, the discussion of the anarchopunk band Crass in Cross (2010: 1–20) and Lohman and Worley (2018)).

Unfortunately, punk's impact on popular culture is often reduced to music; however, that impact has been significant. Punk's DIY aesthetic and strategies have been adopted by other music scenes from independent rock to electronic music (cf. Bennet, 2001: 45–62; Luvaas, 2009: 246–79; Gilbert, 2009). Punk's support for and popularization of black music, chiefly Jamaican sounds like roots and dub reggae and also ska, is well known, but punk has also certainly impacted on the development and popularization of hip-hop and soul[3] (Gilroy, 2002; see also Marshall, 1990; Barrow and Dalton, 1997: 395). Interestingly, academic literature often neglects the certain division within punk that still exists and affects the ways in which punk functions today. This is the split between 'street punk' and what was called in the beginning 'art school punk'. In the academic literature, this division has been recognized in punk since Hebdige's seminal *Subculture: The Meaning of Style* (1979), but the focus has been on the latter in the literature. The former has always been dominantly related to the working-class culture through the glorification of football, violence, male aggression and drinking, while the latter is sometimes very experimental, existential and philosophical, and often finds an alternative output in cinema, art or poetry.[4]

Hardcore music is a further development of US punk (Ward, 1996: 155–84). It is faster and rawer than the punk of the 1970s, but is also more political on a lyrical level. While the beginnings of UK punk are popularly believed to be in a dominantly working-class youth rebellion, in punk-lore US punk is associated more with middle-class youngsters. The roots of hardcore are largely in a teenage protest against US suburban middle-class norms and lifestyle. Later hardcore evolved and split into several styles, some of them proponents of a militant veganism, but others romanticizing 'street life' as described in Chapter 7. This music style and associated fashion styles are, in underground circles, considered to be the American contribution to punk. Hardcore has influenced but also borrowed from heavy guitar music, especially metal. Today, globally, there exist several overlapping hardcore scenes with their own dress codes and specific music styles, some of them politically extreme, some not. Maybe one significant difference from punk is that hardcore is more strongly ideological, emphasizing in song texts resistance, brotherhood, localism and anti-bourgeois sentiments more explicitly than is the case with punk. Hardcore also tends to glorify masculinity, aggression and group solidarity. Therefore, the global hardcore culture tends to be organized on a basis of groups of friends that are called 'crews', which in some hardcore subscenes could be extremely violent (Haefner, 2007; Büsser, 2007; Ward, 1996; Mullaney, 2007; Mader, 1999). This is also expressed in the look of the hardcore fans. Preferred is the so-called casual or street style like baggy trousers, trainers and oversized jackets, but elements of the Cholo style[5] can also be very popular. Some subgroups like New York hardcore sport a somewhat criminal look, sometimes donning leather blazers and trilby hats that can be combined with military garments and boots. Interestingly, in the world of the underground, hardcore is often accused of elitism. Fans of hardcore are called 'hardcore kids' irrespective of their age by the scene insiders and outsiders.

If punk is a phenomenon that is difficult to define comprehensively, then skinheads are even more controversial. Skinheads are popularly associated with violent right-wing neo-Nazi thugs and there is a certain element of truth in this. However, the whole phenomenon is more complicated and multilayered. Skinheads as a youth subculture appeared in England in around 1966–67 as descendants of hard mods. They were the UK's first multiracial subculture where mainly white working-class youngsters copied the style and music of Jamaican youth culture, the rude boys. The first wave of skinhead style was very heterogeneous; they wore military and Dr Martens boots and bleached jeans, but also suits, Crombie coats and loafers. Musically Jamaican music (ska, rocksteady and early reggae) and US soul were their favourites. Skinheads were notorious for their violence against Asian immigrants, for example, through so-called Paki-bashing, despite the fact that many skinhead gangs were of mixed race. The peak of the first wave is considered to be in 1969, which also witnessed a certain commercialization of the subculture.[6] The subculture faded out in the early 1970s, only to come back in the late 1970s. The beginning of the second wave is directly related with the appearance of Two Tone British ska and a subgenre of punk to be widely known as street punk or Oi!

This was a time of stylistic but also political divisions of the skinhead scene. The traditional skinheads are more followers of the music and dress code of the 1960s and early 1970s, while the adherents of the Oi! music style adopted a more militant and uniformed appearance that is currently and stereotypically associated with the subculture – tight jeans, high boots, flight jackets and shaved heads. When the subculture arrived in the United States, American skinheads became followers of hardcore music and later adopted elements of the subcultural style, like trainers, baggy trousers and sportswear. Politically, the British radical right-wing movements, such as the British National Party or British Movement, infiltrated part of the skinhead scene and successfully initiated the emergence of neo-Nazi and right-wing skinheads. Simultaneously, some of the skinheads aligned themselves with left-wing organizations to become left-wing skinheads or redskins. In between the two political groups, there still exist skinheads who call themselves apolitical or even anti-political. The skinhead attire of all subgroups is extremely fashion- and detail-conscious, and the 'right way' of dressing is a constant matter of discussion within the scene.

Punk moved over to Germany by the end of the 1970s and established itself quickly in West Germany. There are people who argue that the music was introduced to the GDR by the legendary BBC Radio 1 DJ John Peel, whose shows were also broadcast on the radio for the British troops in Germany (Sobe, 2008); others argue that West German radio stations were mainly responsible for the spreading of punk (Westhusen, 2005b). Later, punks from the 'East' or from the 'Zone'[7] asked their Western relatives to send them records and clothing. Nevertheless, as was typical of all socialist countries, punk records were difficult to find in the GDR and they circulated among friends who taped them on either cassettes or reel-to-reel tapes. The particularity of punk in East Germany was that it existed very much under the roof of the Lutheran church due to the autonomy the church had at that time. For that reason, the church was a place where several dissident groups like environmentalists, hippies and oppositional intellectuals were able to meet, and punks quickly found their way there. The contact with such groups was the reason why many punks developed an interest in alternative poetry, art or theatre. Churches were also places where punks were able to organize their concerts. It seems that organizing concerts or being in a band could get one into legal trouble and several East German punks were indeed incarnated for such activity (Westhusen, 2005a, 2005b; Galenza and Havemeister, 2005, Horschig, 2005; Kohtz et al., 2012; Mohr, 2018). Nevertheless, as the older Halle punks told me, the arrangement with the church was a marriage of convenience because there were no other autonomous institutions in the GDR where punks could go and avoid the watchful eye of the state security or Stasi. As soon as it was possible to establish their own space, punks left the church. This moment came with the collapse of the GDR and German reunification. It must be noted that unlike punk in the West, socialist punk – and not only in the GDR – applied a special kind of irony. One way to laugh at the state and the system was to wear badges and symbols of youth organizations or the army. Punk bands performed songs by communist youth organizations or wrote lyrics that praised building socialism, fulfilling economic five-year plans and so forth. East German bands, for example, often performed songs by the East German official youth organization FDJ. This was all done to mock the official rhetoric and ideology, but very often confused state officials (Simpson 2004).

On the GDR map of punk, Halle was in the premier league. Halle and the surrounding region were the birthplace of several important GDR-era punk bands like Müllstation, Menschenschock and KVD (Westhusen, 2005a) and the scene was very large for the time (the Stasi or the state security of the GDR had counted approximately 150 punks; see Westhusen, 2005a: 85). Moreover, Jana Schlosser, the singer of the one of the most popular GDR punk bands Namenlos, originally came from Halle. She moved to Berlin in the early 1980s and formed the band (Mohr, 2018: Part II; Westhusen, 2005a). Travelling to other cities for punk concerts or just visiting friends was usual for GDR punks and due the proximity to Leipzig, Halle was well known on the punk roadmap (Mareth and Schneider. 1999). This was probably also the reason why the Stasi became very suspicious of such 'degenerate' youth, put them under surveillance and had several informants among local punks (Mohr, 2018: 208–12). On Saturday 30 April 1983, the first ever punk festival in socialist Germany took place in Halle's Christuskirche ('Christ Church' in English) featuring bands like Größenwahn, Namenlos, Wutanfall, Reststand and Planlos.[8] What happened in the GDR was a typical reaction to punk in different socialist countries, although punk musicians were not incarcerated everywhere (for the repressions of punks by the Stasi, see Kohtz et al. (2012)). One of the reasons for the institutional alarm seems to be the interpretation of punk in the media and among officials in socialist countries; since punk was a protest movement, they argued, and in socialism there was no need to protest against anything, punk was truly misplaced in these societies. Indeed, band names like Größenwahn (idea fix), Namenlos (nameless), Wutanfall (rampage), Reststand (leftovers) or Planlos (aimless) sounded too nihilistic to fit into the socialist concept of culture.

On 22 October 1983, another event occurred that irritated socialist officials: a punk meeting that unexpectedly drew approximately 600 guests from all over East Germany. A remarkable number of skinheads (Westhusen, 2005a), who were mostly punks who shaved their hair, participated in this event. At the beginning, the GDR skinheads did not differ particularly from punks; they were 'one floor deeper' (ibid.: 39) or in a deeper underground or less known and more closed group then punks, but were not particularly political, as they would infamously became years later. Punks had their problems instead with football hooligans (ibid.: 53) and the antipathy was mutual (Farin, 1996). While in East Berlin the right-wing sympathies of the skinheads slowly increased (see Hasselbach, 2001), in Halle skinheads were often ex-punks who maintained their links to the punk scene despite having changed their look. In fact, the skinheads' right-wing views and punks' views on skinheads as neo-Nazis seems to be an import from Berlin (Westhusen, 2005a: 56–59). The radicalization of skinheads is very well described by Ingo Hasselbach (2001), a once-infamous neo-Nazi leader from East Berlin. This process culminated with an attack by West and East Berlin neo-Nazi skinheads on a punk concert on 17 October 1987 in East Berlin's Zionskirche (Hasselbach, 2001: 70).

Most East German punk bands did not record more than basement tapes that circulated among their adherents; the most infamous example is the West German release of the Schleim-Keim (given on the record as Sau-Kerle) and Zwitcher-Maschine split record *DDR von unten* (*GDR from Below*) on the West Berlin label Aggressive Rock in 1983. The Stasi for some reason overreacted to the release of the record and punished several musicians (Mohr, 2018: Chapter 21). Only a few punk bands – Die Skeptiker, Feeling B, Die Art and Sandow – made compromises with the GDR state record company Amiga and were able to release their records officially (Sobe, 2008; Westhusen, 2005a; Simpson, 2004). Therefore, these bands were often seen as not 'real', as were their fans (Westhusen, 2005a: 85).

In the early 1990s Halle had several punk squats that regularly organized concerts. This was also a time for conflicts and skirmishes with the emerging right-wing scene. Several of my punk informants were part of a group called the Red Bombers, a militant group of left-wing skinheads known for their red flight jackets. After the German reunification, many of the Red Bombers switched their allegiance to hardcore music and became the first hardcore fans in Halle.

This was a time when people in Halle established a large alternative scene, which was very active when I arrived in 2000. Apart from squats and clubs, the city had several record stores for underground music and shops for punk, skinhead, skater and psychobilly clothing, and had a history of being the home of at least two important local punk record labels.

At the time of my fieldwork, Halle had at least four centres for local punk and skinhead life. A group of punks usually hung out in one of the city's central squares – the Händel square. These people, usually called Händel punks, were in their early twenties and were pretty much looked down on by others because they were infamous for begging for money from passers-by. It was not known where Händel punks spent their time during the winter and bad weather, but they were sometimes seen at punk concerts. A home for the older generation of Halle punks was the VL club-bar. These people were politically active and they ran an information centre and a Volksküche[9] in VL. VL also existed as a concert venue, hosting concerts covering a range of musical styles, from reggae to punk. The youngest generation of punks were regulars of the club Reil 78, or Reilstrasse 78. This club was not very far away from GiG, my main field site, and hosted more DIY hardcore bands than any other local alternative club. The fourth important club during my stay in Halle was La Bim, a club with a cinema venue. Since La Bim was neither a squat nor had a regularly open bar, it did not have regulars as the other venues did. Nevertheless, there was a certain group of people around the La Bim, mainly those who worked at the bar, organized concerts and ran the venue. Activists who ran these clubs knew each other and were generally on good terms. There existed a serious coordination of organizing musical and political events among these clubs. I was told many times that people in VL had a book where all clubs noted down their planned concerts. The purpose of this notebook was to avoid two or more concerts from the same genre on the same day so that clubs would not compete with each other for an audience. For political rallies or solidarity concerts, activists from all these clubs often organized and promoted events together. Nevertheless, this did not prevent the clubs having a separate identity from each other, so that most punks in Halle were associated with a particular location.

ROTER FADEN

The German expression *Roter Faden* is translated in English as 'red thread' or 'red yarn'. As far as I know, it has no equivalent meaning in English, especially when it is translated directly. The meaning of the expression in German is simple: a *roter Faden* is a topic, question, argument or position that goes through the whole text and is a certain conceptual backbone of a book or article. There are two such threads in this book. One is East German identity and the other is East German class. Why are these topics especially relevant to understanding the punk and skinhead lives in an East German town? Tricia Rose notes as follows on black hip-hop culture:

> Without historical contextualization, aesthetics are naturalized, and certain cultural practices are made to appear essential to a given group of people. On the other hand, without aesthetic considerations, Black cultural practices are reduced to extensions of sociohistorical circumstances. (Rose, 1992: 223–27)

I believe this statement is also relevant in the framework of this book. In order to understand what is going on in the East German punk scene, I will put it into a wider context, including a historical one. The topic of East German identity will be covered in two chapters and therefore I will not go deeper into this here. However, it must be stressed that the East–West German differences cannot be completely eradicated and, as I will show in Chapters 2, 3 and 4, keep popping up regularly. There are people who foresee the demise of East German identity, but it simply does not vanish.[10]

After the German reunification or *Mauerfall* (fall of the Berlin Wall), or *Wende* (the turn) as it is popularly known in Germany, the enthusiasm transformed relatively quickly into social pessimism regarding the merging of East and West Germans, and East and West Germany. In the beginning, there was a remarkable economic and lifestyle difference between West Germans and their former socialist fellow citizens. The economic disparities remained and the lifestyle differences did not fade out completely. Despite all the media images, a decade after reunification, 55 per cent of West Germans and 67 per cent of East Germans thought that there were psychological and cultural differences between East and West Germans. Two-thirds of East Germans saw themselves as neglected by society and 25 per cent thought that they were 'second rate citizens' (Dennis, 2000: 87–105). In the early 1990s it was very popular in Germany to speak about the 'wall in the head' (*Mauer im Kopf*), indicating that the physical Berlin Wall has vanished, but that it persists as an imaginary wall in people's minds. I have not heard this expression for a long time, but the East German identity seems to be like the secret knowledge of the Saramaka people from Surinam. Saramaka call it First Time and it is an orally transmitted historical narrative that is fundamental to their identity. This is a knowledge that is only transmitted orally in order to prevent non-Saramaka from learning more about the secrets that are important for the Saramaka identity and organization (see Price, 2002). The East German identity narrative and the counternarrative is constantly reproduced and for many East Germans, it is often like a secret knowledge that West Germans will never understand. This is the experience of the socialist era and it is transmitted to the next generations orally. This oral narrative very often differed from how the GDR and life there was and is depicted in writing or on TV. The counternarrative seems to be that West Germans often (and notwithstanding the public denial that any essential differences between West and East Germans still exist) draw the line between the Easterners and Westerners. I recall reading one report about the private life of then-Chancellor Angela Merkel in 2014. One thing struck me and is still on my mind – namely, when the journalist wrote that in the morning Merkel makes a simple coffee for her and her partner by pouring boiling water on a mug in the coffee powder lies, he added 'this is how you make coffee in the East [Germany]'. East Germany as a certain category lives, and this can be much more than just 'another 'regional identity, as will be demonstrated throughout this book.

When one studies former GDR-era industrial towns, the local proletarian atmosphere and colouring is impossible not to notice. In the academic literature, the nostalgia for the GDR, or *Ostalgie*, is well studied from different angles (Dennis, 2000; Berdahl, 1999: xiii, 294; Berdahl, 2011; Berdahl et al., 2000: vi, 252; Castillo, 2008; Rethmann, 2009: 21–23). It is assumed that apart from economic inequality, the social meaning attached to being unemployed in the East has led to a growth in dissatisfaction among former East Germans. The socialist enterprise was a 'total social institution' (Clarke, 1992), providing not only employment but also leisure activities and social care for its workers. Consequently, East German workers identified themselves very strongly with production and enterprise. Moreover, work was a 'duty' and 'honour', a person's main purpose and the essence of life (Berdahl, 2011; Eidson, 2003; Eidson and Milligan, 2003). As a rule, in socialist countries unemployment did not exist and it was extremely difficult to be unemployed: nonworking was punishable by law in most socialist countries, while dismissing someone was very complicated for the enterprise. As such, it seems that people miss the security of the socialist political economy. My argument is different – namely, that the lack of prospects and stability makes people manifest their East German origin as a sign of protest and resistance. The punks and skins I studied were too young to be raised in the spirit of the socialist cult of proletarianism. The reason why they were embarrassed, angry or critical was because the ideology of self-sufficiency is something that belongs to the working-class ethos. In short, they found being unemployed or underpaid shameful because that runs against what they could be proud of and against the values they grew up with.

Class in Germany is a very interesting and contested term. In fact, the word 'Klasse' or class is seldom used in German, as I will argue in Chapter 4; the preferred term is *Schicht*, a social layer, which is a softer term. Moreover, class in Germany is understood purely in economic terms and is measured in income. According to German sociologists, the middle class starts from an income that is 70 per cent higher than the average salary in Germany, while the limit between the middle and upper classes is an income that is 150 per cent higher than the average salary.[11] In the British approach, the definition of class is less strict and more realistic. The distinction between the 'class as culture' and 'class as economic role' (Lawrence, 2000) helps us to approach the latent antagonism between different social groups. Cultural practices can be heavily class-based (Bourdieu, 1984) and in certain situations this is crucial for mutual sympathies or glass ceilings (cf. Friedman and Laurison, 2019). In Chapter 3, I will show how a gap exists in Germany between the 'state' or 'objective' class and the 'self-ascribed' class (ibid.: 313, 316). My research shows that people who are officially classified as 'lower class' or 'precariat' stick with their self-identification with the *Arbeiter* – the worker or working class. In my analysis of East German punk and its wider context, I lean on a Weberian reading of class, where the status of a group is defined through three components: wealth, prestige and power. This triad offers a perfect framework to speak about the substitute society of a subculture.

NOTES

1. The documentary is called *Punk Rock vs Sharia Law* and was made by Noisey, the music channel of *Vice* magazine. This is about the punk scene in Aceh, Indonesia's only Sharia law province. The documentary is available on Noisey's YouTube website as Episode 5 in a series of 'Music World' – see https://www.youtube.com/watch?v=6Sbne-qCNzU (retrieved 28 February 2020).

2. http://www.halle.de/en/Home (retrieved 28 February 2020).
3. Both US and UK 1970s punk bands like Blondie, Bad Brains, The Trowsers, Generation X, The Meat Puppets, Wire, The Clash, Pere Ubu and The Ruts merged reggae into their music, and this trend continues today. Reggae was in this era seen as a rebellious and largely underground music that made it attractive to punks (see Letts, 2008; Lydon, 1993; Needs, 2005). Many older reggae DJs I met in Berlin in the 1990s became interested in reggae by listening to white punk and reggae bands. The Clash covered several original and already-forgotten roots reggae songs like 'Two Seven Clash' and 'Armageddon Time' and gave them a second life. At the end of the 1970s, the Two Tone movement merged musically punk and Jamaican ska. The Clash also experimented with hip-hop elements and bands like Redskins or Dexys Midnight Runners played their own fast and raw versions of 1960s northern soul music.
4. It is not the topic of the book, but in the punk scene, working-class street punk is believed to have its roots in the British football-infected lad culture, therefore musicially street punk relies on early lad rock and pub rock combining it with football terrace chants. This was the background of Sham 69 and Cock Sparrer, followed by Angelic Upstarts and later a whole wave of bands too numerous to list here. Art-school punk has its origins in the art schools, as several members of The Sex Pistols, The Clash, etc. studied art. It should be noted that the definition of who is on which side is very much *post factum* in punk lore, as the dividing line is continuously created and maintained even now, through band interviews and nonacademic books.
5. Cholo is a US-Mexican criminal gang subculture, which is especially widespread in the southern states. For a good overview of the Cholo style, see Mendoza-Denton (2008).
6. In the UK, skinhead clothing shops and the popular young adult pulp novels of Richard Allen targeted the new skinhead (i.e. skinhead reggae) market.
7. 'Zone' (in English 'the zone') is still a tongue-in-cheek colloquial term for East Germany in the German punk scene. It derives from the name of the pre-GDR 'Ostzone' or 'eastern zone' that marked Soviet-occupied territory after the Second World War.
8. I was unable to track any study or autobiographical work that had the full list of bands that performed in the first punk festival of the GDR. Apart from the bands mentioned here, Wikipedia also lists HAU and Unerwünscht. See http://www.parocktikum.de/wiki/index.php/1.Punkfestival_der_DDR (retrieved 28 February 2020).
9. In Germany, 'Volksküche' or people's kitchen is usually a left-wing charity initiative that cooks and provides free or very cheap food to people in need.
10. https://www.spiegel.de/international/germany/the-eastern-german-identity-has-disappeared-a-919110.html (retrieved 28 February 2020). The article in the *Foreign Policy* journal about the state elections in the autumn of 2019 proved to be illuminating. The analysts argued that the political setting in Eastern Germany is very different from that in Western Germany, where voters' preferences are more 'traditional'. The article also speaks about the political 'normalisation' in the country's east, indicating that the states that were part of the GDR still belong to a twilight zone: https://foreignpolicy.com/2019/03/11/when-communists-lie-down-with-christian-democrats-germany/?utm_source=PostUp&utm_medium=email&utm_campaign=11803&utm_term=Editor
11. https://www.deutschlandfunk.de/oben-mitte-unten-sozialwissenschaftler-vermessen-die.1148.de.html?dram:article_id=329444 (retrieved 28 February 2020).

On the other hand, confusion exists in Germany about how to define the upper class. For one part of the group, the well-paid academic from a wealthy background, some researchers use the term ‘Ultra-Elite’. See https://www.tagesspiegel.de/wissen/exzellente-oberschicht-die-ultra-elite-stammt-aus-bestem-hause/12067856.html (retrieved 28 February 2020).

CHAPTER

1

THE TRANSFORMATION OF EAST GERMANY

Wende and the Socioeconomic Framework for the *Ossi*-Identity

This was no reunification, this was a sell-out!
—Thomas, 3 October 2010, on the Day of German Unity

The Berlin Wall was a symbol of the Cold War and its disappearance signalled the end of the Eastern Bloc and the Cold War. The German Democratic Republic (GDR) was an unusual socialist country for many reasons. First of all, Germans were the only people in Europe who were divided between a capitalist and socialist country that bore their name. After socialism, the GDR did not transform into a democratic state or fall apart, but was sucked into its neighbouring capitalist Federal Republic of Germany (FRG), being the only former socialist country that joined another state. East Germany was, if not the country with the highest living standard among socialist states, then one of the wealthiest. By the end of the GDR, the socialist side of Germany was an advanced state in Eastern Bloc terms, with respected universities, stylishly dressed people on the street and a relatively high living standard. Moreover, the GDR was the only socialist country with the Wall.[1] The moment of collapse of the GDR and reunification with the FRG is colloquially referred to in Germany as *Die Wende* (the turn).[2]

The aim of this chapter is not to offer another analysis of these events, but to provide a certain framework for the following chapters. Therefore, this chapter will not provide an in-depth look at the *Wende*, but will examine the social, cultural and economic changes in East German society after the collapse of socialism that are relevant for this book.

The GDR existed from 17 October 1949 to 3 October 1990 as a socialist Soviet bloc state and part of a divided Germany. It was established on the basis of the Soviet-occupied zone and therefore it was smaller than the capitalist FRG (ca. 17 million inhabitants in the GDR in contrast to 60 million in the FRG in the 1973 census (ENE, 1975: 47)). During my school days in Soviet Estonia, I often heard the rumour that the Soviet Union planned to create a model socialist state of the GDR and, indeed, the economy and governmental structures of East Germany were seriously reformed from 1949 onwards (EE, 1995: 325). The GDR became an industrial state, with more than 60 per cent of its economy based on the industrial sector, including heavy machinery production, the chemical industry and energy production (mainly brown coal extraction) (ENE, 1975: 48). The GDR was also admired for its modernity, being for instance the state that introduced fashionable plastic into everyday use (see also Gorsuch and Koenker, 2013, p.12). Alongside Hungary, Poland and Czechoslovakia, the GDR was oriented towards so-called 'consumer socialism', providing its citizens with the best living conditions and rewarding them materially for their achievements in the work place (Gorsuch and Koenker, 2013: 11). Ironically, notwithstanding a short-lived flirtation with the ideology of a nonconsumer-oriented 'alternative modernity' in the late 1950s, the socialist society was as consumer-oriented and materialistic as Western society (Gorsuch and Koenker, 2013: 11; Peteri 2008: 934, 937). However, the policy of satisfying people's needs was unsuccessful in the GDR, as was also the case throughout the Socialist Bloc. In fact, citizens in East Germany were not only disappointed by the quantity of goods but even more so by their quality, which was clearly inferior to the goods smuggled in from West Germany (Dennis and Kolinsky, 2004).

Before the *Wende*, the GDR was a socialist industrial state where industry contributed approximately 60 per cent to the national income and employed a workforce three times that of the agricultural sector, which provided less than 15 per cent of the state's production (ENE, 1975: 48). One of the main branches of GDR industry was the chemical industry (which accounted for 15 per cent of national industrial production) centred in the area of Leipzig and Halle. In the 1950s, the state-owned VEB Leuna-Werke Walter Ulbricht was established south of Halle and the city served as one of the living places for the enterprise's workforce.

Ruptures in the Socialist Bloc started with the reform policies of the Soviet leader Mikhail Gorbachev. The goal of the *perestroika* policy was to strengthen the Soviet Union and the Socialist Bloc in general (Gorbachev, 1987, 1993, 1995), but unexpectedly it initiated a series of popular pro-democracy movements in most socialist countries and caused the collapse of 'actually existing' socialism.[3] The GDR was one of the last to join this wave. Apart from Berlin, another centre for big democratic street protests and demonstrations in the GDR was Leipzig, only 30 kilometres from Halle.

It should be noted that not all Germans were united in the end goal of the democratic movement in the GDR. The majority obviously supported the idea of German reunification, but there also existed quite strong scepticism as to its outcome and even people who opposed it. The research shows that some youth in East Berlin were afraid that in the event of reunification, East Germans would become second-class citizens in the reunified German state (Leidecker, Kirchhöfer and Güttler, 1991). Moreover, some East German intellectuals formed the so-called Third Way movement, arguing that the GDR should be maintained as an independent state and a reformed socialist state (Berdahl, 2011: 37). During my fieldwork, I encountered sentiments that the Third Way could have been successful. In 2011 one left-wing skinhead told me:

> The GDR could have been a well-functioning state. We had very good industry and a well-organised economy. There should have been some redistribution of property but not in the way it was under Capitalism. I mean, more state owned smaller enterprises. Probably we all still would have jobs, with smaller salaries than in the West, but still working places. (Discussion with Mütze, field notes, 2011)

For the Third Way intellectuals, German reunification represented a 'selling out' to capitalism with the GDR being bought by Western capitalists (Berdahl, 2011: 37; Neubert, 2008: 383–84). Sadly, it must be noted that at least some of their warnings came true.

On 9 November 1989, the Berlin Wall fell, which was 'the beginning of the end of the GDR' (Lange and Shackleton, 1998: 5). The GDR and the FRG existed for a short time as a twin-state in monetary and social union until 3 October 1990, when the GDR officially joined the FRG and subscribed to its constitutional order (see Dennis and Kolinsky, 2004: 1). This was also the beginning of the *Wende* period, the above-mentioned transformation of the socialist society into a capitalist democracy. A reunified Germany continued to exist as the FRG, maintaining the institutions and official symbols (flag, coat of arms) of the former West Germany. East Germany was 'sucked up' (Solga, 2006; Ventsel, 2012) and had to go through far more radical reforms than its Western counterpart.

RESTRUCTURING OF THE FORMER GDR

First of all, East Germany had to undergo structural reforms. In this way, it was changed radically in order to be incorporated into the existing FRG. However, most of these transformations were 'top-down-reorganization' or decisions made at governmental level with very limited consultation with the people (Kollmorgen, 2005). In retrospect, it can be noted that this was the very beginning of East–West German tensions, with people from East Germany having the increasing feeling that they were thrown into turmoil and where they had very little control and participation in the ongoing transformation (Berdahl, 1999).

The old 15 Bezirk (district) system was reformed and five bigger Länder (or Bundesländer) were established, hence the popular term for the former GDR in the 1990s – *neue Bundesländer* or new federal districts. The East German universities were also reformed in a process called *Abwicklung* or implementation (Kollmorgen, 2005). The process of *Abwicklung* seems to have been especially radical in Berlin, where departments and faculties of West Berlin universities were unified with East Berlin universities and vice versa, with the aim of integrating Eastern academia with Western academia. Another result of the *Abwicklung* controversy was the re-evaluation of the former GDR academic staff. Notwithstanding that most former GDR professors believed that they were treated unfairly, the transformation brought with it changes in tenure, including positions with five-year contracts, downgrading former professors to assistants, former academic staff not being rehired and replacing East German professors with West German academics (Pritchard, 2004: 131).

However, the changes most strongly felt by everyone were those that related to the economy. After the introduction of the West German Deutsche Mark in what was known as the *Währungsunion* or currency union on 1 July 1990, East German products were rapidly replaced with Western consumables (Neubert, 2008: 385). The subsequent reunification quickly turned out to be a disappointment. While welcomed by citizens of the former GDR (who for a long time desired access to goods they knew mainly from West German TV), a change in prices ruined hopes (Berdahl, 2011), even among the punks. 'We had saved money for a long time to buy a new guitar amp. Something proper, Western, a Marshall amp. We almost had our money together and we knew someone who was willing to sell his amp. Then the *Wende* came, the money we had saved was worth nothing. Goodbye, guitar amp!', one older informant told me. However, access to Western goods generally meant that punks in the GDR spent their first Western money on items related to their subculture. 'You know, before the Western Deutsch Mark was introduced, every East German was entitled to the *Begrüssungsgeld* [greeting money]. This was 100 DM they gave you when you entered the FRG. Everybody went to buy clothes and so on. We went to the first record store and spent everything we had on records', one of my informants recalled with a smile.

The reform that affected more or less every East German inhabitant was the restructuring and privatization of the former socialist planned economy. This planned transformation was as ideological as it was economic. The ideological goal was to replace the socialist one party-ruled GDR economy with the free market, a private sector and democratic thinking (see Domdey, 1998). Simultaneously, it was believed that the GDR mode of production was unprofitable, outdated and nearly bankrupt. The state privatization agency Treuhand played a crucial role in the process of economic restructuring. 'Treuhand destroyed the industry in the East, they sold out everything for a penny', claimed Thomas, a punk in his mid-thirties in 2010. Treuhand remains in the narrative of the *Wende* as the central actor and its name is related to various myths and stories about injustice.

Treuhand existed between 1991 and 1994 as a controversial state agency of the FRG for the privatization and restructuring of the former GDR economy. In short, it was the largest holding in the world whose task was to privatize more than 8,500 or 95 per cent of former GDR enterprises with ca. four million employees (Roesler, 1994: 505). Treuhand was created to prevent 'insider privatization' to GDR *nomenklatura*, a task that was both ideological and economic (Siegmund, 1997: 6). The policy of the agency was to privatize enterprises as cheaply as possible in order to motivate new owners to invest in the newly obtained property. Enterprises that were not suitable for sale were broken up and sold off or liquidated. The expectations of the flow in investments and immediate economic growth were, in retrospect, unrealistic, but in the early 1990s managers of Treuhand apparently believed in it because they sold some enterprises for a symbolic one dollar price (Gibbon et al., 1995). On the other hand, it should be noted that there existed no precedent in terms of how to successfully privatize and reorganize a former socialist economy that also created a certain trial-and-error aspect in Treuhand's strategies. Controversy still remains about the evaluation of the success of the agency in the restructuring process. When Treuhand ended its operations, it had amassed 270 million DM in debts, which was arguably caused by the low market value and poor shape of the former socialist enterprises (Nellis, 2007). Apologists of Treuhand argue that only via this 'shock therapy' was the state agency able to successfully privatize the former socialist state property and that without Treuhand, unemployment, which hit the former GDR hard after the *Wende*, would have been even higher (Carlin and Mayer, 1995; Pickel, 1997). The positive aspects of the privatization are believed to be the speed of the process, the complexity and scale, and 'the creation of the institution and performance of these tasks when previous privatisation offered little guidance' (Lange and Pugh, 1998: 56–57). Moreover, the supporters of Treuhand argue that the comparison with the Czech Republic shows that as an independent state, the former GDR economy would have obtained far lower levels of investment. For example, the increasing unemployment was part of the postsocialist transition process all over the former Socialist Bloc, but only East German unemployed and retired people were compensated by annual subsidies at such a high level (Lange and Pugh, 1998: 71). However, some experts argue that the low price policy and the subsidies of investments in former GDR enterprises were contributing factors to the rise in unemployment (Siegmund, 1997: 28). The opinions of the critics of Truehand confirm the common belief that Treuhand 'de-industrialised the world's tenth-largest industrial economy by deceiving the nation and selling out the East Germans' (Gibbon et al, 1995: 20).

Treuhand's role in contributing to the narrative of deindustrialization could end here, were it not for another controversial practice applied by the agency. Namely, Treuhand officials preferred West German buyers because it was considered that this way, there would be fewer problems with language and culture (Seliger, 2001). This sales strategy was accompanied by the appointment of West Germans to managerial positions in East Germany, not only in academia, as noted above, but also – and especially – in the larger economy. In 1996–97, only 2 per cent of East Germany's top managerial and administrative positions were held by East Germans (Solga, 2006: 153). Such 'Western imports' (Solga, 2006: 153; see also Koch, 1999) was simultaneously a 'straight East-West transfer of power' (Domdey, 1998: 46). Moreover, West German enterprises also profited from the shift more than their East German counterparts. The monetary value of West–East 'exports' grew more than three times in 1991–92, while growth in the movement of goods from East Germany to West Germany was insignificant. The privatization provided access to state subsidies and investment orders for West German enterprises. Therefore, within the first three years following reunification, West German manufacturers received two-thirds of state investments (Domdey, 1998: 47).

These processes would have passed without initiating deep negative feelings had they not been accompanied by a rapid increase in unemployment. The entire workforce at the moment of German reunification was 10 million, but within a year it had shrunk to 6.6 million (Flockton, 2004: 39). When Treuhand took over responsibility for the former GDR industry, it also became the employer of 4.1 million workers (Domdey, 1998: 45). In the privatization process, only one million employees out of four million kept their jobs. It should be noted that unemployment was 'virtually unknown in East Germany in 1989' (Roesler, 1994: 51). Moreover, people who had grown up in socialist Germany also grew up with the notion that work was a 'duty' and an 'honour', which brought meaning to their lives (Berdahl, 2011; Eidson, 2003). The shock caused by the loss of work and the accompanying shame turned people against the privatization process and the associated Western companies. 'The main reason for all this, Treuhand and so on, this was to buy up Eastern enterprises. The Western companies bought their competitors, closed them and took only a few specialists to the West.

This was contrary to all the rules, they had to develop and invest in the new enterprise, but no one cared', explained one of my East Berlin politically active skinhead friends who was in his forties when we discussed the *Wende* in the late 1990s. His statement was not the only one I have heard on the topic and it shows that grievances were still very much alive twenty years after the *Wende* began. These sentiments were fuelled by real life events that are still remembered today. A notorious case involved the optic company Carl Zeiss that existed both in West and East Germany. The West German Zeiss bought out its East German counterpart in 1992. After it was announced that only 2,800 of the original 25,000 workers would retain their positions, thousands of workers went out into the streets demanding the end of privatization. After the protests, the state of Thuringia repurchased 20 per cent of the assets and established the state-owned Jenoptik in order to save 6,800 jobs (Roesler, 1994: 513). However, even this intervention was not able to prevent jobs from being lost. According to Jenoptik's website, in 2014 the enterprise had approximately 3,500 employees and that number increased to 4,043 in 2018.[4]

THE BIRTH OF *OSSI*

The economic, social and political transformation of the former GDR not only meant that the East became 'an extended work-bench' for the West German economy (Solga, 2006: 155), but also led to the development of a distinctive regional identity – the *Ossi*. *Ossi* is a German colloquial term for East Germans; the inhabitants of West Germany are referred to as *Wessi*. However, these terms do not only mark a regional affiliation.

While throughout the Cold War era German families struggled to keep ties with their relatives on the 'other side' (Borneman, 2000), the solidarity eroded soon after the *Wende*. During my numerous fieldwork periods, I discovered that, in general, local punks did not express any warm feelings toward their relatives in Western Germany. On the few occasions when relatives were mentioned, it was also emphasized that they were *Wessis*. The desire to draw a line between two branches of a family was obvious. The sense of distance was well voiced in a story I was told by Olli in Gig:

> My mother just got out from the hospital [where she was for cancer treatment]. All of sudden these *Wessi*-relatives from Hamburg appeared. They just came to visit without any warning although they should have known that she just came from the hospital. They came in, had a chat and then demanded something to eat. My mother just told them that she was too weak to prepare something and had no food at home anyway. These *Wessis*, they were really rude so my mother had to throw them out. (Field diary, 22 October 2017)

I have my own doubts about the accuracy of the representation of this episode, but the tone is a good description of the alienation inside one family. However, this alienation is not specific to my informant's family, but can be seen in the complex relations between the West and East Germans in modern Germany.

First of all, tensions go back to the uneven and unequal economic positions of West and East Germans, combined with a different interpretation of the results and costs of the reunion. On the Western side, the *Wende* meant slowly decreasing living standards, whereas the East was confronted with unfulfilled expectations for prosperity. In the early 1990s, German people were assured that 'the GDR will pay for unifications ... from her own pocket' (*Wirtschaftswoche*, cited in Roesler, 1994: 507). Helmut Kohl, the Chancellor at the time of the *Wende*, promised *blühende Landschaften* (blooming landscapes), whereas Helmut Haussman, his Economics Minister, was convinced that after the introduction of the Deutsche Mark, East Germany would become an 'economic miracle' (Flockton, 2004: 39). The German government announced that 'no rise in taxation would be needed to pay for the task of rebuilding in the new states' (Flockton, 2004: 39). This turned out to be untrue when new taxes to finance East German restructuring were introduced in 1991, such as the solidarity tax or Solidaritätszuschlag, which constituted 7.5 per cent of all individual and corporate income (Flockton, 2004: 43: cf. Ventsel, 2012: 349). The typical West German position was succinctly expressed by a motorist who picked me up close to the Dutch border when I was hitchhiking in the mid-1990s. He was an entrepreneur who ran a company in the former GDR and when discussing the reunification, he said: 'East Germans are ungrateful. When the *Wende* happened, we [West Germans] did not have any unemployment, our state budget was full but now all the money went to the East.'

While the West German perspective is characterized by disappointment, the approach from the East German side is more complicated. As was mentioned above, many East Germans were sceptical about the German reunification even before it took place. The growing unemployment added another dimension of scepticism that soon grew to a level where it became a public issue. One expression of these tensions were the derogatory terms that came into use during the 1990s: while East Germans were often referred to as *Jammerossi* (whining Easterners), West Germans were called *Besserwessi* (*Wessi* who knew everything better) (Carlin and Mayer, 1995; Berdahl, 2011). DeSoto (2000) concludes that the use of the term *Besserwessi* symbolizes the power imbalance between East and West Germany, which is certainly true to some extent. However, the term also expresses the alienation and anger over the arrogance of West German managers. Cracks also appeared among the East German population, with a few people – winners of the transition

(*Wendegewinner*) – profiting from reunification, but most people ending up on the losing side (*Wendeverlierer*) (cf. Berdahl, 2011: 94). I recall all these terms being in active use throughout the 1990s in Berlin, a city that was still divided by the 'wall in the heads'.

The notion of *Besserwessi* signalled the beginning of an unannounced cultural war between West and East Germans. Daphne Berdahl (2011) demonstrated that the main reasons for the *Ossi–Wessi* divide were not only differences in prosperity, but also the ridiculing of the GDR past and culture. In the 1990s, when I lived in Berlin, and as a student worked in temporary jobs, it was not unusual to hear how West Germans dismissed East Berlin architecture as 'ugly', East German cars like the Trabant as 'silly'[5] or East German products as 'crap'. Therefore, it is not surprising that many East Germans viewed the Western 'takeover' as a form of colonization with themselves as second-rate citizens (Berdahl, 2011: 94; Dennis and Kolinsky, 2004: 8). Researchers argue that the assumption of being disadvantaged in German society was, for the majority of East Germans, understandable to a certain extent. First, there was the economic imbalance (Dennis and Kolinsky, 2004). Drawing on Shafir (1998), Comaroff and Comaroff (2000), de Garzia (1996), Daphne Berdahl (2011: 91) argues that citizenship is directly and indirectly linked to an individual right to participate in mass consumption and concludes that, 'since reunification, consuming has continued to be a particularly important means of defining an East-West distinction'. Lower living costs in Eastern Germany during the 1990s obviously did not compensate for the living standard gap caused by lower wages.[6] Berdahl argues that another factor was lesser or different 'cultural competence' (Bourdieu, 1977). She describes how former GDR citizens were lacking confidence concerning new products and tools that appeared in their shops and were unsure of how to follow Western fashions. However, this insecurity quickly faded away, East Germans learned how to operate colour TVs or to combine brand-label clothing, and the perception of lack of 'cultural competence' was soon transformed into a semi-mythical 'GDR mentality' that hindered people in coping with a Western lifestyle and production process. A deeper discussion on the 'GDR mentality' will be given in Chapters 3 and 4, but it must be noted that as late as 2005, German economist Robert Böhmer (from the Technical University of Dresden, East Germany) argued that the biggest obstacle to successful economic transformation in Eastern Germany was the continued existence of that particular 'GDR mentality' (Böhmer, 2005: 265). The third reason for the feeling of bitterness was arguably the degradation of the social and cultural GDR environment. Socialist enterprises were, as a rule, 'total social institutions', providing social security and a sense of belonging to a collective (cf. Clarke, 1992). The enterprise took care of children's holiday camps, organized social events or provided employees with holiday trips to resorts. Consequently, East German workers identified themselves very strongly with production and enterprise. The social function of enterprises disappeared, as businesses closed or were restructured (Berdahl, 2011). This also changed the status of the worker. According to the socialist ideology, the working class felt privileged compared to other segments of society. This privileged status was not always reflected in higher living standards,[7] but in public celebrations, rhetoric and the ideological focus.

The cultural answer from the East Germans to the East–West imbalance was *Ostalgie*. The word is a combination of *Ost* (the East) and *Nostalgie* (nostalgia). *Ostalgie* means 'the supposed longing East Germans feel for the past' (Rethmann, 2009: 21) and marks a variety of cultural production, consumption practices and use of former GDR symbols. First of all, *Ostalgie* was demonstrated by the astonishing success of films like *Sonnenallee* (1999) or *Good Bye, Lenin* (2003) that visualized the lifestyle, politics, culture and social relations in the GDR. However, years before these films, so-called *Ostprodukte* (Eastern products) began their revival in supermarkets in East Berlin. The *Ostprodukte* were revived consumables and brands from the former GDR, such as certain brands of soft drinks, ice cream, coffee or even soap. Suddenly, white labels with green letters announcing proudly *Ostprodukt* appeared on shop shelves. The triumph of apparently long-missed GDR products was vividly discussed in the media and hailed by East Germans. Petra Rethman (2009) describes the nature and history of an *Ostalgie* hotel in Berlin, and 'old time' bars appeared all over Berlin while previously existing ones became increasingly popular. Simultaneously, former GDR music became available on newly released CD samplers and was used as a soundtrack for numerous *Ostalgie* club nights as early as the end of 1994. Some GDR symbols achieved an almost iconic nature. While in the early 1990s the GDR home-produced car, the Trabant made of plastic, was not adequately valued and could reportedly be exchanged for a six-pack of beer, by the end of the 1990s, Trabi – as it was called colloquially – became a symbol of *Ossi*-identity. Trabi-rallies were and still are organized in various East German towns, and the car itself is a collector's item today. Another marker of East German identity was the growing popularity of the GDR coat of arms. T-shirts with this symbol were on sale at merchandising stalls in rock festivals and many of my punk informants still have the GDR flag hanging on their living room wall.

CONCLUSION

Ostalgie has been analysed in both English and German academic literature. As a retro-wave, *Ostalgie* was the first nostalgia wave in former socialist countries, appearing very shortly after the demise of the GDR. The meaning of

Ostalgie is doubly charged, containing an element of irony, but – as is typical in a 'joking relationship' – it is a serious exposure of identity. It is argued that *Ostalgie* is a form of resistance to West German cultural, political and economic domination (Berdahl, 2011, Rethman, 2009). Daphne Berdahl (2011: 38) argues that *Ostalgie* was and is the embodiment of the 'Other' that East Germans were in the Western viewpoint.

Most studies on *Ostalgie* stress, in one way or another, the emotional connection of East Germans to the GDR, a certain revaluation of something that has become the 'happy past'. This might be true for many older people, but my informants in this study were in their early teens or even younger when the Socialist Bloc collapsed. Therefore, it is an exaggeration to assume that they miss the society of which they have only a vague memory. 'Everything I know and has been told to me about the GDR ... I think this is a state I would not want to live in', a young skinhead told me whilst sitting on a couch under the GDR flag hanging on the wall. However, the *Wende* and the accompanying social and economic transformation are relevant as a narrative in the still-existing *Ossi–Wessi* divide. As will be demonstrated in Chapter 5, the GDR played a role in the reformation of identities for punks and skinheads in Halle.

Recent studies by German sociologists prove that the East German youth still feel alienated within the FRG, but this does not automatically mean they want to return to the GDR. The word *Ossi* still contains unpleasant overtones and is in East Germany understood as an insult. However, the adjective *ost* (eastern) is used with pride and marks the line between East and West Germans. The multilayered meaning of the term *Ostpunk*, which has become a self-description for the East German punk scene, draws from the history of the *Wende* and is connected to the processes that are related to the appearance of *Ostalgie*.

Notes

1. Some people I have met in Germany during the last twenty years argue that the symbol of the Cold War – the wall around West Berlin – was just one part of the 'socialist defense wall', as it was called officially in socialist Germany, and that there existed another wall between East and West Germany.
2. The fact that the GDR was the only socialist state to join another state and adopt its structure, organization and methods of governance means that the GDR avoided the long path of experiments, reforms and cataclysms experienced in other former socialist countries. This unusual historical development also means that East Germany seems to be academically somewhat less postsocialist than, for example, Poland, Hungary or Latvia. While in the English language there exist a myriad of anthropological studies discussing postsocialist transformation in every country from the former Soviet Bloc, the list for the former GDR is much shorter. There are even

fewer scholars who conducted their fieldwork during the reunification period. The most important scholar is, of course, Daphne Berdahl, who has published a series of works on the GDR during and after the *Wende* (Berdahl, 1999, 2011), but somehow anthropologists did not catch the momentum of the turn. However, there exist a myriad of studies written by sociologists, economists and historians focusing on changes in the GDR.

3. 'Really existing' or 'actually existing' socialism was a Brezhnev-era ideological expression and was used to demonstrate that socialism as a political and economic formation 'had won' in several countries despite the skepticism of Western critics.
4. See respective annual reports on Jenoptik's website: http://www.jenoptik.com.
5. When I moved to Germany in 1994, I quickly realized that jokes about the Trabant were painful and humiliating for East Germans. As I was told more than once, to get a Trabi in socialist times was extremely difficult; people had to wait for a decade or longer to own a car. Overnight, these people discovered that their personal automobile was not something precious, but just a 'plastic soap box'.
6. The difference in living costs between Eastern and Western Germany was especially obvious in Berlin. During the 1990s, depending on your address, you had to pay either eastern or western tariffs for insurance, a city transport monthly ticket and rent.
7. In the GDR, blue-collar workers usually earned more than white-collar intellectuals, but their income was nevertheless lower than that of the management at the time (Engler, 1999).

CHAPTER

2

PUNK ROCK

Living Music

> There have been attempts to connect punk with techno. After a punk concert, DJs played techno music. But it did not succeed, punks were too conservative and disinterested.
>
> —Steven Dewar, 1994

Steven Dewar, a guitarist of Wrax, a long-forgotten straight-edge punk band from Göttingen, told me this. It was 1994 and I had arrived in Göttingen to attend a compulsory German language course at the Goethe Institute. After my arrival and a short period to adapt, I explored the local underground scene to find a youth club, where I also discovered Wrax and befriended Steve. Techno was booming globally in those days and many people in the German punk scene became interested in experimenting with electronic music. The audience, however, did not show any appreciation for the attempts to merge these two music styles, and probably their following. The underground scene around the local youth club in Göttingen seemed more open and colourful than I had experienced back in Estonia. Typical of the German small-town scene, new age hippies, punks, skaters and skinheads hung around together and enjoyed each other's music. Nevertheless, there seemed to be a red line where a certain kind of music, and everything related to it, became unacceptable.

This chapter focuses on punk music and related music styles, and how these are regarded on the scene. In the popular imagination, punk (and other subcultures) is associated first and foremost with certain forms of music and a way of dressing. The academic approach does not differ radically. Numerous sociologists, cultural studies scholars and even musicologists have written extensively about various aspects of punk music and the outlook, so much so that these topics seem to dominate academic studies on punk. There is also a logic behind it – sonic and visual styles are the first markers of the subculture, being relatively easy to recognize and classify. Each subculture is a collective of individuals, but there exist huge discrepancies in terms of what these individuals accept and what the subculture is ready to accept. The first thing to consider is the music. When I became involved in the skinhead scene in Berlin, I discovered that most of my friends owned records and CDs of different genres of music, be it techno, calypso, jazz or even right-wing rock. Gavin Watson, a renowned skinhead photographer, confessed to me in an interview that during his skinhead period, he mainly listened to classical music. Some punks in Halle are dedicated Depeche Mode fans and at least one of them has an extensive collection of Lady Gaga, Madonna and Beyoncé CDs. This musical eclecticism is accompanied by a variety of modes of dressing that makes it difficult, if not impossible, to pin down the definition of 'What is punk?' It might seem that scholars from a post-subcultural approach are right in arguing that subcultures have been annihilated and have disappeared because it is impossible to reduce these phenomena to a clearly defined style. As some scholars have shown, young people switch between different outlooks seemingly deliberately and without any concept, so it is reasonable to assume that what were known as subcultures were just consumption trends. However, more than dress or music preferences, post-subcultural reasoning questions the relationship between the subculture and the working class. There are other voices that delicately argue against these positions. For example, Blackman (2005) criticizes – among others – David Muggleton's seminal book *Inside Subculture* (2000), which claims that subcultures are nothing more than a 'surface' for individual identity-seeking. Blackman argues that under the 'surface' of the post-subculture structures, subcultural mentality is alive and well: 'However, if you look at the case studies presented by Muggleton (2000), the mods and the punks, it is clear that they conform to precise subcultural regulations' (Blackman, 2005: 10). Dedman (2011) shows with the help of British grime culture that the notion of coherent style is outdated, but the subcultural insider status is gained through cultural knowledge and creative engagement. Other authors have argued that it is too early to bury socioeconomic factors as one determent characteristic when looking at subcultures (Shildrick and MacDonald, 2006). In line with this, subcultural authenticity has been interpreted as working-class resistance against the dominant culture (Clarke et al., 1976) where stylistic resistance is applied to demonstrate separation from the dominant commercial mainstream (Leblanc, 2001) or a conscious self-stigmatization by appropriating the symbolic style of a poor, dirty and stigmatized inner-city underclass (Traber, 2001).

The concept of homology – developed by Dick Hebdige (1979) – states that in a subcultural world, there exists a semiotic relationship between music and style, which also includes a certain ideology and practice. Later research has shown that different subcultures can also have their own ways of speaking or have created their own forms of slang (Bucholtz, 2011; Jones, 1988; Kitwana, 2005; Middleton and Beebe, 2002). When subcultural studies connected the appearance of subcultures with working-class rebellion, the following post-subcultural studies questioned that argument in particular. In the modern 'supermarket of styles', almost every individual is able to find a suitable resolution for how to express themselves and to which community to belong. The question posed here is: 'Why certain individuals choose punk?' The main goal of this chapter is to discuss why the street punk style – a conglomerate of hard punk, hardcore and skinhead styles – is suited to the working class and to a certain extent can be understood as a rebellion against mainstream conventions. The demography of regular visitors to GiG support the assumption that street punk is attractive to people from a working-class background. As I was told by Pieps, one of a number of masterminds behind the GiG club: 'It used to be very mixed here [in GiG]. Students, artists, different kind of people came here. Now there are mainly working-class youth (*Arbeiterkids*) [among GiG regulars].' In the subcultural world, popularity of styles, music genres and locations is constantly rotating. After the explosion of the alternative scene in Halle in the 1990s, the actuality of what GiG had to offer waned in the early 2000s and many regulars 'moved on'. Therefore, it does not seem incorrect to argue that particular forms of punk include something that motivates people with a working-class background to remain loyal to this style. Two elements of the expression of street punk – music and style – here come under closer scrutiny.

SOUNDS OF PUNK

'Music is not a symbol of identity so much as way of living it', writes John Street (2012: 116; see also Rapport, 2014). Music is indeed essential when talking about subcultures and subculturalists, as it is probably the first incentive that attracts the attention of a modern youngster to a particular style. Later the apprentice discovers through that gateway a whole semiotic world that is defined as homology or 'the symbolic fit between the values and lifestyles of a group, its subjective experience and musical forms it uses to express or reinforce its focal concerns' (Hebdige, 1979: 143). Looking at the primary importance of sounds and rhythm for the recruitment of new subculturalists, it is therefore justified to begin the analysis at this point.

Punk music has a long history and is fragmented into several – often warring – genres and subgenres. In general, the music is characterized as an embodiment of rage combined with texts 'written out of anger', in contrast to more sophisticated rock music styles, where seemingly more advanced musicianship is required. The academic writing on punk tends to be engaged with the ideology, message or semiotics of the music, whereas scant interest is paid to the sonic qualities that are very important from the position of the listener (see also Rapport, 2014). The discussion about the political message or commercial nature of punk music seems to overlook the fact that punk in different forms and derivatives (McNeill and McCain, 1996: 324) is, among other things, a youthful, energetic and vivid music. Punk is a rhythmic, fast and loud form of music: it is generally easy to move one's body to it and it is extremely suitable for collective entertainment. Keith Negus (1999: 94) explains the success of rap as 'an emotional performative sound event', which should not be reduced only to race, lyrics or images. Punk is not so different, offering a platform for expression but also collective enjoyment (see also Rapport, 2014: 44). When one reads the autobiographies of punk musicians, one encounters the opinion that energetic punk music was a perfect sonic cure for the 'frustration' of the era (Albertine, 2014; Letts, 2008; Lydon, 1993; Savage, 1991). This pseudo-medical explanation also pops up in interviews with German punk bands, where love for the music is often explained through the aspect of being a certain kind of energizer against a boring and monotonous everyday life (see various band interviews in fanzines like Dropkick Murphys (2000); Maurice (1998); Sandler (1997); Steel and McNasty (1997)). By its nature, punk is a very tight form of music, where guitars, bass and drums play in relative unison and the listener is confronted with 3–4 minutes of relatively simple melodies, where different fragments rotate in a logical order. Most punk, hardcore and ska songs of this world have a predictable structure, a concrete beginning and an end, and very few loose elements, like the long improvised solos of progressive rock or virtuoso solos (often performed on two or more guitars) that heavy metal is known for. In this sense, punk is rightfully a 'straight-in-your-face' music or a 'stripped down rock and roll' (as expressed by Charlie Harper, the singer of the U.K. Subs in his interview for a fanzine *Wahrshauer*; see Maurice (1998)). These sonic specifics are combined with the ambitious side of punk when it comes to the lyrics. In a private conversation, legendary punk singer TV Smith told me that it is a rather complicated task to write a text that tells a story within a few minutes.[1] And of course, he simultaneously complained that this skill is nowadays in decline. Nevertheless, when reading autobiographies of the artists from the 1970s and early 1980s or biographies of bands from the same era, the punk music and newly emerging scene is depicted as 'exciting', 'fresh' and 'creative' (Letts, 2008; Marshall, 1990, 1993; Savage, 1991; Turner and Bushell, 2010), and there is a presumption that the making of punk music requires a healthy dose of irony and humour – 'good fun' (Savage, 1991: 200; Turner and Bushell, 2010) – but paradoxically even in this early period there already existed a notion of 'real punk' (Davidson, 2010: 63).[2] People who saw punk bands for the first time were impressed by their attitude and their 'I don't care' stance (Savage, 1991: 141, 170).

STREET PUNK OR OI!

When there was a dominant music style in the GiG circuits, it was a rough subgenre of punk, called Oi! or street punk. This style is often associated with right-wing youth culture and has received very little scholarly attention. Usually this music is mentioned in studies of neo-Nazi skinheads, with very little analysis of the bands and the music scene.[3] Punk folklore and academic writing, in a rare case of consensus, acknowledge that a certain division had already occurred during the genesis of punk music. In academic writing, punk bands with an art school background – The Clash, The Sex Pistols, The Damned, The Buzzcocks and Joy Division – are discussed more often and in detail, but another side of the early punk, popularly known as a working-class or street punk, has largely remained beyond the academic radar (see Brake, 1985; Haefner, 2007; Hebdige, 1979; Marcus, 1989; Nehring, 2007; Rapport, 2014; Savage, 1991; Williams, 2011b).[4]

Almost the only existing forms of literature on street punk are the autobiographic books and interviews with musicians or fans involved in the scene. It is widely believed that Oi! developed from a style played by a number of English bands from working-class backgrounds with a focus on issues relevant to working-class youth. These issues were, among others, football violence, class issues, drinking, politics from the perspective of the working class or a critical stance to the government and its institutions. Generally, the beginnings of Oi! relate to the London band Sham 69, although there are other bands – like Cock Sparrer – who argue that they were playing this kind of music even before the emergence of punk in 1976/77 (Mader, 1996). Stylistically, notwithstanding the lyrics, Oi! is rougher and often faster than classic punk, and Oi! songs usually include singalong choruses, reminiscent to football chants.[5] The name for the genre comes from four iconic compilation albums from the early 1980s, when a British music journalist Garry Bushell decided that new exciting working-class punk bands deserved more attention than they had received and released the samplers *Oi! The Album*, *Carry on Oi!*, *Strength Thru Oi!* and *Oi! Oi! That's Yer Lot*. Because 'Oi!' is nowadays associated with the sound and song structures of British bands from the early 1980s, and the press in many countries regard it as a neo-Nazi music genre, many such bands prefer to describe their music as 'street punk' or 'Oi!/street punk'.[6] Oi!/street punk is released by independent punk record labels and the scene is – as is the case with other subgenres of punk – internationally well connected. This also includes the swift dissemination of music, constant touring abroad and relatively easy access to new releases.

The egalitarian nature of the genre is stressed through the interaction between musicians and the audience; very often people from the audience climb onto the stage to sing along with the chorus. What makes street punk distinct from many other genres of punk is an emphasis on the masculine performance aspect of the concerts. Sooner or later, several people from the audience take off their shirts and one can see lots of bare-chested men on the stage or in the front rows of the crowd. In small smoke-filled clubs, sweaty bodies rubbing against each other, a plethora of tattoos and an aggressive but nevertheless carefully practised pogo create a specific feeling of the brotherhood or 'one gang' as it is referred to in many songs.[7]

SKA AND HARDCORE

Another popular music style in the German punk-influenced underground scene was and still is ska. Ska is a music style that – depending on whom you talk to – emerged in Jamaica either at the end of the 1950s or the beginning of the 1960s. It is a mixture of previous Jamaican popular music styles like mento, quadrille and march music, with American rhythm and blues and jazz (see Barrow and Dalton, 1997). At the end of the 1970s, ska made a comeback in Britain, where several bands appeared that merged it with the punk tempo and guitar-playing techniques. This ska revival is generally known as Two Tone, taking its name from the 2Tone label that was a flagship of the genre.[8] By the beginning of the 1980s, ska jumped over to Western Europe and the United States, although its popularity was brief and it faded out in just a few years. Since then, there have been several waves of 'comebacks' and currently ska is a globally known and performed genre, which is apparently particularly popular in Latin America. The initial idea of this wave was to produce political dance music and promote racial harmony, a premise questioned by the British scholar Les Back, who is not convinced as to whether the adoption of elements of Jamaican culture by white youth really means racial integration (Back, 2013: 12; see also Back, 2000). Ska is a joyful and danceable music that for some reason has never received the commercial success it deserves in Germany or across Europe.[9]

I would like to examine several reasons for this failure of ska to catch on, at least in Germany. First of all, good ska bands are big, including a wind instrument section. From the financial side, a large line-up makes the wages of ambitious ska bands considerably higher than those of much smaller rock groups. This is probably one reason why very few ska bands in Germany have reached the league of successful professional bands and ska has remained largely a semi-professional music where musicians need another income in order to finance their musicianship.[10] In the 1990s, Germany housed several annual ska festivals, domestic and foreign ska bands toured actively, and there existed several large and small record labels issuing ska on vinyl and CD. Yet despite the ska boom of the 1990s, in Germany ska music remained underground and only rarely crossed over to the mainstream. In essence, ska is a relatively conservative music style that does not easily fit into the constantly changing sounds and trends of the popular music. Apart from a few attempts to merge ska with electronic music or metal, the audience does not accept radical changes to ska's soundscape.[11] Modern ska contains several subgenres – retro 1960s-leaning traditional ska, a faster and rockier modern version and extremely punky skapunk or skacore – but there seems to be a clear limit for how far experimentation in ska can go. This conservativism is mirrored in the stage image of ska bands, where the dominant so-called rude boy style is created consciously by the bands from the first Two Tone wave – dark suits, button-down shirts, Dr Marten boots and many items associated with the skinhead or mod wardrobe like Harrington jackets .[12] The bigger problem of the genre, limiting its popularity, has probably been its skinhead following. I recall how in the 1990s journalists from the mainstream music papers always asked ska bands about it and the negative reaction it caused in the Berlin skinhead scene when musicians avoided a direct response or reluctantly admitted to having 'different people coming to our concerts'. When I visited a ska festival in Leipzig in 2010, I noticed that the situation had not changed much – the majority of the audience were still skinheads. In an interview, Gavin Watson commented on the dynamics of the 1980s British skinhead scene: 'Most of us went to Nazi concerts because this was the place to listen to Oi! bands. But when ska appeared, skinheads made a turn and started to go to ska [concerts] because this was where the girls were.' This generalization is of course anecdotal and based on individual memories, but it contains a certain element of truth. In terms of gender, ska concerts are more mixed, and while at punk concerts pogoing is almost exclusively a male pastime, ska gives women the possibility to leave the fringes and be in the middle of the dancefloor.

Hardcore began in the late 1970s in the United States and was the American response to punk (Thompson, 2004; Ward, Stokes and Tucker, 1986). The sonic line between heavier and faster punk and the more melodic hardcore is blurry, although in general hardcore is much faster and the division is more stylistic than musical. When looking at the song lyrics of hardcore, there is a constant repetition on the notion of 'being united', forming a 'brotherhood' or being 'proud'. Hardcore bands – as a rule – do not glorify alcohol consumption, as occurs in street punk,[13] and violence is thematized more often than not as pure aggression, but as a form of defence against the dominant society that allegedly attempts to destroy the hardcore lifestyle.[14] There is a movement within hardcore – called straight edge (see Haenfler, 2014) – that propagates vegetarianism and abstinence from alcohol, tobacco consumption and casual sex.[15] The main objective behind this ideology is to enforce self-control, animal rights and anti-mass-consumption behaviour. The dress style of hardcore fans is deliberately minimalistic and uniform: sweatshirts, baggy jeans, trainers and skate shoes, baseball caps, simple rain jackets and band T-shirts. The fans attempt to portray themselves as a 'brotherhood'. However, it must be mentioned that the hardcore community, especially in East Germany, was until recently relatively small. One brand mark of the genre is stage diving – or climbing onto the stage in order to jump back into the crowd –although this also happens in punk concerts. The people encountered during my fieldwork tend to dismiss the more recent popularization of the genre that has happened when certain American bands started to merge hardcore with more metal sounds[16] and view this type of the music as 'commercial'. It should be noted that hardcore has a long history in the Leipzig area as a music for a small but close-knit community. As Pieps told me: 'In the late 1980s or early 1990s, when you saw another man in camouflage trousers, Chucks[17] and black hood you knew that he was into hardcore. You walked up to him to greet and exchange a few words.' Bands that are popular in the GiG circle are lesser-known 'old school' hardcore bands like 4Shivits, Tangled Line and Verstärkertod. These bands play a fast and robust 1980s-style music, release their records themselves or via small underground labels and rely almost completely on their personal network. In 2006 I followed 4Shivits on their tour through Poland, the Czech Republic and Slovakia, and in 2007 I helped to organize their tour in the Baltic States. This segment of hardcore relies on the personal connections to organize concerts in small clubs. Such touring –where bands do not earn much money – is seen as a proof of a commitment to the 'lifestyle' and symbolizes egalitarianism in the scene, where 'bigger' bands support and treat 'smaller' bands equally. However, as a form of live music, hardcore was rarely represented at GiG, but was often played as a soundtrack from cassettes or a computer. Ska bands also performed in Halle (or Leipzig) in other venues, but the ska concerts were popular as the occasion for a party, and not because people were that fond of ska.

PUNK'S CONSERVATIVE APPROACH

I recall the following conversation with one of my friends in the late 1990s in Berlin. We discussed, as was often the case, the newest records and I said: 'Ska is pretty conservative music. You do not experiment much with it, people [the audience] will not like it.' My friend replied: 'But this is the same with Oi! It was and is conservative, you do not depart from the classic sound.' While Thompson (2004) explains the cult of past sounds in punk rock as nostalgia, Reynolds (2011) talks about 'punk's reactionary roots' or radical obsession with the music styles of the past. The latter argues that such 'retromania' was a 'striking move' when punk appeared (Reynolds, 2011: 261). Many people – scholars or not – argue that after the few first years, punk became 'repetitive' in the sense of Attali (1985), something 'predictable' where musical expression is oriented to reproducing stereotypical sonic qualities and structures. The aforementioned music genres indeed look back to past decades, radical musical innovation is almost excluded and if it happens, it moves the artist quickly into the orbit of another audience (O'Connor, 2008).

In street punk, ska and 'old school' hardcore, commercial success remains unrealistic when the bands stick to the original style. There are very few German harder punk bands that can make living from their music. In most cases, this is not the goal. I was told variations on the following quote by many musicians over the last fifteen years: 'I know we could make more money when we would sign with a big record label, but then it would mean we should make different music. Currently I am happy with the situation when I go to work and then make music I like.' The refrain from musical innovation positions street punk and other linked styles at the periphery of the music business. Whatever constitutes 'mainstream' or 'alternative' music, the aforementioned styles are, as a rule, ignored by the respective media and event organizers. The outsider status gives the music a certain aura of authenticity, which aligns with how the musicians see themselves. The musicians of the Klabusterbären, Halle's undisputed most important punk band, told me in an interview:

> K1: Our songs are 95% about what happens in life, but we see it from our point of view. We interpret it mostly ironically and make fun of it and that is what people like pretty much. What sucks [or] what we like.
>
> K2: And the remaining 5%?

K3: That is the description of everyday.

(Klabusterbären interview, field notes, 2010)

The assumption of solidarity is not only expressed through song lyrics and the practice of stage diving, but also in the very ritualistic speeches of musicians between songs where they thank people for coming and 'supporting' the band. Also important is the tradition of ritualistic fandom in street punk and hardcore – to some extent, bands can be compared with football clubs. Every German city with a punk scene has at least one local band with a devoted following who travel with the band to their concerts in other cities. The self-image of such bands is as voices of a local scene where locality is emphasized in the song lyrics.[18] The bond to the locality and community is a uniting phenomenon in punk, part of a global trend against globalization as it were. For instance, Klabusterbären has a hit song praising the city with the singalong chorus 'Halle! Halle! Halle!' The performance of the song is obligatory in their concerts and marks the climax of the event. Locality is extremely important in German culture where local patriotism is understood in a narrower sense – a bond to the city or village, to its dialect, cuisine, local beer and community (see also Ventsel, 2010). Street punk with its glorification of a connection to the community is a 'visible' music (Tagg, 2011). Bands like Klabusterbären are well known for singing in a local dialect about 'everyday life' in a form where everyone in the audience can participate and relate to the celebration of common identity.

LOOKING FOR THE MEANING OF STYLE

In 2014, Viv Albertine, a former guitarist of the punk group The Slits, published an autobiographic book *Clothes, Music, Boys: A Memoir*. The pecking order in the title shows the importance of the outlook in youth cultures. Subcultures are classically defined through their style. Academically, the style of subcultures is understood as a semiotic construct where available material is combined to create new meanings. This process is analysed through the concept of bricolage associated with Lévi-Strauss (1966), borrowed by Hebdige to analyse the punk style (1979: 102–6). The essence of bricolage is explained well by Bucholtz: 'In French, *bricolage* roughly means "do-it-yourself" or "improvisation": according to theories of style, the bricoleur, or improvising stylistic agent, takes whatever resources are ready to hand to create new styles' (2011: 11). The problem is that scholars of subcultural theory prescribed a shock value to the style. This was true in early punk, as can be seen in the autobiographical memoirs of the people from that era (Albertine, 2014; Letts, 2008; Lydon, 1993). These authors also find that the shocking nature and innovative moment of the punk style faded out pretty quickly, paving the way for a copycat movement. In post-subcultural and later theoretical schools, subcultural style was seen as having a certain limit – these scholars questioned whether the subcultures existed at all because they were observing how different styles merged (Bennet, 2004; Hesmondhalgh, 2005; Muggleton, 2000; Thornton, 1996).

As was mentioned in the Introduction, Halle had several hubs of punk-underground culture. The most spectacular of these were the people called 'Händel punks'. They was a group of twenty to thirty punks in their late teens who sported a stereotypical punk look – leather jackets, mohawks, combat boots, chains and tight trousers. During the warm weather, they usually gathered in a central Händel Square (hence the group's name). Another name for them was '*Schnorrer*-Punks' or 'begging punks' because one thing they loved to do was to ask passers-by for cigarettes and small change. Another club – VL – was a centre for politically active left-wing people who were also much older than all the other groups in the Halle underground and therefore dressed more modestly. It is difficult to describe their style – one common denominator was a preference for second-hand clothes. Reil-78 people were the youngest, and sported (as was typical for the radical left youth globally) a 'crusty' look, or hooded sweaters, baggy trousers and skate shoes, very often combined with dreadlocks.

The style of GiG regulars is difficult to define. On the one hand, most people had their own individual style and yet there were certain common stylistic aspects. When Muños and Marín discuss 'the search for one's own style' in Colombia, they conclude that such a search serves as a motor behind the 'subjectivity building' (2006: 133). The 'GiG style' stressed the individual personality, but there, nevertheless, exists an almost undefinable stylistic framework. Paraphrasing Hebdige, who said that punk was distinguishable in the 1970s because it was 'conspicuously scruffy' (1979: 123), I would say that the visual expression of GiG regulars is 'conspicuously anti-fashionable'. 'Fashion' can here be understood both as the stereotypical leather-clad look of the Händel punks and as mainstream fashion.

The way in which men dressed was more coherent. The preferred look was the 'clean and neat' outfit of loose-fitting jacket, plain or band T-shirt or polo shirt, or button-down shirts of different brands, baggy trousers or Levi's 501 jeans. Bright (especially neon) colours are unusual for men and women alike, as in Germany, these are associated with techno, hipster or student culture. The footwear of choice is usually certain brands of trainers and skater shoes or Dr Marten boots. It is important that most of the details could be associated with various punk, hardcore, skinhead or hooligan styles. Harrington jackets, which in Germany are associated with a skinhead and football hooligan style, are very popular, as are work jackets from Dickies. Only a few men wore leather jackets and only on rare occasions. When I asked Olli why he was not wearing his leather jacket, he responded: 'Because I have a quiff people think I am a rockabilly.' This demonstrates how the subcultural identity is important for one's inner self, for the above-mentioned 'subjectivity building'. There is a certain limit on how much a subcultural person wants to be disassociated from his or her peer group. Identity is, among other things, 'a performance or construction that is interpreted by other people' (Benwell and Stokoe, 2006: 4). Here we can turn to the concept of homology, which in this case can result in building a different identity in the eyes of a stranger. A leather motorcycle jacket carries certain markers that in combination with a quiff could have sent, in Olli's eyes, an incorrect message. This is probably the reason why sweatshirts or hooded sweatshirts were especially popular when they were decorated with a band logo. For an insider, a band logo demonstrates a person's musical interests and through that shows the subcultural background of the wearer. Men tended to wear flat caps (before it became a mainstream fashion) due to their association with the working-class style, 'old school' baseball caps (preferably with a band logo)[19] or ski caps (often with a band logo).

From a working-class subculture perspective, the symbolism related to brands seems to be especially important, and such 'brandedness' is more relevant to men. Especially popular during the period of my fieldwork were three brands – Fred Perry, Lonsdale and Ben Sherman. All these brands are related to the skinhead and football hooligan culture and are still very expensive to buy. The symbolism related to these brands is complex and is a combination of several aspects. I have explained it elsewhere (Ventsel, 2014), but a very important factor in the adoption of these 'holy trinity' brands, as I call them, in German and in global punk-related culture is that they were linked to the notion of Britishness and a 'genuine working-class background',[20] they were exclusive (traditionally on sale only in specialist shops) and not everybody was able to afford them. Most Fred Perry, Lonsdale and Ben Sherman products look good, they have a certain minimalistic design and these brands have until recently not been very fashionable among the mainstream audience. Things have changed in the last decade or so and all brands have become now what Hilary Pilkington referred to in a private discussion as 'just a high street fashion'. The answer of the subculture was to stick with 'classic' models and 'leave' more fashionable models to the mainstream audience. Identity building through the 'conspicuous' consumption (Partington, 2014: 9) becomes especially obvious looking at the 'holy trinity'. When the German branch of Lonsdale started to sell cheap clothing with a questionable design (for instance, 'Lonsdale' written with pink letters on a black sweatshirt) in cheap stores like Aldi, these were rejected by most people who wore Lonsdale in GiG and people continued to travel to Leipzig to buy more stylish but also more expensive Lonsdale polo shirts in specialized 'scene' shops. When Fred Perry became a high-street fashion in Germany, the cult of 'classic' models increased in the punk and skinhead scene, leaving more 'modern' models to the 'Normalos'. Fortunately for the underground, Ben Sherman has never enjoyed much popularity in Germany and this gave many underground fashionistas a refuge. 'Fred Perry is so expensive and bad quality now, I completely stopped wearing them and now buy Ben Sherman', explained one man who was working in a punk-skinhead clothes shop in Potsdam in 2008, and I was able to observe remarkable brand switching in both Halle and Berlin.

Women are more playful in choosing their outfits. I have observed a lower level of addiction to the 'holy trinity' amongst women and a significantly wider stylistic variety. Franzi could dress herself in a 'hardcore style' (band T-shirt, baggy jeans and trainers) and turn up at the next event with a more 'new wave look' (white shirt, tight dark skirt, narrow tie and shiny shoes). Women tend to be more dressed up for concerts, wearing more make-up, styling their hair and dressing differently from their 'normal day'.

Like men, women like to wear T-shirts and sweatshirts with band logos. As with the men, through their music preferences they signalled their subcultural affiliation – a wearer of a punk band T-shirt is logically most likely a punk, whereas the logo of a rockabilly band shows that the wearer is a rockabilly. What distinguished women from men was their stronger enthusiasm to remake their clothes. Usually men added patches and badges to their jackets or trousers, but very seldom the stripes of tartan or imitation leopard skin to their jacket collar or sleeves that some women used remodel their purchased clothes. Sandra, a former girlfriend of Olli with a preference for rock'n'roll, loved to add leopard skin imitation to the shoulders and collars of her blouses and jackets. Irene, the next girlfriend of Olli, loved to remake trousers and add zips, sew tartan miniskirts and add different details to her jackets. When I visited her, Irene was constantly sewing and remaking clothes or accessories. In the winter of 2010, I interviewed a woman tattoo artist, who had a new tattoo studio with a few other female friends. I noticed that her pink sweatshirt had several new additional details. She had added small ears to the hood, so she looked like a cat, and the hood had a new pocket and a few patches. Some of the girls enjoyed visiting concerts in self-made dresses where they generously combined black and red colours with leopard skin-replica fabric. For some reason, black and bright red are associated with heavy rock music, whereas leopard skin is related both to the rock'n'roll outfit but is also preferred by *Biedermädel* or flamboyantly dressed working-class girls in East Germany.

Women were overwhelmingly more experimental, combining sports, hiking and work clothes with boots or dresses bought in shops that specialized in underground fashion and used a bricolage-like strategy to express their individuality. Their visual expression was especially reflected saliently in what Moore (2004) calls 'the double quest of punk' – a quest for an authenticity and deconstruction. By combining different styles and kinds of clothing – punk accessories and hiking jackets, for example – they signal 'a quest for authenticity and independence from the culture industry', but simultaneously 'have turned signs and spectacles against themselves' (Moore, 2004: 307) by taking clothes out of their prefabricated context. Several commentators (Moore, 2004; Wolf-Meyer, 2006) find in such a strategy an element of irony where 'outside' clothes are turned into 'inside' clothes (Wolf-Meyer, 2006: 268). The latter is true, whereas the former is doubtful in the case of GiG regulars. People under study did not stick out with their extravaganza, their style was more designed to be insistently modest and anti-fashion, emphatically average and timeless. By looking at pictures, the style seems so static that it is difficult to say in which year these were taken.

The dynamics of haircuts was volatile and not exactly experimental, but people tended to change them all the time. The majority of men in the GiG circuit had a short cut, which could be modelled to a crew cut or small mohawk and then back. Few people had long hair and only one regular had long dreadlocks. Olli and a few others sported a quiff. Women wore their hair in different lengths and styles. Franzi and many other younger women preferred a 1950s-style ponytail, which could be remodelled into braids when necessary. At the beginning of the 2000s, some women tended to wear dreadlocks, but they ceased to visit GiG before I started my research. Shoulder-length hair was very popular, restyled or tied in a small ponytail at the owner's will. Women also dyed their hair more often than men, who – with two or three exceptions – seemed to be satisfied with their natural hair colour.

Hair and tattoos are important expressions of the individual style and therefore are carefully managed. Simultaneously, hair and tattoos are most difficult to hide when one has to participate in 'normal' life. Tattoos are discussed in Chapter 3, but it should be noted that due to the importance of day jobs to the 'GiG folks', people had to consider carefully how to find a compromise between the subcultural identity and the 'ordinary' look needed in their day job. For example, Wenke, a hairdresser, once told me: 'I need to look respectful. Some of my customers are conservative. That means I must put on something that covers my tattoos.' An absence of specific visual details was helpful when one wished to blur subcultural borders. In 2010 I had a discussion with Olli on why there seemed to be a sudden explosion in the number of young skinheads in Halle and Leipzig. One of his arguments, which I would carefully consider plausible, was: 'It is easier to pick up girls. You just put on trainers and you can go to a techno club.' Probably the reason is not always the opposite sex, but a more neutral haircut allows one to adapt more easily into another subcultural milieu.

Last but not least, several footwear brands like New Balance, Vans and Converse were preferred for different reasons, but a common factor was that punks in Germany tend to prefer 'old school' models, which in a street narrative are associated with the past styles of underground cultures – New Balance with football hooligans and the others with American skate punk. While trainers and skate shoes were favoured, Dr Marten boots (mainly eight to ten holes) could be spotted. However, boots were more popular among the GiG regulars who felt a stronger stylistic affiliation with skinheads.

CONCLUSION: YOU SHOULD LOOK AT THE DETAILS

At the end of my fieldwork, I attended a punk-rockabilly concert in one of Halle's underground clubs. Irene worked at the bar and for some reason we started to chat about styles. Suddenly she pointed at a girl who also worked with her and asked 'What do you think, who is she?', meaning obviously the subcultural identity of the girl. I remember looking at her carefully. She had a combination of a quiff and ponytail and wore a dark denim jacket with some unidentifiable embroidery on the back and tight black trousers. After hesitating, I responded: 'She's a rockabilly.' Irene started laughing, saying: 'She is a goth! You should look at the details!'

Academically, there seems to be a very careful reading of a group's style where the watershed seems to be an Adorno-lesque approach of the passive consumption. This position is eloquently illuminated in Dedman's discussion on British hip-hop and grime:

> Wallace and Kovatcheva make an analytical distinction between the terms youth culture and youth subcultures. The former is ' an element of media-conveyed culture of consumption' (Wallace and Kovatcheva, 1998: 154) whereas the latter possesses a more clearly defined sense of stylistic specificity. This is a significant concept here as it clearly divides the terms youth culture and subculture. Within the fieldwork, the distinctions within hip-hop and grime culture were clearly apparent. Another contentious distinction can also be made between these forms. Subcultures rely on the idea of agency and self-determination in qualifying their own sense of self. It can be argued that agency helps distinguish between the relatively passive consumption of rap music enjoyed by a significant number of the hip-hop audience, compared to the assertive, active, and creative participation engaged in by subculturalists. (Dedman, 2011: 511–512)

I believe that studies demonstrating agency in subcultural styles as a central marker are correctly captured as one of the essential characters of what

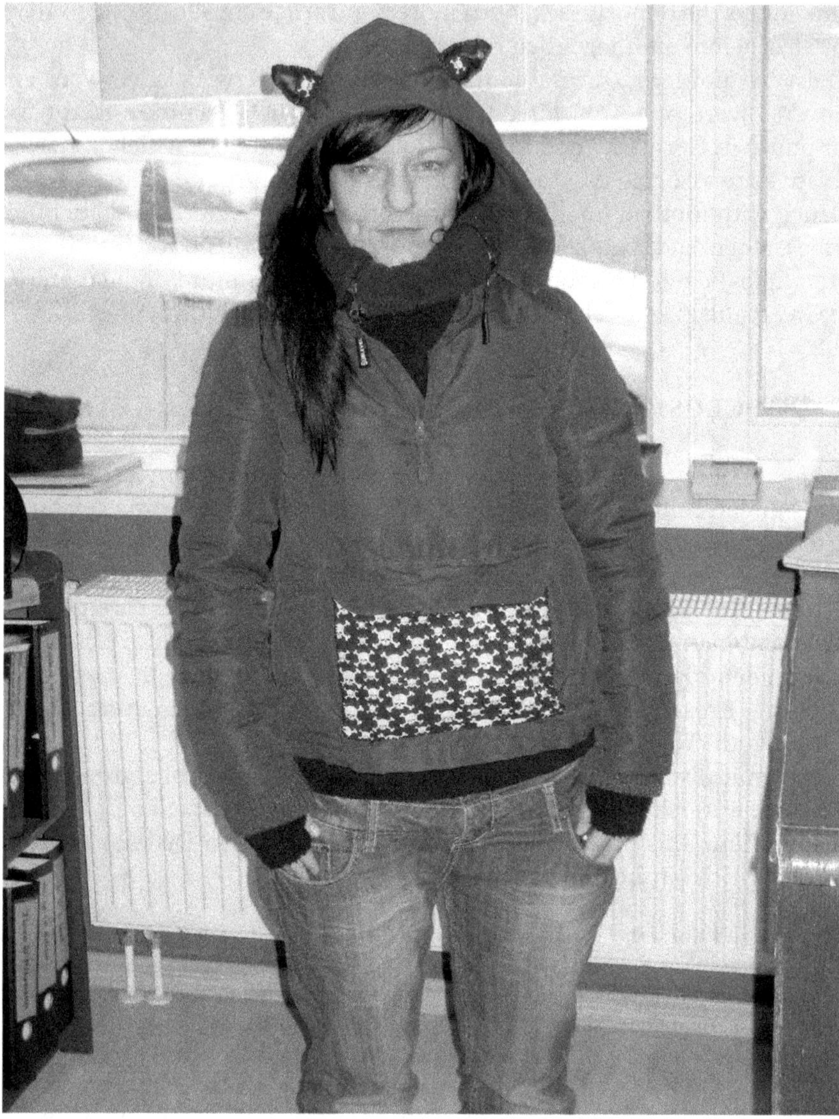

FIGURE 2.1. 'You should look at the details'. Photo by the author.

Paul Willis calls 'grounded aesthetics', which is an everyday culture created through imagination and active practices that the same author calls 'symbolic creativity' (Willis, 1990). Nevertheless, for some authors, the creativity of punk is gone. In a lament about the decline of the punk style, several voices have stated that punk suffered from 'hyperinflation' (Clark, 2003) because subculture 'freezes' quickly (Hebdige, 1979: 96), so punk became 'highly predictable' (Henry, 1989). This book questions such an approach. Indeed, punk is 'far more than a brief moment in popular music history or sartorial style' (Worley et al. 2014: 3) and there must be a reason why it attracts people. Punk in the form expressed in GiG has very little in the nature of a 'spectacular' subculture that more than often gains media attention (see, for example, Dedman, 2011; Hodkinson, 2011; Kahn-Harris, 2004; Nayak, 2006; Potter, 1995; Williams, 2011a). Visually the dominant style here can be defined as an 'emphasised average', some kind of 'anti-aesthetic' that 'rather ... [is] a critique which destructures the order of representations in order to reinscribe them' (Foster, 1983: xv). As described in Chapter 6, punk aesthetics challenges the dominant perceptions of 'normality' through creating its own anti-fashion. In a time where high-street fashion has become increasingly colourful and spectacular, not least through the designer adoption of 'punk' elements like studded belts, mohawks, leather jackets or 'PUNK' written in gold letters on a T-shirt, an option to distance oneself from this is to despectacularize the style. There is no doubt that mainstream fashion affects subcultural style, via a constant reshaping of shirt collars or 'classical' jeans models like the Levi's 501, but the 'symbolic creativity' also helps to combine from available clothes as nonfashionable a look as possible – hence the cult of the 'old school'. Therefore, the British motto 'Style before the brand' is also present in German underground punk. Most people I know from the Halle scene pay a lot of attention to their look just before stepping out, and look in most cases as if they were out of the fashion loop and therefore don't care. Discussing the fashion of independence in postcolonial Argentina, Regina Root (2005: 35) writes that 'the vocabulary of fashion made it possible to identify the ideology of the wearer', which in our case has unmistakable roots in working-class aesthetics. I recall a concert in one of Halle's underground clubs in the summer of 2009. Among the crowd, I spotted a young boy, no older than nineteen. He wore a buttoned-up checked Ben Sherman shirt not tucked in his baggy jeans, spotless new 'old school 'skater shoes and a black snapback cap. At this moment, I remembered that many people I knew preferred to button up shirts, as I have noticed in working-class districts in England. This person had a certain aura of 'earthiness' and reversed flashiness, where his whole outfit was new, 'clean', stylish and a monumental anti-fashion statement. This style is in opposition to the constantly changing working-class mainstream fashion of thick gold chains and seasonally changing pullovers, but, on the other hand, also shares the masculinity and a different style from that associated with students or middle-class Germans. The research on fashion shows that 'fashion reflects economic tensions' (Partington, 2014: 10) where 'unity is hidden under diversity' (Bourdieu, 1984: 95). Although Bourdieu in his *Distinctions* focused on middle-class taste, he acknowledged the 'class trajectory' of taste (ibid.: 105). The reading of *Distinction* induced some researchers to the interpretation of style as a distinctive 'invisible fence' to contour social boundaries (Gullestad, 2002; Manderscheid, 2006). In this respect, the style followed in the GiG group had certain qualities that bridged the local mainstream fashion, but simultaneously juxtaposed it. Local, rather middle-class student or 'hippie', proletarian *Normalo* and subcultural styles were in constant development where 'fashion codes were produced by consumers' (Partington, 2014: 7, 8) and in this interplay certain items were adopted, avoided or claimed. In a period during which I loved to wear baseball caps, I went to a concert with Olli. When we were about to leave his apartment, he looked at me and said: 'Lift the brim or otherwise you look like a young hooligan!' Indeed, I preferred to draw the brim deep down over my face, similar to what was often associated with young fashionable *Ossi* hooligans. On another occasion, I recall that when Olli spotted a flashy mainstream girl wearing a pyramid belt, he exclaimed: 'What is she wearing? She has no right to wear such clothes!' (see also Ventsel and Araste, 2015). Cultivating the 'predictability' as an anti-fashion statement combined with mingling it with various sports, skate or working clothing, punks around GiG created an 'inside style' that was a 'subversion of outside style through inside reflection' (Wolf-Meyer, 2006: 265). This helped people to manifest their working-class aesthetics while maintaining a subcultural identity. Several students of subcultural style have emphasized irony in such a 'double quest of authenticity' in punk (Hebdige, 1979; Moore, 2004; Wolf-Meyer, 2006), but this was very seldom present in the group that I studied. Appropriation of outside clothing was not ironic; rather, it was similar to the aggressive and quite serious claiming of outside clothes that were then 'subculturalized' via the addition of tartan or leopard skin fabric, patches, buttons and chains (cf. Sarabia and Shriver, 2004: 278). The irony of 'commodification of identity' through claiming certain brands (like Lonsdale or Fred Perry) (see also Sarabia and Shriver, 2004: 279) by an anti-commercial subculture was not an issue as long as these brands were exclusive and limited in use. The image, demeanour and vocabulary of a subculture (Brake, 1985) is homologically associated and then expressed by certain genres of music. Keith Negus is right when he states that we should be careful in relating music genres to certain identities (Negus, 1996, Chapter 4). The conservative backward look and manic DIY cult (see also Moore, 2007) helps to keep ska, Oi! and hardcore out of the mainstream music press commercial vs. alternative music axis. These musical styles were seldom mentioned or reviewed in numerous German 'alternative music' magazines, making them a perfect cultural platform of the proclaimed anti-fashionista. The audience, 'sharing the singers' opinion', 'converted' the lyrics into a symbol of common identity (Negus, 1996: 119, 122). Music is the factor that brings the irony into punk. It is difficult to make sense of songs glorifying alcohol, violence and what can be interpreted as sexism (see Chapter 6) when one ignores the fact that they were rebellious, protesting against mainstream ideas of decency and dominant left- or right-wing political discourses (Büsser, 2007: 127; see also Worley, 2012). Simultaneously, these themes addressed the ethos of a working class where masculinity is related to aggression, durability in drinking and sexual prowess. These qualities are also valued by women, as are the notions of self-control and loyalty. Music and style together formed a semiosphere (Lotman, 1999) of resistant protest where precariousness is made into a virtue.

Here we can return to the nonexistent alliance between techno and punk that Steve complained about. The remark was made at a time when techno was hailed as the biggest German underground culture that was simultaneously played in fancy clubs, involved a solid business ethos and was associated with the biggest open air festival of time, the Love Parade in Berlin. The visual style of techno was hedonistic, flamboyant, androgynous, designed and prefabricated. Musically, techno music was constantly moving, looking for new sonic expressions and technical solutions. Techno was the music that glossy music magazines wrote about in their 'alternative music' pages. In its connectedness to the commercial music business and stylistic expression, techno was a world away from what punk was successfully acclaimed to be – musically conservative, consciously affordable, socially cognizant and a purist grassroots style. There was and is no chance that these worlds can intermingle.

Notes

1. Quote from 17 October 2013 in Tallinn.
2. Needs (2005: 163–64) described how many fans did not accept The Clash's third album *London Calling* because of its more experimental and less straightforward direction.
3. David Schwarz (1997) dedicated a whole chapter to Oi!, where he describes it as a music 'produced and consumed predominantly by socially and economically marginal white men' and relates it directly with violence. Bohlman (2003: 54) correctly sums up the message of the chapter: 'A disenfranchised youth subculture coming of age in that culture turned to music that explicitly recalls the images of death and genocide. "Skinhead music" and "Oi" thrived in the subculture of the radical right during the 1990s, not simply providing texts for complaints about minorities competing for employment, but also instigating violence and memorializing it in forms eerily consistent with the century of unimaginable destruction.' In other academic texts Oi! is mentioned as a favourite music of 'neo-fascist' racist and misogynistic skinheads without going into this more deeply (Moore, 1993: 46–54; see also Shaffer, 2013). A notable exception is the work of British historian Matthew Worley (2012, 2013), who has published several papers about politics and street punk, arguing that most Oi! and classical punk bands from the end of the 1970s and begin-

ning of the 1980s were sceptical about both left- and right-wing politics, and showed little enthusiasm in allying with either side. In the meantime, nonacademic writers deny the direct connection between street punk/Oi! and skinheads, arguing that although skinheads were heavily represented in the audience, neither musicians nor the whole scene consisted solely of skinheads (Marshall, 1993; Mader, 1996; Büsser, 2007).

4. Gordon (2012: 13) calls it: '[A]n almost obsessive fascination with the Sex Pistols and Malcolm McLaren.'
5. Garry Bushell postulated that Oi! is 'harder music on every level, guitar driven, terrace choruses' (Petridis, 2010).
6. Within the punk scene, certain disagreement exists as to whether to use the term 'street punk' or 'streetpunk'. At a certain stage of writing, I consulted my colleagues from the United Kingdom and the United States, but also musician friends from Germany. The generally preferred term seems to be 'street punk'. Thus, 'streetpunk' is understood as a style for late 1990s American punk bands that were fast but not rough, often had mainstream commercial success and appeared pretty soft in comparison.
7. For example, Dropkick Murphys – 'The Gang's All Here', Trinkerkohorte –'Till Death Us Do Part' and Loikamemie – 'Oi! That's Yer Lot'.
8. The 2Tone label was established by the front man of the most successful ska group at the time – The Specials. Other bands related to the champions of the wave were The Selecter, Madness, Bad Manners and Bodysnatchers. Some argue that the sudden popularity of ska was linked to the decline of punk and the appearance of new revivalist subcultures – mods and skinheads – (Hebdige, 1987: 82–83), while others see British ska as being part of the punk revolution (Marshall, 1990). Nevertheless, many nonacademic authors agree that the unique moment in British ska was the shift from DJ-dominated club dance music to concerts of new dance bands (Black, 2011; Panter, 2007; Reynolds, 2005).
9. For some reason, I was unable to find academic studies on ska after the 2Tone era and outside of the United Kingdom. The exception is Traber (2013).
10. There are, and have been, several successful German ska groups in underground terms – Bluekilla, Butlers, Busters, El Bosso und die Ping Pongs, No Sports, Blechreitz and Skaos to name but a few. Many of the German ska groups have toured internationally, performing in underground clubs or supporting commercially successful German pop acts at home. The only group that seems to have really 'made it' is a poppy ska-punk group Sondaschule and the artist Dr. Ring Ding, who began his career as a musician and a singer in ska bands and then moved on to dance hall reggae. Dr. Ring Ding still periodically records new ska albums.
11. There have been several attempts to merge ska with electronic music – see, for instance, a sampler '21st century ska' (Free Radical Sounds Records, 2001) – but these records were quickly forgotten. I can vaguely also recall a concert of the group Big 5 in the late 1990s, whose mix of metal and ska was so unconvincing that they were booed off the stage.
12. There is lots of evidence that the Rude Boy look was consciously created and cultivated by Two Tone bands, especially by Jerry Dammers, the frontman of The Specials. Dammers' goal was to develop a youth movement with a distinctive identity, based on music, politics and outlook (see Panther, 2007: 68, Reynolds, 2005: 289, see also Marshall, 1993: Chapter 4; Marshall, 1990; and Black, 2011).

13. The Business – 'Guinness Boys', Menace – 'Live for Today', Pöbel und Gesocks – 'Bier, Bars und Bräute' and Loikaemie – 'Trinkfestigkeit'.
14. Terror – 'Always the Hard Way', Sick Of It All – 'Fred Army' and Agnostic Front – 'Gotta Go'.
15. Minor Threat – 'Straight Edge' and Wolf Down – 'Stray from the Path'.
16. Groups like Terror or Hatebreed, for example.
17. Converse Chuck Taylor All-Stars Shoes.
18. Einsatz – 'Berlin', Pöbel und Gesocks – 'Ruhrpott', L'Attentat – 'Leipzig in Trümmern' and Kollateralschaden – 'Westend'.
19. The 'right' style of baseball cap is a complicated issue. Different forms of baseball caps are associated with different music styles and respective subcultures. The accepted form and colour of the baseball cap also depends on the constantly changing mainstream fashion that, on the other hand, utilizes underground fashion. By the beginning of the 2000s, in Germany so-called *Vollcap* (full cap) was in fashion. It differs from the *Basecap* (baseball cap or base cap) with the closed backside. While on a classic base cap, the wearer can adjust the size of the cap using a strap at the back consisting of two pieces of plastic that snap together, the *Vollcap* lacks this option. *Vollcaps* were categorically dismissed in punk and skinhead circles because they were seen as part of hip-hop style. A few years later, trucker baseball caps appeared and became part of so-called punk'n'roll style – a style that was later absorbed by one part of the hipster culture – wife-beater shirts, 1950s tattoos, key chains and beards. These trucker baseball caps were relatively popular because some German bands from that decade sported the look. The snapback cap came to fashion in around 2006–7. This is a baseball cap with a large flat brim and the same adjustable strap at the back. This cap is regarded as too mainstream fashion and/or hip-hop and my informants in GiG avoid wearing it.
20. I describe the official narrative of these brands and its subcultural reflection in Ventsel (2014). Fred Perry is widely believed to be established by a working-class tennis player who was despised by his upper middle-class contemporaries because of his origins. Lonsdale as a brand was established by a nobleman, but was mainly associated with boxing, an extremely masculine working-class sport. The adoption of Ben Sherman is somewhat more complicated. As a brand, it was never especially working-class-related, but was aware of its skinhead following. Ben Sherman advertisements include skinheads from the 'classical' skinhead era. Moreover, the brand seems to be 'unchanged', i.e. they make a conscious effort to produce shirts, cardigans, pullovers or even suits in a 'classical' 1960s 'mod style'.

CHAPTER

3

OSTPUNK – ARBEITSLOS UND STOLZ! (UNEMPLOYED AND PROUD!)

> Do you remember during the time of the GDR we received parcels from Western relatives? When you opened them, there was this smell! Now we are in the West but the smell is not there anymore.
>
> —Nadine, 2010

The German elections of 1998 were somehow surreal. I had the feeling that too many nonsense parties were on the ballot. On the other hand, as a non-citizen I had always had very little interest in the elections, and the only reason I paid any attention was because for the first time, I had a TV set. I recall a television programme that reviewed obscure parties participating in the process, with little chance of making it to the Bundestag. For example, there was the Grey Party (Graue Partei), which represented pensioners and whose main demand was that rain and bad weather should be forbidden forever. Then there was a conservative Christian party Christian Centre (Christliche Mitte), which campaigned under the slogan 'For Germany following God's laws' (Für ein Deutschland nach Gottes Geboten). However, the main thing that attracted my interest in the marginal parties was that one of them was directly related to punk. The party was called the Anarchist Pogo Party of Germany (Anarchistische Pogo-Partei Deutschlands or APPD). During the research undertaken for this chapter, I discovered that the party had existed since 1981, when it was created by two punks in Hamburg, and had hovered for decades on the fringe of Germany's political landscape, before suddenly appeared on our horizons in 1998.

During these elections, the APPD was very active all over Germany, organizing free concerts with the most popular ska and punk bands to promote its cause. According to German law, a party that gains 0.5% of votes receives compensation for money spent on the election campaign. The APPD promised that if it received this money, this would be spent on free beer for its supporters. It came up with absurd slogans that did not seem to make sense. Its most popular promotional slogan, decorating various T-shirts and badges, was 'Work is Shit!' (Arbeit ist Scheiße!). Another very popular APPD promotional line was 'Stupidity Is Not a Crime!' (Dummheit ist kein Verbrechechen!) and 'Boozing, boozing!' (Saufen, saufen!). To my mind, the most popular APPD T-shirt of the era sported the message 'Antisocial Elements to the Power!' (Asoziale an die Macht!). The APPD was not only a party of absurd slogans; it also tried to link a political programme to its slogans. For example, the party advocated a *Jugendrente* (youth pension) for young people over the age of eighteen, arguing that because 'working is shit', everybody should be entitled to have a state-guaranteed income in order to avoid any contact with work. At the end of the day, the APPD received less than 0.5% of votes cast and the free beer failed to materialize.

In retrospect, the rhetoric of the party was so ambivalent that it was difficult to understand whether it was satire or a sincere attempt at political participation on a mainstream level. It should be mentioned that such ambivalence was unusual in German politics during this time. However absurd the programmes of the fringe parties were, they took it seriously even when everybody understood that forbidding the rain or similar demands were not supposed to become a reality. This is probably the reason why the APPD received more media attention than all the other marginal parties combined. When the media exposure hinted that both journalists and the audience were confused, the potential electorate understood intuitively what was going on.

In the punk scene, people instinctively sensed what it was all about and enthusiastically joined in. APPD T-shirts became extremely popular, as were the 'election campaign events' with the accompanying tongue-in-cheek election speeches of the party candidates. In contrast to the serious manner of political posturing, punk has a parallel dimension of irony and mockery that came to the fore through the APPD. My guess is that the party would have had very little chance of support if its sense of irony and self-mockery was not widely understood and shared by people in the German punk scene.

When writing this chapter, I understood I was addressing an extremely unique and subtle topic. I had the feeling that while it is easy to understand the provocative stance of the APPD, it is an altogether trickier thing to theorize and conceptualize. It seems that in the academic literature, there is a lack of tools to theorize tongue-in-cheekness in the subcultural landscape. The point of the APPD was understood in the German punk scene as a reflection of something that also exists among 'ordinary' punks and skins – the hard-to-place irony and sarcasm where the outsider cannot tell whether it is serious or not. In academic discussions on punk, the 'success and failure' of punk is frequently linked to 'introducing new codes of dress and behaviour' (Cartledge, 1999: 151) and it often seems like the creative phase ended with the classical late 1970s punk era. To some extent, this is true: punk music, fashion and behaviours have transformed and changed in recent decades, but not in a radical or revolutionary way. Compared to the late 1970s and early 1980s, punk has barely initiated any stylistic revolution on the subcultural landscape in the way that it did in its 'heyday' (Hebdige, 1979). What this chapter shows is how the stylistic framework is used for a specific local cause, to address regional and social identities. Part of the punk movement has constructed a conservative stronghold for itself and this chapter shows that what keeps punk going is its insulation from the dominant society.

There are sociologists who have analysed irony in subcultures, but have failed to show its controversial and multilayered nature (Schiermer, 2014; Williams, 2011b). An ironic approach can in some cases be an expression of covert resistance and rebellion, as in the case of the Halle street punk scene. On the other hand, it is not always easy to say what the extent of the rebellion is and to whom it is addressed. Below I will share an excerpt from my field diary to illustrate this point:

> When I entered the Waschhaus café, I heard a noise and saw the owner dragging Bernt to the door to throw him out. 'And never come back!' she yelled after him. Pyro watched it with a smirk and, turning to me, he explained: 'Bernt does not drink on working days but then starts boozing at weekends. Then he becomes unbearable. In many pubs people make bets for how long he manages to stay inside.' (Field diary, 6 June 2010)

Why is Bernt, who is otherwise a lovely person, behaving in such a way and provoking conflicts? Why is this kind of behaviour seemingly approved of by his peers? In the sociology of subculture, there is a debate on whether youth subcultures should be deemed an instrument of rebellion and resistance, and to what extent the social class belongs to it (e.g. Bennet, 2011; Hesmondhalgh, 2005; Muggleton, 2005). In this chapter I want to go deeper into the side of irony and protest in punk rock and show how this can be instrumentalized as a strategy of passive resistance for a marginalized and demonized working class. Early British subculture theory directly associated subcultures with the above-mentioned working-class rebellion (see Hall and Jefferson, 1986), while later works rejected such notions (see Willis, 1993), arguing that subcultures are anything else but a working-class-based phenomenon offering a platform of protest against the dominant middle-class society's norms and lifestyle (Bennett, 1999; Hodkinson, 2011; Thornton, 1996). After more than two decades dominating post-subculture theory (Muggleton and Weinzierl, 2003), some scholars skilfully argued that in some situations, when talking about youth and their cultures, the factor of (working) class cannot be excluded. My position is – similar to those of Shildrick and MacDonald (2006) and Blackman (2005) – that it is too early to throw out the subculture theory and how it links to the concept of working-class resistance. In this chapter I will try to establish this connection and analyse how working-class alienation and resistance is expressed through the language of a subculture.

In doing so, I assume that we have to revise several theories and concepts related to subcultures and youth cultures in general, and for punk in particular. First of all, the reading of punk is too closely related to the reading of music, and especially with the British and US first wave of punk (Moore, 2004; Rapport, 2014; Sabin, 1999; Stratton, 2007).[1] Punk and its offshoots have changed and transformed in many ways during the twentieth and twenty-first centuries. Multiple styles have developed that are sonically and attitude-wise only loosely related to what is called 'original 77-punk'. Another important aspect is that modern punk in the Western world has generally lost the initial shock value that researchers and other writers love to emphasize (Haenfler, 2014; Hebdige, 1979; Williams, 2011a, 2011b). In its musical and visual expression, punk is no longer a radical and revolutionary movement, something that a few decades ago caused a moral panic. Moreover, punk subculture has become standardized in its music and style, and is an inward and backward-looking culture rather than something that can be related to the ongoing musical revolution (see also Bennett, 2006; O'Connor, 2008; Reynolds,2011; Sklar and DeLong, 2012; Thompson, 2004). These days, punk is seldom about changing or destroying the 'system', but more about keeping the 'system' out of the scene, or creating and maintaining *Freiräume* (see Chapter 5). Therefore, the emphasis on the nihilistic aspect of punk, which is so important in many academic publications (Bahrova, 2008; Baulch, 2002; Hebdige, 1979; Moore, 2004; Ward, 1996), is rather overstated (and in fact quite dated) and does not apply to many modern scenes. Yes, provocation is inherently a part of punk culture (and hopefully will be forever), but self-destructive nihilism is very atypical of most German skinheads, hardcore fans and punks[2] who were the subjects of my fieldwork. I would interpret their provocation rather as a joyful tongue-in-cheek, and often satirical, strategy of protest.

It is problematic looking at subcultures as a phenomenon of their own, existing in isolation from the rest of society. The reason is that the majority of students of subcultures are more interested in the local adoption of a transnational subculture than in looking at the local social, cultural or national element in this transnational scene (for example, see Pilkington, 1994, 1999; Pilkington and Johnson, 2003; Simpson, 2004; Yurchak, 1999). One of the main arguments of the British subcultural theory was that youth cultures are an expression of social conflicts of their parent culture, i.e. conflicts between the working class and the dominant middle-class society (see the theoretical part of Hall and Jefferson (1986)). However, in their work, the sociologists of the era detached youth culture from their parent culture. Apart from claiming that skinheads attempt to symbolically re-establish the decaying working-class communities they spring from (Clarke et al., 1976) or demonstrating that working-class girls followed fashion common for working-class women (McRobbie and Garber, 1993), there is a very little analysis on how British working-class culture is expressed through subcultural style and practices. One rare exception is the book by Paul Willis, *Learning to Labour*, which shows how social norms are transferred from one generation to another and how inherited working-class norms shape the understanding of resistance and rebellion among the youth (Willis, 2000). With only a few exceptions (Maira, 2002; Wade, 1999), such an approach is either missing or weakly represented in studies discussing subcultures of neglected racial or ethnic minorities (Alexander, 2000; Brigg, 2012a, 2012b; Glaser, 2000).

This chapter speculates on how and why *Ostpunk* (Eastern punk) can be a demonstration and manifestation of East German identity. I will look here at two sides of *Ostpunk* – *Ost* identity and subversion. *Ostpunk* itself is a contested term. It has at least three meanings: during the Cold War, it meant punk from the GDR – in that era, some alternative/punk record labels issued albums and samplers of punk bands whose tapes were smuggled out from the GDR. This music was referred to as 'Ostpunk'. In a wider sense, *Ostpunk* also means punk music from Eastern Europe, but this connotation is rarely used. *Ostpunk* in such contexts is more or less a musical reference, indicating that Eastern European bands have a different sound from their Western counterparts. Very often, the music of Estonian, Polish, Russian or Croatian bands is distinguishable from the rather canonized way of playing punk music in the West. Eastern European bands had a more hectic way of songwriting, a lower quality of recording and less musicianship. This was the case until the early 2000s. Another difference was the language, as many Eastern European punk bands sang in their native language, making their music even more exotic for Western listeners. The last and most relevant meaning is regional, such as the current punk scene in former East Germany. I understood the importance of that connotation when I was presented with a black polo shirt featuring a red label 'Ostpunx' embroidered in a design similar to the legendary Lonsdale logo. The present was produced by a short-lived alternative clothing brand from Halle and its purpose was to emphasize local, regional and subcultural identity (see Chapter 2).

A HIDDEN CLASS IN GERMANY

Before I discuss *Ostpunk*, I will provide a certain socioeconomic framework for the chapter. During my ten years in Germany, I came to understand that German society is very rigidly socially stratified, so rigidly that one can speak about a well-developed class system. Paradoxically, German society saw itself as rather egalitarian, where different social strata are well integrated with little or no class differences. This is already expressed in the public terminology. The word 'class' (*Klasse*) was not often used in a public discourse; instead, more milder expressions were in use. For example, in the 1990s and the beginning of the 2000s – to mark upper, middle or working class – terms like 'Überschicht' (upper layer),[3] 'Mittelschicht' (middle layer) and 'Leute aus dem Arbeitermilieu' (people from the workers' milieu) were employed. I always found the idiom 'milieu' in that context rather amusing because it has a certain romantic and positive connotation. The terminology had changed when I returned to Germany around 2009 for the second part of my field research. At the centre of the public discussion, new words had appeared. Middle class remained 'Mittelschicht', but the working class was indicated with the more popular 'Unterschicht' (lower layer/class) or sometimes as 'bildungsferne Schichten' (literally 'social layers far from education' or plainly 'noneducated'). Measuring class is problematic (Giddens, 2006: 305) and this can be especially tricky in Germany, where officially social groups are measured in terms of income rather than their social identity. By some calculations, members of the middle class earn 80–150% of the median income and this group comprises approximately half of the German population.[4] Statistically, Germans are divided into different 'income classes' (*Einkommensklassen*) and no clear consensus exists as to where the line between different classes should be placed.

Nevertheless, there does exist a social identity that is expressed in terms of class and by a different lifestyle, level of education, position in the labour market and in all the aesthetics that Bourdieu defines as taste. The social distance between the middle and working classes in Germany is visible and largely geographical, where all cities are divided into more or less respectable districts, wealthy areas and ghetto-like concrete suburbs. This division is especially observable in the east of Germany and especially in Halle. In Halle, there are old socialist concrete districts (so-called *Plattenbautenbezirke*), which are more or less exclusively populated by the working class and increasingly by people drawing social benefits. In contrast, there are the districts of private homes or inner-city old apartment houses that demonstrate the remarkable wealth of their inhabitants. Moreover, a very important status symbol in Germany is the car and by looking at cars parked on the street and the condition of the buildings, one can pretty easily understand the social status of people living on any street.

The social hierarchy in Germany is very well illuminated by one anecdotal case. In 2010 I visited my friends, a working-class couple, in Berlin. The wife was a caretaker in a kindergarten and she offered to show me her workplace. My impression of the kindergarten was that it was cosy and friendly. When I visited them a few months later, she told me that her colleagues had asked her who the visitor was. 'When I told them that you are a friend of mine from Estonia and a scholar, they made big eyes. "How you know such people?", they asked.' When I told the story later to Olli, he shrugged his shoulders and said: 'Here, simple workers [*Arbeiter*] don't communicate with people like you.' Thus, stratification can most simply be defined as structural inequalities between different groupings of people (Giddens, 2006: 296).

Chapter 1 gave a short overview of the restructuring of Eastern Germany's economy and society after the *Wende* and its consequences. A commonly observed result of the process was the increase in unemployment. This was also the case in Halle, where the former manufacturing town suffered rapidly from deindustrialization. When I visited the city for the first time in 1996, my strongest impression was that Halle is grey – the old eighteenth- and nineteenth-century buildings dilapidated, the socialist-era blocks were not in great shape and people looked, as my friend said, 'voll im Osten' (fully Eastern German, in this connotation referring to the socialist era). When I began my Ph.D. in the town in 2000, it seemed like the city had not improved. To my surprise, a large number of residents still drove Trabants and Wartburgs, both East German socialist-era cars, which in Berlin were driven only by freaks as a sign of their alternative lifestyle. The greyness was still there, yet now one began to find small picturesque alternative shops, bars and venues in backyards and small record shops in the old town, which all made the city's atmosphere more joyful. Economically, however, things were far from perfect. Halle's local construction industry took a battering at the end of the 1990s, when German building giant Holzman went bankrupt. The company declared its insolvency in 1999 and was supposed to fire 25,000 employees. At the last moment, the then Chancellor Gerhard Schröder interceded and convinced creditors and banks to work out a recapitalization plan. Schröder created a huge publicity stunt out of his participation, making speeches to Holzman workers in front of television cameras ('Schröder was even in Halle, but it did not help much!', said Olli bitterly). The Chancellor could only postpone the bankruptcy for a few years and in 2002, Holzman ceased to exist.[5] The insolvency had a huge

FIGURE 3.1. Working class: Olli and Thomas. Photo by the author.

impact – many of Halle's small construction companies were connected to Holzman and they lost substantial revenue. Olli's private firm was hit deeply, resulting in bankruptcy, and Olli ended up being in debt to many of his friends (see Chapter 4). The Holzman bankruptcy did not help to improve Easterners' opinion of the *Wessies* and it also contributed to the image of the *neue Bundesländer* as a region of scroungers. In November 2012, after the end of my fieldwork, the unemployment rate of Saxony-Anhalt was the fourth-highest in Germany,[6] while the official unemployment rate in Halle was in the same month nearly 11% of the working population, accompanied with 17.2% underemployment.[7] In reality, the numbers are much higher because German statistics excludes the unemployed who participate in various re-education programmes (*Umschulung*) or people engaged in so-called short-term employment (*Kurzarbeit*). Both are interesting strategies for how to reduce unemployment figures. I am sure the motivation behind the retraining or other measures was laudable, but the results are questionable.[8] In cases where jobs are literally not available, the professional retraining did not help much. I have met people who became qualified in four or five professions, mainly low-skilled jobs, like a restaurant waiter or assistant teacher for the kindergarten, but were nevertheless unemployed.

One important factor that impacts social mobility and fosters social segmentation is the German school education system. As with many such things, the structure of the school system in Germany is democratic and egalitarian, yet in reality it mirrors the general social fragmentation. Under the current law, children go to school according to the district they live in, and there is very little their parents can do to choose between schools. Therefore, in theory children from different social strata go to the same school when they happen to live in the same district. However, in 2006, the OECD Programme for International Student Assessment (PISA) published study results stating that 'in Germany and the partner country Bulgaria, variation in performance between the schools in which 15-year-olds are enrolled is particularly large, about twice as large as the OECD average between-school variance' and 'in Germany, about three-quarters of the difference in student performance across schools is accounted for by socio-economic factors' (PISA, 2006). According to the OECD, Germany has above-average strong socioeconomic disparities (*Sozioökonomische Disparitäten*) when it comes to school education, and in the German school system there exists a strong correlation between the educational achievement of students, the quality of school and socioeconomic indicators of the parents. To put it plainly, in Germany, the children of wealthy parents tend to go to a well-equipped school with good teachers. Therefore, the results of such students are far better than those of schools where pupils are from a less affluent background and who go to a school that often lacks good teachers and money. The quality and problems related to school education have been a topic of conversation with my informants and friends, especially those I have known for a long time. I have known some of my friends long enough to have witnessed how they raised their children and sent them to school. From our conversations, I learned that the apparently democratic German school system has its hidden tricky side. One watershed that impacts on the social mobility of young people is whether the parents are able to afford to hire a private tutor, which many people argue is necessary to guarantee that the child passes exams and is accepted into a gymnasium. This factor, in terms of being decisive in children's educational progress in the school is also mentioned in the PISA 2006 report.[9] The OECD study also reports that 'funnelling some students to more academic secondary schools and others to vocational schools' is something that cements social segmentation in Germany[10]. According to other studies, German 'lower-class' students tend to receive a worse education than middle- or upper-class students, which also affects their chances of achieving a successful career (Jugendstudie, 2010; Lenz, 1995; Schubarth and Speck, 2010). Due to all these reasons, OECD reports have demonstrated for several years that Germany has had one of the lowest, if not the lowest, levels of social mobility among the OECD countries.[11]

APPEARANCE OF THE PRECARIAT

One symptom of low social mobility is the rhetoric related to the precariat (*Prekariat*). When I returned to Germany in October 2010, this was the word of the season. I do not remember the word 'precariat' being widely used before that year, but suddenly it was on TV talk shows, in respectable journals like *Spiegel* or *Focus* and in the newspapers.

The word *Prekariat* also started appearing in academic studies. The patronizing tone that some of these studies employ is surprising. The reading of various German academic works confirms the impression that the unemployed 'precarious' working class is often seen as a passive mass of people who expect to be ushered out of their misery by state institutions (see Böhmer, 2005; Dennis, 2000; Engler, 1999; Fischer et al., 2000; Kollmorgen, 2005; Willisch and Eckert, 2012). Arguing that 'being unemployed is fate', studies directly accuse the 'lower class' of 'social fatality' and conclude that existing class differences are deepening, and they see very little chance for the 'lower class' to attain any upward mobility (Jugendstudie, 2010). One reason for the lack of prospects for the 'lower class', according to German sociologists, is the failure of 'lower-class' schools to teach their students the principles of *Leistungsphilosophie* (performance philosophy): how everyone in Germany is individually responsible for shaping their own future (Hurrelmann, 2012).

The discussion about unemployment in Germany was obviously biased: it was considered to be first of all a problem of the working class – or the 'lower class' – and is often linked with presumptions about certain moral qualities. The year 2010 also marked the occasion of another scandal. I arrived in Halle a few months after the scandalous book by Thilo Sarrazin, a former member of the Executive Board of the Deutsche Bundesbank and senator of finance for the State of Berlin, was published. The media was resentful of how in his book *Germany is Destroying Itself: How We Gamble with Our Country* (*Deutschland schafft sich ab. Wie wir unseres Land aufs Spiel setzen*), he described Turks and Arabs as genetically unable to integrate into German society. Paradoxically, what was completely ignored was Sarrazin's rant against the working class. Looking for reasons as to why Germany's unemployed were overweight and with a low education, he came to the conclusion that this is due to the inherited low intellect of what he called the 'lower class' (*Unterschicht*) or 'education-distant population' (*bildungsferne Schichten*) (Sarrazin, 2010: 175). Sarrazin also noted:

> Availability of 'cultural and social means' is an obfuscating expression. In plain German, this should be put [as follows]: those who only have 'small cultural and social means' (to use politically correct EU-speak), are not sufficiently intelligent, educated and stable in their behaviour. By this formulation of the EU, the poor, defined in this

> way, is disburdened of the responsibility for their situation and relieved of the moral pressure to try to alter it. (Ibid.: 113–14)

Throughout the book, Sarrazin argues that money received as social benefit is enough to buy healthy food (ibid.: 117), free time should be used for educating oneself and not watching TV (ibid.: 112), and that in Germany there are people who earn less than the unemployed receive from the state, but who nevertheless do not give up working (ibid.: 172).

In December 2010, I was told by a long-time unemployed punk in Berlin: 'Currently there is a new guilt complex [*das neue Schuldgefühl*] rising in Germany. People believe that when you have no work then this is your own fault' (field diary, 2 December 2010). There is no need to wonder why many people in such a climate of 'class racism' (Balibar, 1991), in order to escape from the destructive 'shame in poverty' (c.f. Chase and Walker, 2013; Walker et al., 2013), turn to a source with an alternative view of the working class.

German punk has a long history of glorifying the working class. Since the beginning of punk music in West Germany, there has been a regular supply of songs juxtaposing workers with the mainstream society and the state.[12] Partially, this is of course just copying stereotypical song texts of many American and British punk bands. In many cases, the 'cult' of the working class has been turned by some German skinhead bands into a cliché, but the fact is that these topics pop up regularly in songs.[13] In many cases, it seems that punk is, and has always been, the only voice that offered young people a positive interpretation of being working class, and this is one reason why it is embraced by many adherents.

SUBVERSIVITY

Germany is a country with a global reputation for its environmental policies. Therefore, in the early 2000s, a new regulation for bottles with a refundable deposit was introduced. One consequence of the law was that beer in cans almost vanished from shops and kiosks. One of the wittiest complaints about it I heard was: 'Thanks to this law it is impossible to be punk anymore! You cannot throw beers cans around!' Years later, I discovered an ambiguity in this statement. Breaking norms is considered to be an essence of punk globally. One of the most popular slogans in the German punk scene is probably: 'Ich mach was ich will!' (I do what I want to!). Very often, the urge to break rules is combined with a provocation against the *Spiesser* (petite bourgeoisie) that is often expressed by a dress code, music and behaviour designed to offend the conservative Otto Normalbürger (Joe Public). Being drunk, brawling and throwing around beer cans are such forms of behaviour. However, this provocation cannot go too far. Smashing beer bottles is seemingly the red line one should not cross, because such a deed would provoke a more critical response from bystanders, a fine by the police and – last but not least – harm to the dogs of punks (see Chapter 7). In this way, we can say that punk provocation has its limits and does not rush towards a full confrontation with the state. In Chapters 4 and 5, I will demonstrate how punks try to avoid directly criminal activities in their shadowy business and in some cases even cooperate with law enforcement officials from the local police department. German punks, as my research shows, are surprisingly law obeying and only slightly – notwithstanding all the stereotypes they love to believe – law breaking. As will be shown in Chapter 5, punk is placed within the existing social and legal framework and does very little to contradict it.

Therefore, one strategy to rebel and show resistance to the lifestyle of the dominant society is what I would summarize as different forms of subversive practices. Such practices clearly demonstrate a certain deviation from the general norms supported and nurtured by the *Mittelschicht*. One of the subversive practices is to apply irony to the degree where it becomes unclear to the bystander whether it is meant seriously or not. In the Russian tradition, this form of irony is called *stiob* or *steb*. According to Alexei Yurchak, *stiob* 'differed from sarcasm, cynicism, derision or any of the more familiar genres of absurd humor', in that it 'required such a degree of *overidentification* with the object, person, or idea at which [it] was directed that it was often impossible to tell whether it was a form of sincere support, subtle ridicule, or a peculiar mixture of the two' (Yurchak, 2006: 250). In another place, he writes that: 'One of the key characteristics of *stiob* irony was that its identification with its object was unaccompanied by metacommentary on its ironic procedure. In other words, *stiob* was a "straight", deep caricature that usually did not signal its own ironic purpose' (Boyer and Yurchak, 2010: 181). He uses the term 'performative shift' (Yurchak, 2006: 24–26, 74–76), 'a communicational turn away from constative (literal or semantic) meaning and toward performative meaning' (Boyer and Yurchak, 2010: 182). *Steb* practice is not limited to the politics of the APPD or to a seemingly lone maverick like the above-mentioned Bernt. First and foremost, the subversivity is expressed in song texts, but can also take other forms.[14] For example, in Halle and Berlin there was the well-known 'mafia boat trip' of Potsdam punks and skinheads, where once a year a group of people rented a boat and enjoyed their day dressed like American Mafiosi from the 1930s. I recall confused articles of the event in a local Potsdam daily. It was hard for the journalists to understand what the punks were doing and why, but the event was worthy of coverage. In this way, the controversial message is on public display and is performed in front of the rest of society.

Mocking general social norms and hierarchies is traditionally part of a subcultural ethos in general and punk in particular. In our case, the irony has been turned into the weapons of the weak, an easy way to show their empowerment. As James Scott shows, one important part in resistance is 'resistance as thought', the idea of resisting hegemony, something he defines as 'normal resistance' (see Scott, 1985: Chapter 2). Contrary to the argument of the post-subculture theory of scholars that dressing in youth cultures is a mere act of consumption, the outlook delivers the agency to the wearers (cf. Bucholtz, 2011; Lowney, 1995; Mendoza-Denton, 2008; Selfhout et al., 2008; Ventsel and Araste, 2015) because one of the easiest and most powerful mediums through which to convey a message is always clothing. This is an especially powerful medium in a conservative town like Halle. Many of my informants have complained that Halle is a place where 'you are constantly stared at'. Donning a T-shirt with a slogan 'Work is shit!' directly irritates Otto Normalbürger.

Working and not working are crucial issues in German society. In a period when unemployment is publicly thematized, the dominant opinion about people on benefits is that they are *Schmarotzer* (scroungers). In Chapter 4, I will argue that most punks do (or want to) work, because according to their working-class ethos, working and self-reliance are crucial for their self-confidence. The problem is that these people do not want to work at any cost, for low pay and in what they see as inhumane conditions. During my fieldwork in Germany, there existed several schemes directed at decreasing unemployment. One of them was the ABM measure, where the state paid the first six months' salary for a job offered to an unemployed person. One of my acquaintances explained how employers use this for their own benefit: 'I worked in a kindergarten, and the job was paid from the ABM programme. They wanted to hire me but I was told that "I must fire you because after your ABM position is over we must pay your salary on our own. It is much more reasonable to fire you and take another ABM-applicant".' Another form of employment was working for a *Lehnarbeit* or for a company that leased workers. This meant working for minimum pay without any control over where one works. Some of these jobs were tough, like preparing frozen pizzas on a factory line equipped only with thin gloves. Other forms of undesirable jobs were the more or less compulsory work placements in order not to lose one's social benefits. Namely the Arbeitsamt had the right to oblige unemployed people to work regularly for €1 per hour and this occurred when the applicant had turned down several job offers or was unemployed for more than six years. These jobs lasted several weeks and were mainly low-skilled manual work, like cleaning parks or public green areas. Therefore, tricking the Arbeitsamt in order to receive more benefits (free dental treatment, additional subsidies), but avoiding any obligations or engagement under such conditions was not seen negatively. Punk's ideological and placative anti-statism delivers a justification for these strategies, as will be demonstrated in Chapter 4, providing a flair of anti-systematic resistance to similar practices.

The reputation of unemployed people in German society is low, but punks turned it publicly into a badge of honour. Moreover, they address their position loudly, in an in-your-face way following the tradition of absurdity – like parading safety pins or controversial sexual garments publicly as the early punks did in the United Kingdom (Laing, 2015: 118). By deconstructing dominant power hierarchies through irony, punk establishes its 'culture or authenticity' (Moore, 2004) that in a hidden way supports the working-class values of its peer group.

The reversed roles where symbols of contempt are subverted and proudly worn as identity markers are tattoos. There are different academic ways to interpret this body art, but in the context of this research, tattoos were also very strong messages. The research for this book was conducted when tattoos were not in fashion and in the conservative environment of East German former industrial towns were signs of an outsider status. In small towns like Halle, inked skin was associated mainly with deviancy (criminals, bikers and skinheads) or proletarian chic. A very radical way of demonstrating both – putting them in one word *Assi* (asocial) – was to have neck and especially facial tattoos. The latter were less widespread than the former and I have encountered it more among skinheads. Having a facial tattoo crosses the line of general acceptance and irony. In Germany, this is a sign that the person has forever given up the possibility of having a respectable position in mainstream society. Therefore, it is no wonder that I have seen facial tattoos on the musicians of mediocre but more radical (loud and hard with respective lyrics) skinhead bands. A facial tattoo is a direct challenge of the societal pact of complying general social norms and focusing on improving one's social status.

OST-IDENTITY

The phenomenon called *Ostalgie* started in the early 1990s, only a few years after the fall of the Berlin Wall. Paradoxically, East Germans, who in 1991 enthusiastically threw out GDR foodstuffs and abandoned their socialist-era plastic Trabant cars, began to miss it all only a couple of years later. *Ostalgie*, or a yearning for a disappeared state and its culture, is not what *Ostpunk* is about. When I have spoken with my informants, the period they speak about with nostalgia in their voice is the *Wende*, a time when 'everything was possible'. This is the golden age for many punks of the older (thirtysomething) generation, not the socialist era. Punks in Halle do not yearn for the lost state of the GDR and its culture. Nor have I noticed any *Ostalgie* practice among punks from Halle, Potsdam, Dresden or Berlin. With the exception of a few people who still possess East German-era amps for domestic music consumption, my informants do not have utensils from the GDR and make no effort to obtain them. None of the punk clubs I have seen is designed in a fake socialist-era style (cf. Rethmann, 2009) or has any hint of a GDR past. On the other hand, the GDR coat of arms and flag is displayed openly as a sign of regional pride and also as a provocation. T-shirts illustrated with this symbol can be purchased in punk festivals' merchandise shops and I have seen the flag decorating many private homes of Halle and Potsdam punks.

The semantics of the word 'Eas' or 'Eastern' is very confusing in East Germany. The word *Ossi* is clearly prerogative, whether *Osten* (East Germany) or *vom Osten* (from the East of Germany) is pronounced with pride. Again, I remember using the combination 'voll Osten' (it looks like in the East) caused the feeling of being offensive to my discussion partners. There is a controversy that is difficult to explain constructively. A good example is a controversial discrimination case from 2010, where an East German woman was not given a job in a West German company. After employment was denied, the application documents were returned to the woman with the handwritten remark 'Ossi'. The case was leaked to the media and caused a scandal.[15] On the other hand, I documented a phrase that shows the pride of the GDR heritage that distinguishes East Germans from West Germans: 'In *Ostzeiten* ['eastern times' or the time when the GDR existed as an independent state] we learned to use all materials and tools, to make something out of nothing due to the constant lack of everything. This is what *Wessis* cannot do' (Oliver, interview, 14 October 2006).

The word *Ossi* is historically charged with an emotional burden (see Chapter 1) depicting a backward and underdeveloped the Other who turns up in 'normal' society – the capitalist and democratic FRG – and demonstrates his or her partial inability to participate fully. The word *Osten* gives a framework to a local patriotism, filled with necessary content.

Not without reason is modern East Germany but also the GDR called *die Zone* (the zone) by *Ostpunks* in a tongue-in-cheek manner, and therefore in a same manner is the *Ostpunk* referred to as *Zonenpunk* (see also Westhusen, 2005a). The word derives from the Cold War-era rhetoric, where the GDR was called the *Ostzone* in the West German media. The connotation is a reference to the tough life in a socialist country where people had to make more effort to have a decent life in what scholars call an economy of shortage (see Verdery, 1993). The informants of this book are too young to have struggled with the notorious shortage of goods in the socialist East Germany, but they utilize the narrative to create their own identity.

In Germany, local identity is very important. It leans on local dialect, food and beer, but also memories and narratives that tie people to a particular place, and this is also adopted into punk. Not dissimilar to the classical British Oi!, German skinhead and punk cultures also cultivate local and regional patriotism and deliver a template and framework for the *Ostpunk* (see also Ventsel, 2010). In Halle, relatively important to local punk identity is the relation to things that symbolize the 'earlier times' (*wie früher*). Interestingly, these symbols were only a few bakeries, butchers and restaurants that offered the same menu in the same facilities as before the *Wende*. Gudeman (2008: 35) states correctly that '[c]ommunity usually keeps emblems that stand for its presence and identity', and the East German punk scene is a good example of how the present identity is defined though the past and the 'earlier times'. Elisabeth Peacock (2012: 214) writes about the Ukrainian youth discourse of the urban and rural places referring to Vanderbeck and Dunkley (2003):

> Young people are not immune to the role that public discourses about place can have on their social identities, as '[their] narratives of identity often reflect public narratives which construct hierarchies of places.' (Vanderbeck and Dunkley, 2003: 242)

Studies on punk and other alternative rock scenes in former socialist countries have discussed the increase of anti-capitalist and anti-establishment sentiment as a reaction to Westernization (e.g. Bahrova, 2008; Muršić, 2009). However, East German punk anti-establishment ideology is not vented against a vague and impersonal 'West', but often at a very concrete target – *Wessis* and their 'Transition-winner' peers in East Germany. In this, punks are not alone.

The neglect is mainly economic, but is also linked to other spheres. For example, in some economists' work, unemployment is automatically seen as an East German problem. Reading such works, one is given the impression that unemployment exists in Germany only in the eastern part of the country. Public opinion is often felt to be even more polarized. Berdahl (2011: 38) argues that East Germans were the 'Other' from the Western German perspective. In a similar vein, according to my interviewees, many of them felt like the Other in the reunified German state and not only was their Otherness rooted in cultural differences, but their alienation was also caused by the negative emotions about their own prospects in an unjustified, economically disadvantaged position in German society. One engineer from Potsdam expressed this dissatisfaction very clearly: 'There is no reason for lower wages in the East. Living costs are the same if not higher here. *Wessis* just take advantage of the fact that people in the East [Germany] have no work!' (personal communication, September 2006).

This comment was made in 2006, but a few years later, in Halle, where I had heard very little about the *Ossi–Wessi* conflicts, one night in GiG, I overheard a young women next to me at the bar discussing some issues and finishing with a loud 'Scheiß Wessis!' (Damn *Wessis*!) I was quite surprised that her tirade was followed by negative comments about West Germans. Later in the kitchen of the Max Planck Institute for Social Anthropology I asked the opinion of one of my German colleagues about why these old sentiments had re-emerged. Her response was short: 'The wage gap between the East and West [Germany] is growing again.'

In her studies in the remote villages of Kyrgyzstan, Judith Beyer came to the conclusion that being 'abandoned by the state' has not led to disempowerment, but rather to a development of alternative common-sense ideology (Beyer, 2015: 80). The research on gangs shows that when many people are denied a career path according to the rules and ideals of the dominant society, they establish their own world where these rules are turned upside down (Anderson, 2007; see also Cohen, 1955). The students of the state stress that the state is foremost an idea (Graeber, 2004, and Abrams, 1988, in Beyer, 2016: 60) and Berdahl's (1999, 2011) research on early post-Wende East Germany shows that *Bürger von neuen Bundesländer* (citizens of the new Bundeslands) experienced difficulties in adapting to this ideology.

I was in GiG when I heard one skinhead girl complaining: 'Everybody says that I am not stupid. But the company never promotes me, always these new middle-class employees. Despite all the training courses I am never educated enough.' This complaint related directly to what another of my friends and informants told me. 'Sure class differences are getting deeper', said a mother, and metal fan, with bitter irony: 'We as the "lower class" ... if it is up to the rich, we stay where we are. To them, this is our place.' It is widely believed by German working-class people I have spoken to about the issue that there exists a belief among the more affluent strata that low-paid or unemployed people do not deserve better. The punks who were the focus of my study share the anti-West German sentiments of their social peer group (Ventsel, 2012), but are also frustrated by the direct and indirect social discrimination. There is a logic as to why these punks have formed what Appadurai calls a 'community of sentiment' (Appadurai, 1990) in a situation where Germany's reunification is annually celebrated as a historic victory over alien communism. This situation offers itself as a symbol for provocation and direct dissent – this is the *Ost*-identity expressed with a proud display of the GDR coat of arms.

CONCLUSION

The *Ostpunk* way is a caricature of a 'culture of poverty' (Lewis, 1975) where brawling, being drunk, being 'asocial' and unemployed are manifested as virtues. Carolyn Humphrey writes about inequality in Russia: 'Inequality, in this light, is seen as something that can be produced by political emotions and discursive practices, rather than as a fixed situation to be explained in terms of income disparities, unequal rights, or structures of exploitation' (Humphrey, 2001: 332). Having conducted fieldwork both in Russia and Germany, I would say that sentiments in peripheral former industrial towns are strikingly similar. In both places: 'The question addressed ... concerns the generation of a particular kind of inequality through practices of exclusion from a socio-political whole' (ibid.: 332).

J. Patrick Williams states that 'studying the behaviour of subculture participants and coming to understand how they make sense of their own behaviour will shed light on how resistant they think they are' (Williams, 2011b: 95) In their style and practices, an ironic emblematic emphasis on being lazy and asocial is combined with the quest for authenticity as a group outside of 'normal' society where personality and dignity are valued and recognized by other members of the scene. Some studies demonstrate that the members of the German working class are aware of their group identity and consciously juxtapose themselves with higher social groups (Dewe and Scherr, 1995). Unequal access to resources and the demonization of the 'lower class' accompanies the specific interpretations of working-class youth as a source of problems and who some scholars characterize as 'strangers in this country' (ibid.). German 'lower-class' people are the new 'dangerous class' (Standing, 2014) that is unable to manifest 'getting on' and 'getting in', and therefore is not 'fitting in' (Friedman and Laurison, 2019).

In the East German case, punk offers itself as a platform for the social ironic commentary of the 'lower class' to address issues like unemployment, lack of future perspectives and denial of recognition through subcultural and politicized regional identity. In his book on punk and politics, Matthew Worley (2017) shows that punk makes politics through music and the underground media. In fact, punk can be politics when it rejects classic party politics. Keith Negus (1999) uses the concept of 'articulation' to analyse how artistic individual identities and a sense of togetherness are created through music between the artist and the audience. The concept of 'articulation' seeks to explain how 'particular cultural forms become connected to specific political agendas and social identities' (ibid.: 135). In former GDR industrial towns, working-class youth and adolescents are targets for demonization based on their social and regional origin. In response, with the East German street punks, the 'new guilt complex' is articulated on two levels: as a member of the 'lower class' and through the regional semi-political identity of being *Ossi*.

Notes

1. This approach is rightfully mocked by Furness (2012b) in the introduction to his book *Punkademia*. Furness writes about the sloppy analysis of punk by academics and highlights ten 'tell-tale signs' that are often repeated in scholarly writing. These contain 'Little attention paid to punk scenes that fall outside the ostensibly holy quadrangle of New York-London-Los Angeles-Washington DC.' and 'An obsessive fascination with the Sex Pistols and Malcolm McLaren' (ibid.: 12–13).
2. When writing about my critical position on the academic concept of punk nihilism, I recall a discussion I had late in the 1990s with one of my friends, whose background was rather goth. He told me that Autonomen and squatters were nihilists and justified it by referring to the lifestyle of these people. Autonomen in English are better known as anarcho-punks and while there exists some impressive research on their politics and music (Cross, 2010; Drissel, 2011; Lohman and Worley, 2018; Worley, 2017), their lifestyle has not been studied. The interesting argument of my friend was that anarcho-punks have a self-loathing of their own bodies, which is expressed through wearing thick black clothing all year round, even in summer. Summers in Berlin can be hot and I always wondered how could Autonomen – dressed usually in black hooded sweatshirts, with black US army coats over these – bear the heat of over 30°C. One thing is for sure – such a dress code means commitment to the cause and to a certain extent, without evidence to the contrary, this behaviour is indeed nihilistic.
3. In reality, the upper class in Germany is very discrete and therefore the term is not in wide use. The upper class in Germany is considered to be the uber-rich, partly hereditary nobles. This group of people lead very separate lives and only seldom appear in the public discourse, and then more often than not in the tabloid press or on certain specific television programmes.
4. http://www.arm-und-reich.de/verteilung/mittelschicht.html (retrieved 5 March 2020).
5. See https://www.focus.de/finanzen/news/tid-13685/firmenpleiten-holzmann-erst-schroeders-rettung-dann-der-konkurs_aid_381365.html (retrieved 5 March 2020).
   www.pub.arbeitsagentur.de/hst/services/statistik/000000/html/start/karten/aloq_land.html (retrieved 5 March 2020).
6. www.pub.arbeitsagentur.de/hst/services/statistik/000000/html/start/karten/aloq_land.html (retrieved 5 March 2020).
7. http://statistik.arbeitsagentur.de/Navigation/Statistik/Statistik-nach-Regionen/Politische-Gebietsstruktur/Sachsen-Anhalt/Halle-Saale-Stadt-Nav.html (retrieved 5 March 2020).
8. A year or so after I finished my fieldwork, I met an official of the Arbeitsamt at a conference. One night, we had very interesting discussion where we compared views from both sides of the desk – meaning the desk in the Arbeitsamt where the official

sits, with the unemployed person on the opposite side. He told me clearly that 'the purpose of the *Arbeitsamt* is not to provide people with jobs, but to decrease the unemployment statistics' and that 'of course, we know how people cheat in order to get more social benefits, but there is no human resource to fight it'.

9. *Deutschland gehört zu den Ländern in denen der Zusammenhang zwischen dem außerschulischen naturwissenschaftsbezogenen Engagement der Schülerinnen und Schüler auf der einen Seite und ihrem sozioökonomischen Hintergrund auf der anderen Seite besonders ausgeprägt ist.* 'Germany belongs to those countries where the correlation between the students' extracurricula engagement in natural sciences and their socioeconomic background is especially well marked.' The situation has improved modestly. The official OECD report of the PISA results from 2015 states that: 'As in the majority of OECD countries, a more socio-economically advantaged student in Germany scores more than 30 points higher in science (the equivalent of one year of schooling), on average, than a disadvantaged student (42 points in Germany). In Germany, 16% of the variation in student performance is associated with socioeconomic status, which is above the OECD average (13%). However, this relationship has weakened by four percentage points in Germany since 2006.'
10. https://www.dw.com/en/germanys-social-mobility-among-poorest-worse-than-in-the-united-states-oecd/a-44245702 (retrieved 5 March 2020).
11. Seehttps://www.dw.com/en/germanys-social-mobility-among-poorest-worse-than-in-the-united-states-oecd/a-44245702, https://www.fairobserver.com/region/europe/social-mobility-opportunities-particularly-poor-germany and https://www.theguardian.com/society/2018/jun/15/social-mobility-in-richest-countries-has-stalled-since-1990s (retrieved 5 March 2020).
12. One of the classic examples is Slime, with songs like 'Alptraum' (Nightmare), 'Yankees Raus' and 'Polizei SA SS'. The topic has been addressed by Normahl and Daily Terrot, political punk bands, and by Herbärds, one of the first, if not the first, West German skinhead band ever.
13. There is a long list of German skinhead and street punk/Oi! bands that tackle working-class-related issues: Volxsturm, Sondaschule, Emscherkurve 77, Eastside Boys, 4 Promille, Pöbel & Gesocks, Oxo 86, Troopers, Berliner Weisse and Stomper 98. In a slightly older song 'Ohne Arbeit' ('Without Work'), Volxsturm addresses unemployment. Somewhat newer but straight to the point is the song 'Arbeiterpunk' ('Working Class Punk') by the Eight Balls. Very much a cliché are a few songs by a very influential skinhead band from Leipzig, Loikaemie – 'Good Old Rich Kid Bashing Day' and 'Ich komme auf die Welt' ('I Was Born in This World'). Smegma, a cult band from the early 2000s, took it to the extreme and in their songs 'Oi-Punk' and 'Ich bin ein Skin' ('I Am a Skinhead'), where they emphasize a working-class pride typical of some mediocre English skinhead bands of the 1980s.
14. One of the best examples of how such an approach is a public irritant is a song by the German pop-punk band Die Ärtzte. By the end of the 1990s, the band released a song entitled 'Männer sind Schweine' ('All Men Are Pigs') and stirred up considerable protest and criticism from conservative newspapers. Because Die Ärtzte are immensely popular among teenagers, they been often accused of subverting general common sense and decency.
15. See http://www.spiegel.de/wirtschaft/service/diskriminierung-ossi-streit-endet-mit-vergleich-a-723605.html (retrieved 5 March 2020).

CHAPTER

4

ONE LAW FOR THEM, ANOTHER LAW FOR US

The Punk Rock Moral Economy

This is not the punk I know!

—Olli, reaction to reading *The Philosophy of Punk: More than Noise!* by Craig O'Hara, 1995

The material forming the centrepiece of this chapter is where my research on East German punk started in 2006.[1] When I told my colleagues that for the next six months I would study the economy of punk, then they all understood I was going to study punk rock as an element of the music business. I was caught off-guard, because as far as I understood it, the business in and around punk music was mostly run on enthusiasm and generated very little revenue for the participants. When I explained that I would be looking at how people make a living, it was the turn of my colleagues to be surprised. I explained how, in the underground subculture, probably very few people can make their living from music and so require another income, and this would be my focus.

This chapter is an analysis of how ideology, social structure and a subculture's economy are interlinked. My aim is to illustrate that a 'youth subculture' is more than a way of dressing, enjoying music and building groups that follow their own norms. 'Subculture' is also a social group with unique economic practices and social habitus[2] based on an anti-state ideology and inner solidarity, and this together embodies the meaning of punk for people. In this analysis I demonstrate that subcultures establish their own semi-autonomous structures within the state society and can be understood as 'semi-autonomous social fields' exercising their own moral economy.

In the most widespread sense, the term 'youth culture' is increasingly used in connection with youth groups who define themselves through a common music, a way of dressing and distinct social norms (e.g. Hall and Jefferson, 1986; Haenfler, 2014; Gelder, 1997; Muggleton, 2000). It should be noted that this discussion is all too often limited to the above aspects in the study of subculture, in the search for its ideology, identity and politics. Therefore, the approach of cultural studies and the sociology of subcultures seems to me problematic because other important issues for understanding the lifestyle of subcultures are neglected. I fully agree with the classical argument of Angela McRobbie, who wrote that:

> If we look for the structural absences in this youth literature, it is the sphere of family and domestic life that is missing ... few writers seemed interested in what happened when a Mod went home after a weekend on speed. Only what happened out there on the streets mattered. (McRobbie, 1980: 57)

My topic is geared towards the economy because subcultures are also social groups whose members have to earn a living, in most cases outside of the music business. Networks of like-minded friends within the subculture connect people of different professions and, as I will show, are reciprocal. Typical to social networks, transfer of information, distribution of resources and the exchange of services are central to the existence of networks (Castells, 2000; Chang, 2011; Cheal, 1996; Meagher, 2006), and here punk is no exception. The fact that the backbone of a network tends to be an extended and fictive kinship (e.g. Brandtstädter, 2003; Galvin, 2001; Leacock, 1954), also has parallels in the world of subcultures. Due to the importance of economic activities, social relations in studied groups are multiplex and create a 'multistranded' structure that covers several economic sectors with a view to having alternative access to resources (Mitchell, 1969, 1974). However, does this imply that a subculture makes and follows its own laws that are distinct from the state law, establishing a semi-autonomous social field, to use the concept created by Moore (1973)?

THE GENERAL CONTEXT

In this chapter I look at the links between two German cities: Halle, a medium-size university city, and Potsdam, the satellite suburb of Berlin. Formerly, both cities belonged to the GDR and all the people mentioned here grew up in socialist Germany. At the beginning of the 1990s, the alternative scene in the two cities blossomed. Squats mushroomed in both and were a platform for alternative clubs and bars. Contact between the cities was already common, as travelling to concerts and visiting friends was something already practised during the GDR. However, the travelling intensified after reunification due to the fact that the number of concerts and other social events increased. So, almost all the contacts between Halle and Potsdam that are relevant to my study developed after the *Wende*.

As mentioned in the Introduction, the alternative scene in the GDR had an extreme anti-state ideology and this continued after the collapse of Socialism (Kohtz et al., 2012; Westhusen, 2005a). Members of the alternative scene saw themselves as living outside of state law and structures; the squats in East German towns had for many years existed in a world of their own, successfully avoiding interference from the German state. Over time, with the state's control over the space (i.e. restitution of property) strengthening, squats as independent communes vanished (see also Chapter 5). However, the ideology, as I will discuss below, is rooted in this period and can be referred to as 'legal systems' that 'do not derive their legitimacy from the state' (von Benda-Beckman and von Benda-Beckman, 2001: 23–24), but from opposition to the state.

What remained from the early 1990s were numerous alternative clubs and bars in many German cities (including Halle and Potsdam) that still carried the legacy of the squatter world. Many of these places were former squats or were established by people who came from the early squatter scene. I have introduced GiG elsewhere (see Chapters 2 and 3), but a central squat-club for Potsdam was Archiv (Archive). Potsdam had many alternative bars, but only two clubs, most likely due to its proximity to Berlin, where people often went to concerts. The outlook and interiors of alternative clubs in Potsdam was similar to what I saw in Halle and did not differ from what everyone could have seen in other German cities at the time. Archiv took its name from a predecessor in the GDR era, because in the building was located the film storage of a socialist film company whose headquarters was in the city. The club hosted metal, rock, hip-hop, reggae and many other different events, but nevertheless the club was musically dominated by punk rock events, and punks, skinheads, psychobillies and hardcore kids were their main customers.

The focus of this chapter is on the networks of working-class men and their various employment activities in the 1990s. They combined their working life with the scene life, i.e. visiting concerts at weekends or after the work. Socializing within the scene, and buying records and punk and skinhead clothes were key aspects of their life. The people central to this study were construction workers with different skills and specializations.

Connected to them was a loose group of men and women occupied as car or bicycle mechanics, tattoo artists, computer specialists, hairdressers, social workers or hospitality workers. My informants were friends and belonged to a coherent age group (between twenty-eight and thirty-five), and it was common for many of them to be engaged in the informal economy. Many of these people were officially unemployed and received social security money from the state, while others topped up their legal income with illegal work based on opportunity and the network. During my research, I discovered that people who socialized actively at concerts and pubs also belonged to networks that were mainly economic in nature.

In Chapters 5 and 6 I describe the German *Stammtisch* tradition in GiG, and such a tradition also existed in Archiv. The *Stammtisch* groups in alternative clubs were 'close-knit intensive' relations, building 'clusters' within 'cross-linked' bigger social networks (Mitchell, 1974: 287–89). In practice, it meant that none of the networked groups had a closed isolated characteristic, i.e. people communicated with other people and by necessity transferred jobs and services to persons outside of their own immediate social network. It was common for an individual to be familiar with more than one group, which meant that he turned up for many *Stammtisch* in a week. Especially in GiG circuits, but to a lesser extent in Potsdam, cooperation and solidarity seemed to work within one generation despite their musical preferences. What was important was the subculture affiliation associated with the underground. In Halle, communication with older key members of the local hip-hop scene was very active, and also with some people who were more into techno and reggae music. As I was told, this was due to a common background and professional contacts. Punk rock people and hip-hoppers over the age of thirty were the people who started the alternative scene in Halle in the early 1990s. 'In those days, punks went to hip-hop parties and the next day gangsters [hip-hoppers] came to the punk concert', explained Olli, one of my main informants in this research.

A distancing from the state and a semi-legality expressed in cultural practices like organizing illegal hip-hop and techno parties were important unifying factors for people from different scenes. Pieps from GiG explained:

> I still know the older hip-hoppers. We were together in the anti-fascist political scene. It was at the beginning of the 1990s. And we listened to each other's music. Only later, both scenes became bigger and grew apart. But we still see each other with old friends. (Pieps, 2007, interview)

Due to the history of GiG, which was the oldest working alternative pub in Halle, it was the meeting point for many people who had joined the scene in the early 1990s. However, Potsdam was different when it came to cultural coherence. People in Archiv tended to socialize more with people who shared their taste in music or belonged to similar scenes. For example, while skinheads socialized not only with punks but also with fans of metal, I did not come across active contacts with hip-hoppers or other so-called club music scene people. The reason could be the proximity to Berlin, which had a much larger scene, representing multiple music styles. Close contacts within the same music scene in Berlin had already begun in the GDR era and this also meant that personal contacts with other music scenes had been always less active than in smaller towns where the scenes were more 'mixed'.

Common for both cities was that regulars of the same club saw each other as one group or 'crew'. In summer, the crew would often travel to big alternative music festivals, throw barbecues in the parks or organize events.[3] In this way, it was not unusual to gather 15–25 people for the purpose of spending time together.

Travelling to other German cities, especially those in Eastern Germany, was still common. In most instances, visiting friends was linked with going to concerts, continuing in this way the tradition of active communication with other punk communities. It was believed that different clubs had their own atmosphere and even when the same bands played, their concerts had a different 'feeling' in different places. For that reason, it was not unusual to drive to another town for a concert despite the fact that the band might have just played or were about to play in one's hometown.

NETWORKS AND RECIPROCITY

Travelling around the country helped to establish networks of like-minded people and in the following section I will go into the practices and ideology of a punk rock network. This ideology is generally acknowledged as 'common sense' that links to a certain perception of 'appropriate' behaviour and included 'common sense terms', obligations and expectations of the social relationship (Bird-David, 1995: 17–31; Godelier, 1975: 3–28; Goody, 1973; Moore, 1973: 719–46; Nuttall, 1992; Schweitzer, 2000; Ziker, 2002). Subcultural common norms and 'right' behaviour were important in maintaining the reciprocal nature of punk rock networks, in accordance with networks from other regions and settings (Willis, 1990; Frith, 1996; Connell and Gibson, 2003; Hebdige, 1979). Gudeman (2008: 40) argues correctly that reciprocity is related to a shared identity and, leaning on Lévi-Strauss (1969) and Sahlins (1972), is 'the glue of society and economy'. On the other hand, and as will be shown below, reciprocity is a 'risky venture' because it 'establishes mutuality', but there is a 'possibility of breaking it' (Gudeman, 2008: 41). Therefore, the goal of punk networks was to maintain trust and predictability in different life situations where the actors imagined themselves as outside of mainstream society (cf. Cañas Bottos, 2008: 108).

IF YOU WORK HONESTLY, YOU CAN GO TO SHITE!

Analysing networks in organized crime, McIllwain (1999) stated that central to organized crime were 'human relations'. He used the analytical categories of Wasserman and Faust (1994) of 'actor', 'relational tie' (relations between two people) and 'relations' to describe these 'human' relations. In this section I demonstrate how 'human' relations were established within the punk rock network, including social relations between single individuals and within the group as a whole.

As an example, I use the network in which Olli played a central role. This network was established over many years and became fully formed (as much as we can speak about completeness in the network building) in the following way – namely, one person, Kalle, moved from Halle to Potsdam. After doing different odd jobs, he finally decided to open a bar that combined an alternative ambient with petite bourgeoisie comfort. Kalle hired people he knew who were skilled construction workers, but due to the fact that he was short of money, he preferred to hire people illegally for less pay. In addition, he managed to get much of the work done for the *Freundespreis,* i.e. for extremely low pay as a friendship service. I will discuss the nature of these services below; the only thing I will add for now is that later Kalle failed to recognize the obligation this kind of cooperation involves and ended up in conflict with many of the people who helped to build his bar.

However, during the building and designing of the bar, many punks and skinheads from both towns, who came to the building site via a personal acquaintance with Kalle, also became friends with each other due to their common musical interests and social habits. After their working days, they spent time in Potsdam's alternative pubs, especially in Archiv. One of workers, Loofie, who was twenty-eight years old, not only lived in the house of Archiv but also organized concerts in the venue and was responsible for the management of the club's bar. From the beginning of the work on Kalle's bar, people started to travel within Potsdam and Halle at weekends, meeting other people from the local scene. After a while, this relationship embedded more and more economic features so that leisure became connected with the transfer of jobs, goods and services.

Because construction workers are at the centre of this study, it is necessary to describe some of the illegal practices in this business. The construction business is highly specialized. For example, painting walls and ceilings is considered one speciality, whereas laying pipes or installing toilets is another skill, all of which are learned over a long period of time. Therefore, in order to finish a site – whether a house or just an apartment – one needs several specialists. This is also another reason why the construction workers knew each other in the town in which they lived. They were colleagues who met on various construction sites, sometimes even recruited one another to complete building objects or advised their bosses to hire certain skilled specialists. As I discovered, there were extensive communication channels between construction workers of one city reaching beyond their working hours, and this communication created a lot of informal contacts. These informal relations between construction workers helped to form illegal working teams to complete illegal 'after working day jobs' that in Germany are generally referred to as *Schwarzarbeit*.

In the pre-recession autumn of 2006, there was a building boom in Germany. Landlords hurried to finish reparations or construction of their property before the winter started, but, as my informants told me, many property developers and landlords wanted to finish their objects before January 2007, when the new tax law increased the Mehrwertsteuer (VAT) and made building work more expensive. Therefore, it was a widespread practice that all construction workers with the necessary skills worked illegally on various sites after their official working day. And this applied not only to employed construction workers, who did illegal night shifts to earn some extra money, but also to those who were officially on social benefits. When I asked my friend Loofie why it was necessary to work this way, he replied: 'If you work honestly, you can go to shite!' (Wenn du eherlich arbeiten gehest, kannst du kacken gehen!), explaining that the legal work was enough to satisfy his primary needs, but the money for travelling, hobbies and leisure came from illegal work.

Another additional source of income in illegal construction work was stealing building materials on the official job site to use on the illegal construction site. The reason for this was that the customer usually had to pay a previously agreed amount of money for the construction material and work time, and by using stolen materials, the workers were able to earn additional money. To my surprise, the informal network of colleagues served as a supply channel for stolen materials. The problem is that all the necessary materials were not available on one construction site; therefore, builders communicated with each other when they were looking for something specific. I was present when Loofie got a phone call where he was asked to 'obtain' (*besorgen*) 1.5 metres of a particular pipe and he promised to have it by the next evening. In cases where it was impossible to steal the required materials due to more vigilant security at the building site, people who were in need were informed about the location and amount of the required goods, and these items were often stolen at night.[4] Such a 'transfer' between colleagues usually took place without money being involved and was understood as a 'friendship service', whereby the favour had to be returned at a later stage. There is an ironic factor concerning the theft of materials: as many of my informants told me, construction firm bosses were very well acquainted with the practice, and the costs of missing materials were usually calculated into the price. Apparently, in Germany, 20% of the price of every smaller building site – be it an apartment or a house – covers the possible theft of the construction material by workers and is paid for by the customer.[5]

In this informal economy, perhaps more important than the construction material was the transfer of jobs. As mentioned above, the construction work was highly specialized and to renovate a flat or house required workers with various profiles. Therefore, a person who was illegally hired had to contact his workmates and ask them to accompany him to complete the task. As in every network, even in the most egalitarian or 'anarchic' society, punk subculture has some group hierarchy (cf. Pospisil, 1973: 544–45). Certain leading persons – I will call them 'anchor persons' to borrow a term from Mitchell (1974: 283) – had an economically significant position affecting the redistribution within the network. In Halle and Potsdam, I met people who were central figures connected to the allocation of jobs. These people had built up their good reputation as honest workers, delivering good-quality work, and were constantly in demand from various private people, but also from enterprises for larger construction jobs. Such key figures can be described as the 'walking yellow pages' of the local skilled work force because they knew colleagues by their skills and were able to recruit building teams for a particular task. Workers were never constantly available, so the team leader had to know even more people to provide alternatives. Loofie in Potsdam and Olli in Halle were such 'anchor persons' – their good reputation was well known and their mobile phone number circulated around the town amongst people who needed to rebuild, renovate or complete their flats, houses, offices or shops. To be an 'anchor person' was a matter of personal pride because it also meant wider recognition of one's professional skills.

In relation to illegal construction jobs, there were also differences between Loofie and Olli, i.e. between employed and unemployed workers. At the time, Loofie worked officially for a small construction firm, which meant not only access to building materials but also that his time for illegal jobs was limited – only after his regular working hours and on weekends. Besides that, Loofie had to be careful not to turn up to such illegal jobs in his daytime working clothes (emblazoned with the company logo) or not use his company's van when there was a danger of being caught. As he explained, illegal construction work was followed not only by the tax office, but also by competing firms who would then inform the officials.[6]

Loofie was a skinhead and I quickly discovered that his professional and social network in Potsdam was composed mainly of skinheads. And besides work, they also met at weekends, when they travelled to concerts or football matches. I met most of this group one weekend, at the home of a sturdy and heavily built man I will call Maurer. Maurer was a bricklayer in his mid-thirties and had recently bought a house that all the friends helped to renovate. Loofie took me with him to ask if someone would be interested in a weekend illegal job at someone's flat. Later he told me that many such jobs were sourced by a Polish worker who lived in Potsdam and earned money with legal and illegal construction activity, and was rumoured to be building his own house in Poland with the money. To counter the stereotype about the generally racist nature of skinheads, Loofie once said: 'This Polish guy is a top fellow! He makes splendid work and constantly offers me some jobs. And he never cheats, you can always trust him!'

While Loofie had a steady job with a construction company, Olli was officially unemployed and received social benefits of ca. €620 each month. While doing illegal work, Loofie risked losing his job; Olli's risk was losing the state's social benefit money. Nevertheless, Olli worked as much as he could, and during a good month could earn an extra €2,000. He worked on private residences, for people who wanted to renovate newly bought flats or rebuild their private houses and were eager to do it cheaply, i.e. illegally. Some years before, Olli had worked for several small firms, and ten years ago he even had his own small construction enterprise that went bust when one customer refused to pay.[7] He earned his illegal income also doing jobs that were by nature legal. There he had developed various strategies for how to maintain his illegal status. For instance, he had a friend, Stephan, who sometimes needed his painting skills. When Olli worked for Stephan, Stephan altered the records to hide Olli's identity. Sometimes even private customers needed an invoice and for that purpose Olli had many friends who were working legally and were able to produce the invoice. A friend wrote a document under their own name, Olli received payment and paid the tax money of the sum to his friend. This strategy worked well and Olli never had any problems getting the official bill when needed.

Olli, like Loofie, had many friends he could hire for various construction jobs. Most of these friends I knew were GiG regulars. In this sense, GiG and Archiv functioned as illegal job markets where people met when they needed a job or wanted to hire someone. Due to his extensive involvement in the construction trade and being a former business owner, Olli knew the most important construction material wholesalers in Halle and was able to buy construction materials at a cheaper price. This was another reason for his popularity among customers: his services were not only good quality but also less expensive. Over the years, Olli became an illegal entrepreneur who was highly valued by his customers and also an appreciated employer for his punk friends.

One such friend was Ille, a forty-year-old man who always dressed very stylishly. Ille often worked with Olli and Stephan, and sometimes when Olli had other jobs replaced Olli with Stephan. Ille was also a painter and, like Olli, was a specialist in interiors, although he was not considered to be as skilled. Ille was officially also unemployed and, as Olli explained, he was a good construction worker, but lacked the necessary commitment. When extended overtime hours were required (because the object had to be delivered) or the need for a night shift (a very common occurrence with supermarkets, where almost all renovations are done outside of working hours), Ille refused to work. For smaller jobs when Ille was not able to accompany Olli, he used the help of Kai. Olli and Kai knew each other well and played in the same band. Despite their friendship, Olli was quite sceptical about Kai's working skills and even more so about his work ethics. He explained how Kai was someone who worked a few days when he needed money and then disappeared to continue partying. Therefore, Kai was considered by Olli and Stephan as unreliable and was only enlisted for short-term jobs requiring multiple workers.

Stephan is worth remarking on as he was the only one in the network who had no relation to the others via music or subculture. As mentioned above, Stephan was a small-scale entrepreneur who Olli knew from working in Stephan's company some years before. Stephan was greatly respected in the scene around GiG because he was a 'nice lad' who occasionally dropped into GiG for parties and was on good terms with the alternative people (see Chapter 5 on inclusion and community). Olli and his crew respected Stephan because of his extraordinarily sophisticated professional skills; it was rumoured that Stephan was one of the few who 'was able to conduct all construction jobs'. Olli and Stephan had a special relationship. Stephan not only provided Olli with jobs and produced fake invoices for him, but also functioned as a banker for Olli. The money Olli earned by working for Stephan remained on Stephan's account, and when Olli needed it, he called Stephan to take €100. In this way, Olli always had some extra cash, even when other sources – like social security money and income from other illegal jobs – were exhausted. And Olli was the best and most-trusted worker on Stephan's team, who was able to work (and sometimes this was necessary) sixteen or more hours without a dip in quality. In addition, Stephan knew that Olli prioritized working for him and was available any time he needed him.

Since Olli and Loofie met, they often travelled between Halle and Potsdam, combining weekend visits with illegal jobs – for example, when Olli required some materials from Loofie or Loofie needed Olli's professional skills. The usual pattern for such visits was to arrive Friday evening, go to a pub or concert (or both), and then work on Saturday, continue partying on Saturday evening and leave for home on Sunday. As Olli explained: 'This kind of work in Potsdam is like a short holiday. You don't have accommodation costs, you know very well what is going on in town. This [Potsdam] is like a second home.' Such trips occurred approximately every two months.

Reciprocal relations between friends in the network were multiplex. Reciprocity also included numerous small favours. Olli and his friends helped each other by fixing their private flats, and lending tools and vehicles was also common amongst friends in Halle. These kinds of small favours seemed to be spontaneous without anybody keeping a record. I observed that this long-term delayed exchange (Woodburn, 1982: 431–51; 1998: 48–63) did have rules, namely that you should not exploit your friends too much without reciprocating. This was illustrated in the case of Olli's cooker, which led to an argument with his girlfriend after she demanded that Olli ask Stephan for his help with their new cooker. After Stephan had installed it and left, Olli told her: 'But it means I have to work one day for free. You cannot take without giving!' The ideology of reciprocity behind the whole network was that services and favours both in and outside the immediate construction work were treated as equal and connected. As such, doing favours could be a long-term investment. When I asked Loofie why he helped Maurer to build his new house, he replied: 'One day I will have my own house and then Maurer will help me with renovating it.'

Reciprocity played an important role in the punk rock networks and according to the logic, there was a concept of the 'accepted and permitted' but also 'ruled out' behaviour (Pospisil, 1973: 546). Failing to understand the rule of balanced favours could have serious consequences. For instance, many people who helped to build Kalle's bar later avoided him. They explained to me how Kalle had forgot that they built his bar 'more or less for free', yet always charged them full price for drinks. Two years after the bar had opened, Kalle wanted to make minor renovations and asked the same people to come and help him. 'I told him, I have no time' was Loofie's comment on that discussion. The exclusion of a person could be a serious problem and consequently Kalle spent a long time looking for workers.

There is no clear concept of punishment in punk networks. In general, with the end of trust also comes the withdrawal of other people and silent social isolation. This ostracization could include not inviting him to parties or excluding him from work teams. This happened to N., a person who constantly refused to lend his tools to others. I was present in GiG when Olli asked him for a drill and N. only smiled and said: 'I don't have to lend it, do I?' Olli was very upset and never offered him jobs after this. Within a few weeks, Olli's friends slowly but consistently began to limit their contact with N., who was no longer invited to parties or other social events. Via withdrawal, the people in the punk rock network activate its multiple links to bring pressure to bear on someone (see Mitchell, 1974: 283). Although I tried to locate other similar cases involving such conflicts, I was unsuccessful. I want to finish this section with the words of Olli when we discussed the issue, which could have been taken from a textbook on social anthropology: 'The lack of conflicts shows that our network is close-knit and stable. It is good though!'

OTHER PARTICIPANTS IN THE NETWORK

After analysing the above-mentioned networks, it was clear that there were more people involved. The nearest friend of Olli lived directly beneath him, only one floor below in the same house. His name was Alan and he was an acclaimed tattoo artist in Germany, meaning he was good and that it was difficult to book him. Alan was quite an exceptional figure in the alternative scene of Halle. He was quiet and had more or less only three interests – his work, smoking weed and his python, who lived in his flat in a huge aquarium. Years ago, when Alan moved into the house, Olli helped him to renovate his new flat and built the aquarium (which had to be made from a special strong glass and installed with automatic heating). Olli worked on the flat for many nights and weekends, and with the completed apartment, the reciprocal relationship between the two was established. Alan paid for Olli's work with free tattoos and decorated his right arm. Furthermore, their cooperation continued with small but important services. Olli was very mobile, constantly in other cities either for work or concerts, and he often needed someone to walks his dog. Now, with Alan as a neighbour, he no longer had to think about it. Alan needed Olli's help and advice in dealing with bureaucratic matters, i.e. when he had to communicate with the landlord or other formal institutions. There were always small favours Olli and Alan exchanged without even thinking about whose turn it was to pay back the service. Olli explained it to me in the following way:

> You do not count everything in money. We are friends. Of course, you could do it. For example, if I would hire someone to walk my dog, it would cost me €10 each time. And now I save the money. Alan takes care of my dog, keeps an eye on my flat and so forth. And I help him. This is mutual respect! (Olli, 2006, interview)

Olli also had hairdressers, computer specialists and doctors among his friends. When he needed their services, he only had to call them and make an appointment. Therefore, it was not unusual when someone came to visit in the evening and along with the chat and beer fixed computer problems or cut Olli's hair (punks are very sensitive about their hairstyle). Olli's part in the relationship was to provide his skills and contacts when required. As mentioned above, Olli knew many construction material wholesalers and was able to get paint and other items cheaper. It was also not unusual for him to take his tools with him in the evening to do some quick repairs at a friend's apartment.

It was very interesting to observe how a reciprocal social network functioned between Potsdam and Halle in addition to the exchange of building materials and job opportunities. Besides providing jobs for Loofie, the above-mentioned Polish colleague also smuggled cigarettes to Germany. I discovered this was a dangerous business when we drove to his house late one night, parked the van out the front and switched off the lights. We hid our glowing cigarette tips in our palms and waited while Loofie snuck into the house to return half an hour later with a fully loaded black plastic bag. Then we disappeared as fast as we could. These cigarettes were sold later in Archiv and other punk pubs in Potsdam, the customers being Loofie's friends. Some of the cigarettes were taken to Halle, where Olli either smoked them or traded them on at a small profit. Another product that travelled from Potsdam to Halle was diesel fuel. When Olli was in Potsdam, he lived in a house that was commonly known as the School, where he had a friend called Carmen. Carmen was an ex-girlfriend of Kalle, but she and Olli had known each other for a long time, as when Carmen lived in Leipzig, they visited the same clubs and concerts. The School was a huge apartment building near the centre of the city and close to the old town. It was previously a squat, which had been the case for more than a decade after German reunification, and during the time of my fieldwork was now a legalized commune with a rental contract with the city council.[8] A mixture of punks, bikers and hardcore fans lived in the School. One of the inhabitants, Bug, was a free riding biker (i.e. he did not belong to any biker club) who worked illegally as a Harley Davidson mechanic in various motorcycle shops. Bug had many friends who were also active in the car, van or motorcycle repair business. One of his friends had access to cheap fuel (which was also stolen) and this fuel was sold among close friends. Olli had the possibility to buy this fuel for a *Freundespreis* – 50 cents a litre – whereas the official price at the petrol station was approximately €1.5. Bug's contacts were also used for repairing cars and vans. Many people, not only from Potsdam but also from Halle, drove to Potsdam, where their vehicles were fixed cheaply in various legal and illegal repair shops. Characteristic to this exchange was that people acclaimed the whole process to be 'noncommercial'. As was the case with the cigarettes, people who sold fuel or fixed friends' vehicles convinced me that all these practices were pure 'friendship services', which meant that no one profited excessively from the practice. Instead, it was viewed as a way of retaining money and keeping living costs low.

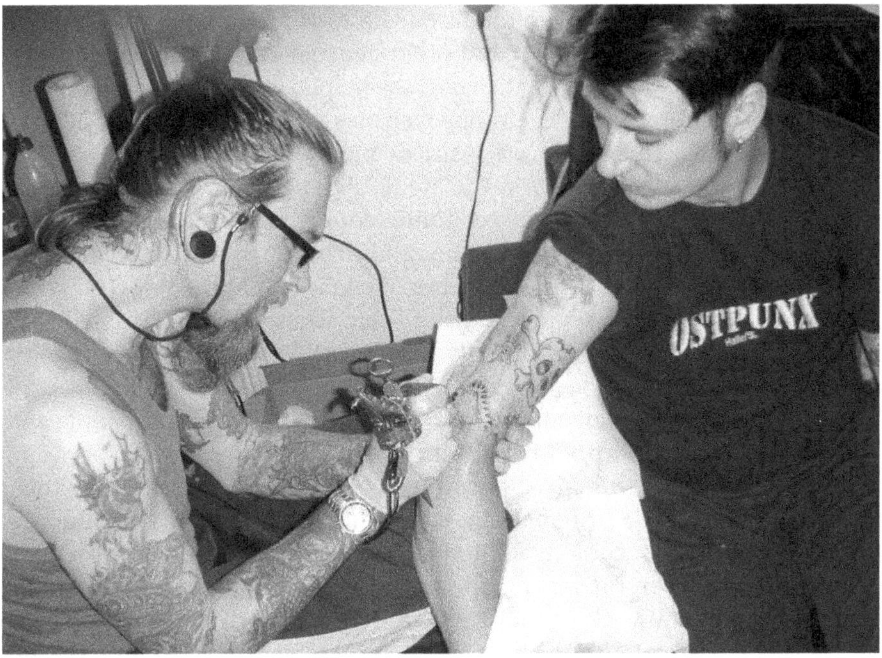

FIGURE 4.1. The moment of reciprocity. Photo by the author.

Another good example of the social heterogeneity of punk networks was a doctor called Kristian. When I met him, Kristian was forty-two and already an established doctor. For a long time, he lived in Halle, where he studied medicine. During the 1990s in Halle, he became involved in the independent record label business and released a series of punk records. He was originally from a small town near Potsdam and after his studies returned there to work as a therapist. There he continued to go to punk concerts and was involved in the independent record business. As a doctor, he had many customers from the punk rock scene from both cities covered in this chapter. Due to the fixed prices for medical treatment in Germany, Kristian was not able to make his services that much cheaper, but he was the doctor who could help when someone needed the Krankenschein – the document for an employer when one was ill. Therefore, it was no wonder that Kristian received great respect in Halle, where he had many friends whom he visited regularly. Another, more atypical person in the network was a woman called Sophia. She was in her early forties and had a house outside of Halle, where she lived with her boyfriend. Sophia was a well-known customer at GiG and had been part of the scene since the early 1990s. When I met her, she was already an established IT specialist working for several companies as a web designer and computer specialist. She often hired Olli to work on her house or used Olli's help to buy cheaper paint and other construction materials from the wholesalers. In exchange for that favour, she helped Olli and other people by fixing their computers and developing websites for clubs and record labels.

At the end of this section, I want to mention gender. As is obvious from my outline of the network, this punk rock network comprised fewer women than men.[9] In terms of economic cooperation, females were also more marginal – there were fewer possibilities for women to be engaged in profitable illegal jobs. The hairdresser Wencke sometimes worked without giving receipts and avoided paying some taxes this way. While many women occasionally worked illegally in pubs, these were only short-term and part-time positions, as for regular hours the employers required legal contracts. With the female jobs it was less easy to involve other people and offer them some significant financial incentives. Moreover, the favours and services that women were in a position to offer were not something their friends (whether male or female) needed constantly. Women often helped by organizing parties, cooking for a small and often symbolic fee or decorating venues. However, the female presence was important to keep the scene coherent and 'punk rock' – they helped organize parties and other social events (taking care of food, distributing flyers, etc.) and their skills were important in terms of the network's economic autonomy.

As in every scene, there was plenty of gossip in the punk rock pubs and one favourite topic was gossiping about other people's relationships. Dealing with the strict nature of social relations in networks, sexual relations play a major role, and I had the impression that people avoided dating within the network and favoured people from 'outside'. As a matter of fact, in the network in question, there were only two couples who were both full members of it. Usually boyfriends or girlfriends of the network members were quickly accepted by the rest of the people, but these people rarely achieved (or sought) the position that 'full' members had. As a rule, the boyfriends and girlfriends had their own close friends and preferred to focus on them. It was widely accepted that couples go to separate concerts or parties, because 'one sometimes needs space'. Such an approach to sexual relationships could be viewed as a strategy – social relationships were more important and people did not want to risk spoiling them by dating within their close-knit group.

FAMILY IDEOLOGY

Examining the punk network, it looks like every other reciprocal economic network that exists on the fringes of illegality. From a purely economic point of view, punk rock networks were also an 'economy of affection', where multistranded relations, long-time loyalties and risk reduction were important to keep the whole structure intact (cf. Meagher, 2006: 571; Mitchell, 1974: 283). Informality and trust clearly exist within the network (and other similar underground scene networks). The same informality and trust relationship also exists within formal structures (cf. Macaulay, 1963). Therefore, what I want to present is how the participants legitimize their behaviour and actions in the underground scene. One motivation for my research was the desire to find out how much the behaviour and everyday life of the punks reflects the ideology of solidarity and anti-state positioning, which is often thematized by the music and the underground press. When conducting interviews with people belonging to the networks I studied, I asked everybody why they prefer to turn to friends and seek support and help amongst them. Besides the usual reasons like 'it is cheaper' or 'I trust these people', I also often encountered one particular expression: 'This way we support each other and the money remains in the family.'

What made this network special was not its economic reciprocity, based on trust and cost calculations, but the ideology of the 'family' and the conscious attempt to keep resources within the network. Here the reciprocal moral support and solidarity, propagated by bands and fanzines (e.g. Jahn, 2006; Luegner, 2005/2006: 104–5; Maurice, 1998: 22–23; NZO, 2006: 2), developed into a practice of economic support. This was why some of my informants took a one-hour drive to visit Kristian instead of going to a doctor in their vicinity. Over the years, the system of favours had lost any obvious ledger, in the sense that people had ceased to observe whose turn it was to repay a favour. It had developed into a delayed-return system of favours where people helped each other and expected the same when they needed it (Woodburn, 1998). Leaning on Mitchell (1974: 183–284), the common sense of the punk rock 'family' contained a strong ideology of obligations and expectations in their social relationships. The economic calculations beyond the family ideology were such that actions will most likely be repaid in the future. As Bug explained: 'The money remains always in the same circles. And I mean with it that when you know people, you can always find further jobs. I make for him [some punk friend] a low price but he brings the next customer to me and then I can take the full price.'

Ideologically such practice stems from the street punk and hardcore music concept of 'unity' and 'brotherhood', but in practice the social relations of people were established via a common biography, shared events and a common geography, i.e. the 'connectedness' of the network was strong (cf. Mitchell, 1974: 282). As has been explained in previous chapters, most of my informants became friends in the 1990s during the squatter period or even earlier during the GDR era. It was a time when the young and vital underground scene presented a radical anti-state position. And the fabric of the network became stronger (Mitchell, 1969: 12), i.e. these contacts were maintained over fifteen years, even when people's lives took different directions – some became white-collar officials, others blue-collar workers. Good relations survived even beyond changes in musical preferences – many people moved from punk to techno or hip-hop. The relationship in the network was 'activated through social action' (Mitchell, 1969: 43), i.e. people met each other regularly at concerts and in certain pubs like the bar area of GiG. The fact that people had learned and practised various professions only helped to give the network a semi-legal economic flavour. To give an example of this, before the end of my fieldwork period, Olli and Ille started their next job outside of Halle in a small village, where their common acquaintance, a prominent figure in the local hip-hop scene, had started his illegal club. As Olli explained: 'He is an old gangster [hip-hopper], we know each other from those days when everyone partied together. He is OK. He has always done his own thing. They built up the scene here.'

The emphasis on 'unity' and 'brotherhood' was an attempt to maintain a sense of egalitarianism among friends. Indeed, there was no clear hierarchy in the network and no clear position of 'culture carriers' (Evan, 1963: 68). However, studying such networks, I noticed that there were one or several aforementioned 'anchor persons' who 'activated social links' (Mitchell, 1974: 286). The 'anchor person' was very much at the centre of the multistranded relations and was able to control and support the 'social redundancy' of the network. The notion put forward by Frankenberg of 'social redundancy' of the personal network means that in 'multi-channel routes alternative channels are available if any one channel should fail' (Mitchell, 1969: 15). Loofie, for instance, was able to transfer jobs to different people. In the case that he could not attend a job (through lack of time or where it was outside of his specialist area), he asked some of his friends to do it.

Here again, the position of the 'anchor person' also meant the obligation to people whom the 'anchor person' engaged in the work distribution process. I remember one evening, after Olli had been ill for weeks and was distressed because he could not work, he said: 'Now when I lay in bed, other people cannot work as well. Some of them have family, you know!' This sense of responsibility was not limited to words. In 2001, when I got to know Olli, he was working hard to pay off his debts. When I asked him what kind of debts he had incurred, he told me that he had hired many friends to rebuild a huge house. The salary they expected was thousands of German Deutsche Marks. But, as was not unusual, the landlord refused to pay. Since Olli had promised his friends a good level of compensation, he felt obliged to pay this money. To fulfil his promise, he worked hard and managed to get rid of the debt within five years. When I asked him why he did this, given that he had no obligation to pay them from his own pocket since no one received money from the landlord, he replied: 'I promised the money to the people. There was no way back for me!'

A combination of the anchor person's 'qualities' and 'achievements' (Moore, 1963: 15), both as a central figure in the economic transfer and resource management and as an important member of the scene, made his position more 'total' (Mitchell, 1969: 12).

PUNK ROCK

One phrase I heard many times during my interviews was 'This or that is punk rock' or 'This or that is not punk rock'. 'Punk rock' itself is a noncodified quality marker for many things like bands, events and locations, and is also a description of a lifestyle and attitude. The other meaning of 'punk rock' was a group with shared social norms, a way of behaving connected to specific cultural and economic interests. Loofie once told me: 'I work hard but I have to go to concerts at weekends. This is what punk rock is!' When I asked 'What precisely do you mean by that?', he said: 'Punk rock is going to clubs and meeting people. This is important because this way you make your contacts.' Olli's explanation was similar: 'Punk rock is ... You go to punk rock concerts to make contacts. And later ... people know each other, they respect each other. And so you can find jobs!' By attending concerts with people, I noticed how important it was for them 'to meet people' in clubs and how often people went to bars because they had 'to make and nurture connections', as Loofie explained. Ille's point of view also clearly describes how music and economic cooperation combine:

> Music plays an important role [in our lives]. During concerts you also make acquaintances with people who either do other jobs where you can be useful, or can be useful for your business, plus you can find out information about people and what they do. And you have a nice balance between this and entertainment. It is so, that you do not meet people over a cup of coffee but over a few pints of beer. (Ille, 2006, interview)

The importance of socializing at concerts went so far that people met to discuss their economic affairs during the breaks between the bands or to withdraw into a back room bar of the club for a quick discussion. As one of one of my informants before one punk concert in Halle told me: 'I have to go to this concert, M. goes there and it could be that he has some job for me!'

From my interviews, I observed that punks were not just music fans who shared a love of common bands; something had evolved and they had transformed into a socioeconomic group. The thin line between music culture and the economy became increasingly apparent while spending time with people and participating in their conversations, everyday lives and activities.

FIGURE 4.2. Discussing business. Photo by the author.

It was not uncommon for people to fluidly discuss their point of view on different topics like music, football and work, jumping without introduction from one topic to another and returning to the initial theme within minutes. So, when people were discussing some work-related topic, no one batted an eyelid when someone said suddenly 'But the concert on Friday was really good!' and after talking a bit about the event, turned to discuss their work, only to switch again to discuss a recent football match. Talking about the music – concerts, bands, records and interviews in fanzines – takes up a great deal of time, and it shows how equally important and interlinked music, sport and work were for people within the punk rock network.

A significant portion of time and financial resources was spent on concerts and driving to concerts outside of one's immediate home town. This passion for music was for many people one marker of their identity, something that distinguished punk rock people from mainstream 'average' people. As one person who worked in GiG said: 'When I meet my relatives at family celebrations, they always wonder and cannot understand how I can still live this life in adulthood. For them, constantly going to concerts is stupid and not understandable.' Besides time, money was spent on music and clothes. In the age of free (and illegal) online music downloads, punk rock people spent a lot of money and time buying records. Rising record prices did not interrupt this practice, but rather increased the amount of time that people spent looking for music – it meant regularly visiting supermarkets looking for cheap CDs in discount boxes, and hours behind the computer trying to buy second-hand vinyl and cheap stylish clothes on sites like eBay.

In conclusion, money was needed to keep the underground culture alive and one conscious reason to earn money was to invest it in items relevant to the punk scene.

AGE COHORT AND RECRUITMENT

As mentioned above, persons in the network I studied formed a relatively coherent age group between twenty-eight and thirty-five (with a few exceptions) of locals who had known each other for a long time. Nevertheless, there were always people who 'appeared just a few years ago', such as Wencke, a female hairdresser. She was a thirty-year-old woman who previously moved around in the goth scene, then approximately in 2004 changed her style and scene to rockabilly. When I studied the scene in 2006 and 2007, she was already a GiG regular and was recognized as a full member of the scene. This meant that she was invited to every party and always had the possibility to go with other GiG regulars to outside concerts. Her contribution to the network's economy was to cut the hair of people in the group, in return for services such as repairing her flat, car or computer. Similarly, she also earned an independent living and was a very committed music fan.

In comparing Wencke's position to that of Stephan, in many aspects it was similar, but there were also differences. Stephan did not share with others a love of punk rock. Despite the fact that he occasionally turned up to GiG, he never participated in other music-related free time activities like attending concerts or talking about the music. What connected him with the punks was trust. Stephan did not hesitate to engage in illegal jobs and he also offered illegal jobs to others, or made it possible to legalize illegal jobs by signing receipts. All of my informants who worked with him held the opinion that Stephan was extremely trustworthy. As Olli expressed it: 'So, we met each other through work. And here it comes to trust, that we help each other when there is need for support, either in financial or work cases.' Stephan, like the Polish worker in Potsdam, was integrated into the network – and this was also the expression my informants used – due to their common understanding of loyalty and support, and wilful ignorance of the violation of the state norms. A common feature shared by all three was their lifestyle – these people earned their living through their work and they were highly skilled in their respective profession. However, such non-subculture-involved people like Stephan and the Polish man were the exception. This shows that music and socialization related to music was important for the integration of the group. Music as a social space (clubs and bars) and social activity (spending time together) brought the majority of the people together and gave them a group identity. Nevertheless, the integration of Stephan and the Polish man shows that socializing in a music-related space does not mean that music was the only criteria for friendship.

IDEOLOGY OF INDEPENDENCE AND THE ANTI-STATE STANCE

Central to the family ideology was to be as independent from the state and state structures as possible. For instance, Ille's response to the question why it was necessary to first hire friends was: 'Then the money remains in the same circles' (Es bleibt halt immer in dem gleichen Kreis das Geld!). And to my question of how important the transfer of jobs in the network was, Olli answered: 'This is the most important thing ... Not to be dependent on the state's money or be in too close contact with the state is good when the money will be distributed among your own people.' However, the influx of money into the economy of the network was necessary and this was frequently earned through jobs with 'outside' people, where illegal income was again preferred to legal income. In this light, avoiding paying taxes became not only an economic strategy but also a political stance.

The view, strategy and ideology of independence in punk networks can appear to be very contentious. Ideologically representing an anti-consumption stance, people still wanted to earn money to spend on music, clothes, cars and other commodities.

Despite the anti-state rhetoric, the practice was very complex and controversial. The punk rock scene was dominated by state law strong enough to make people pay attention to its existence. People avoided being fully fledged outlaws, following many rules, starting with traffic regulations, for example. Moreover, in many respects the punk rock people conformed to the norms and values of mainstream society, while developing a way to justify such behaviour and assimilate it into the ideology of independence. When it came to owning property, this presented a host of contradictions and areas of contention.

Earlier I mentioned Maurer from Potsdam, who had just bought a house and renovated it with the help of friends. He and Kristian were the only ones in the network to own a property. However, plans to buy a house or a flat were not unusual among my informants and a lack of capital was the only obstacle to doing so. In academic research, autonomy through owning a property and financial independence is usually related with the middle class.[10] In Eastern Germany (and not only there)[11] the desire for autonomy cuts across classes and it is common that many working-class people own their own property, especially when they live in villages and small towns. I know that Loofie was saving money to buy a house one day and Olli was very close to owning his home, which only failed to materialize because the landlord sold it to another buyer. When I asked Olli what was the difference between him and one middle-class petit bourgeois teacher, who he criticized constantly, he replied:

> No, this is totally different. The house, you need it so as not to pay money to some landlord, but to invest into your own property and into your house ... For example, when I build my own house and install solar energy, I save a lot of money that I otherwise pay to the state or to its institutions like the energy company. Because I can produce energy for myself. Of course, you have to pay certain taxes, but these taxes [like the land tax and the property tax] you pay anyway, only you pay these taxes via your landlord. You cannot avoid paying all taxes, but it will be less and you do not have to feed some landlord. When you have your own house, you can put money into it and you know where it goes to. (Olli, interview, 2006)

Soon after, Olli installed a wood burning stove, claiming: 'I do not intend to pay money to this Nazi state.' I asked how the oven was connected to the state and he explained that the energy company belongs to the state and by using the central heating, one also finances state structures. When I discussed the topic with Ille and asked him the same question about the difference, he insisted that 'this is not the same, because we live differently'. Upon further questioning as to what the difference was, he came back to the patterns of consumerism, saying that 'the practice of consuming [*Konsumverhalten*] is different.' A punk rocker does not invest so much money in trendy clothes or fashionable items, but spends more money in going to concerts or buying music (both records and equipment to make and listen to music).

Despite the anti-state and anti-consumer rhetoric, I did not meet many people who were extremely effective in their attempt to reach maximum independence from the state, its institutions or bourgeois society in general. For example, people did not always give up their legal jobs and, if they did, they generally accepted social security payments. There were only two people among my informants who were able to finance themselves solely through illegal income without applying for state social security funding, and one of them did not even have a registered address. These two independent people were Bug (mentioned above) and Pyro. Bug was very proud that he did not even have a registered address (which every person living in Germany must have) and on his ID his address was just 'city of Potsdam'. He told me that he had no intention to register himself as unemployed because 'now my life is easier. When you are officially unemployed, they send you to training and get on your nerves'. Another person who managed to minimize his contact with the structures of the state was Pyro in Halle. He lived in the house of GiG and was responsible for booking bands, but earned money as an IT technician. From his room, he designed websites for companies and programmed their computers. In contrast to Bug, Pyro had a registered address, but he had no intention of registering with the unemployment office.

This did not mean that the consumption patterns of such people were radically different from others, but they were able to finance their lives without being employed in legal jobs or receiving money from the government. These two precedents demonstrate that the ideology of punk rock can to a certain extent be less anti-consumerism than anti-state and that maintaining a certain living standard was more important than strict independence from the state. However, people's strategies to achieve their goals demonstrated that legal pluralism 'affects people's behaviour', and 'the way the legislation is implemented' plays its role in the context of punk rock culture (von Benda-Beckman and von Benda-Beckman, 2001: 33).

CONCLUSION: SEMI-AUTONOMOUS SOCIAL FIELD OF A SUBCULTURE

The desire for autonomy, of course, cuts across classes, and niches are carved out in the most unlikely places. I have shown in this chapter that punk rock networks are based on multiple social relations with a system of values and norms rooted in a working-class ethos of independence and self-reliance. In the social networks I studied, people follow certain norms and have a particular ideology. Simultaneously and based on their ideology, the actors have created a punk 'semiautonomous social field' that 'can internally generate customs and symbols and has rule making capacities' (Moore, 1973: 720). However, this social field was neither completely autonomous or in isolation. The dominant role of the state is remarkable in the strategies of the punk rock people and the 'choice behaviour' of actors was not completely free; they had to follow certain state rules. But the state was not capable of exerting total social control over its citizens or of preventing 'subsidiary norm making' (Allott and Woodman, 1985: 23). The opposition was not all-encompassing because the attitude towards the market economy and consumption was less hostile than to the state, i.e. subculturalists did not completely follow their ideology of opposition. Chiba noted that 'there is more than only "state" and "unofficial" law' (1985: 208) and the punk groups studied here balanced these two sides of the same coin.

To distinguish themselves from mainstream petit bourgeois society, punk rock people used an ideology of 'independence' to justify their own consumerism and certain collaboration with the state structures that have power (cf. Griffiths, 2002: 289). Despite this, the distance from the state institution was important and one strategy to achieve or maintain this was to establish semi-legal economic structures that were as independent as possible. Looking at the punk rock ideology, there is no doubt that the actors attempted to follow a self-determining and independent ideology and to adapt it even into the legal, social and economic sphere.

I believe that punk economic networks are reminiscent of how we understand the moral economy. First of all, their ideology serves as a tool to legitimize the practice to fight the immorality of the imagined mainstream ideology and state politics (Thompson, 1964: 62–63). When analysing different contradictory practices like enthusiastic consumerism, property owning or tax evasion, 'we have come upon unsuspected complexities, for behind every such form of popular direct action some legitimising notion of right is to be found' (ibid.: 68)

Another aspect of the punk moral economy is the justification of rebellion. Although punk is not a physical rebellion, it is described as a 'resistance through rituals' that is seen as a 'righteous protest' (O'Brien and Li, 2006) to seek economic justice by what Scott (1976: 3–4) calls 'low classness'. The violation of certain laws like avoiding paying taxes is seen as a rebellious act according to subcultural ideology. Last but not least, the moral economy à la punk provides the actors with agency. People combine central working-class normative assumptions with the street punk rhetoric to see themselves as those who resist mainstream society's norms and give themselves and what they do a subcultural identity. Piketty (2014: 82) argues that 'national psychology' is where 'private motives' merge with 'power motives'. Punk's economic resistance gives power to the socially and economically marginalized working-class punks and the belief that they call the shots. Snyder defines 'law' as a form of social consciousness (1985: 269) that 'have as their [*sic*] generic function the expression, regulation or maintenance of the dominant social relations within a social formation'. In the punk rock scene, solidarity, reciprocity and the anti-state position were an important part of the scene ideology, and this ideology was capable of maintaining and allowing the social group to flourish.

Notes

1. This chapter is based on research in 2006–7, later updated with research in the following years up to 2010.
2. Regarding Bourdieu's concept of habitus, one cannot ignore the work of Alan O'Connor, who shows how class and national background shape the strategies, careers and practices in punk (2008, 2016).

3. In the winter, most GiG or Archiv regulars met at big birthday parties involving dozens of people. Both clubs were also bases for football teams. Several regulars of GiG established a football team that struggled its way through the town's league. Each year, Archiv organized a football championship in which teams (usually groups of friends) from Potsdam and Berlin participated. At this event, volunteers gathered together a team that had new players almost every year. This championship always ended with a concert and a barrel of free beer.
4. The other side of the coin was that I heard stories of how the same workers, who were responsible for completing the object with a deadline, had to spend nights on the site shortly before it was finished, to prevent theft where it would have been too time-consuming to replace stolen material and equipment.
5. Since I never interviewed entrepreneurs, I cannot confirm whether it was true or not.
6. During August 2006, the following story illustrates the harsh competition in the German small-scale building business. Loofie helped his colleague by finishing a private house on the outskirts of Potsdam. The colleague has turned up in the company's van and Loofie had parked his private car behind it. People from the competing construction company, who had suspected that this house was going to be renovated illegally, took pictures of Loofie's colleague's van and reported the event to the *Innung* (guild). Loofie's colleague got into trouble with his boss and had to compensate the company for the stolen building materials. He kept it secret that he was not alone in building the house. Loofie's car was parked behind the van, but the photographer did not have a picture of its number plate and so Loofie's involvement remained undiscovered. The background of the story is that the competing company offered to rebuild the house. According to Loofie, the offer was as cheap as possible, within the limits of legal building work. But the offer was turned down and when the work began in the house, people from the other firm knew it must have been an illegally conducted job.
7. This is a long and sad story, but according to many of my informants, was rather typical of the construction business. The customer who ordered the work declared bankruptcy and subsequently avoided the payment. Because the house Olli worked on was registered in the name of his wife, there was no chance of getting money for the work and after a long legal process, the workers remained without any pay.
8. This is quite typical for German squats. At the end of the 1990s, most squats were either closed by the police or became legal governed institutions that had a collective contract with the local city council. The general meeting of inhabitants was responsible for paying rent and communicating with the municipal institutions. The internal affairs of such communes were also discussed in the general meeting. For instance, in most houses, a new inhabitant gained permission to move in only when all the people living in the house approved it.
9. Rock scenes tend to be overwhelmingly male-dominated (see Frith, 1983; Hjelm et al. 2011, Kahn-Harris, 2004) and although some of my informants argue against it (see Chapter 6), this also tends to be the case with the punk, skinhead and hardcore scenes in Germany.
10. Interestingly, James Scott links middle-classness (or rather the classical petite bourgeoisie subsection of it) to autonomy in his book *Two Cheers for Anarchism* (2014), arguing that people aspire to become small property owners due to the perception that this confers autonomy (and social standing) (see also Heath, 2003). Another

side of the coin is currently to enhance the middle-class autonomy and again social standing through what Currid-Halkett (2018) identifies as 'conspicuous consumption', an elitist habit of associating cultural knowledge with consumption, and, for example, a preference for organic food and materials, yoga classes, etc.

11. For example, there exists substantial literature on postsocialist Russia from the perspective of how the working class is seeking, struggling and sometimes failing to achieve autonomy in a capitalist economy (Morris, 2016, 2018; Morrison and Schwartz, 2003: 553–74; Ashwin and Lytkina, 2004: 189–206). For the autonomy-seeking British working class through property ownership, see Jones (2011).

CHAPTER

5

TOLERATED ILLEGALITY

I can say that we live here in tolerated illegality!
—Pyro, 12 November 2010

GiG or Ganz in Gegenteil (its full name) is a picturesque building on the outskirts of Halle's city centre. As mentioned in Chapter 6, the punk scene of the city is divided geographically: punk groups were defined through their locations, which in most cases were related to the clubs themselves. The location of GiG is a concrete four-floor building, built most likely after the Second World War. On the street, the wall of the first floor was once coloured green and is now covered with graffiti and posters announcing concerts, and decorated with the initials and logo of the club. What distinguishes the club from other similar locations in the city was that the back half of a Trabant car is set into a wall above the main entrance. The wooden door to the bar and club area is located a few metres from the main entrance gates, which is typical of German apartment buildings that have an inner courtyard. The door is thick and massive, with a peephole in it, a remnant from the 1990s political street battles when right-wing groups were expected to attack the club.

On entering the club, to the left-hand side the visitor sees the bar desk and a piece of a cardboard attached above it where it says 'Ausschank nur für Mitglieder der e.V.!' (Sale of alcohol only for members of the association!). When I saw it for the first time, I asked what it meant, and someone explained that although the club has no bar licence, it is registered as an association of limited liability (*eingetragener Verein* or e.V.) and is allowed to sell alcohol only to its members. I did not ask anything else, because in Germany alternative bars and clubs usually get around restrictions limiting the sale of alcoholic beverages in this way.

This chapter looks at how Halle punks establish their illegality in a framework of legality or how they use laws, gaps in the law or simply tolerance from the side of state institutions to keep their *Freiraum* going. *Freiraum* (*Freiräume* in plural) is a German word that is often used in fanzine editorials to describe the goal of punk: to create and maintain a social, cultural and geographical autonomous space, literally 'free room'. It is a strong cliché that punk is a subculture that opposes the state institutions, fights them and tries to live independently outside of an institutional and legal framework. Germany has a long tradition of displaying what Matthew Worley (2017: 149) calls 'punk's implicit oppositionism' or the opposition to the state and especially to the police, most often expressed through music and activism. Collectors and lovers of 1980s and 1990s German punk music probably know songs where expressions like the 'Nazi-Staat' (Nazi state) or 'Bullenschwein' (copper pig) were shouted with great enthusiasm.[1] These songs were recorded during the decades when Western Germany had an active squatting movement where punks played a more or less leading role. After German reunification, the movement bled over into the former GDR, where due to confused property relations, squats and autonomous culture centres were established in literally every town. Berlin was the city that proudly hosted a large number of squats and *Wagenburg* (illegal trailer parks) during the 1990s. This all changed when conservative politician Jörg Schönbohm became the Senator of the Interior of Berlin from 1996 to1998. This was the time when the German government was officially relocated from Bonn to Berlin. Schönbohm promised to clean the capital of squats and he was indeed very successful in keeping his promise – most squats were closed or transformed into different forms of legal housing (in many cases the inhabitants managed to buy the house and converted the squat into a co-op). What this transformation shows and what is also the main argument of this chapter is that punk exists not outside or against the official state laws, but rather adapts to it and uses the possibilities provided by the legal framework.

French scholar George Balandier, one of the great names of political anthropology, writes that according to the views of 'conservative theoreticians', 'The widest interpretations see the state as an attribute of all social life, a mode of social arrangement that operates as soon as the state of culture is established' and that the state is in this interpretation 'the very essence of human nature' (1970: 124). Here it looks like the state is an inevitable result of human progress that is supposed to satisfy all. Balandier, however, is critical of such a naturalistic approach and refers to different theories of state in his programmatic book *Political Anthropology*, which questions the total suitability of the state for all its inhabitants. Nevertheless, there is one thing that such critical authors like Émile Durkheim, Lucy Mair or Max Weber have in common – they relate to the state as a political formation with the domination of the majority over the minority. Balandier seems to be especially impressed by the theorization of state power by Weber and dedicates long sections to Weber's concept of the 'legitimate domination' through bureaucratic structures (Balandier, 1970: 45–46). He adds that apart from bureaucracy, one attribute of the functioning state is 'the existence of more or less complex organic structures on which the political unit is based'. In the context of this book, the police and different officials in Halle's municipality are the forces mainly embodying the state for members of the local punk scene. The association of the state with power, domination and hegemony is far from unusual, whether it be in the writing of Foucault, Bourdieu or Gramsci. However, the area in which I share Balandier's fascination with Max Weber is that Weber's 'ideal state' also contains 'the gap between official and private relations, the degree of potential dynamism' (Balandier, 1970: 45).

It must be noted that scholars of legal pluralism see this 'potential dynamism' as a rather one-sided vector. Often the state and nonstate normative orders are viewed as a relationship of enforcing and resistance or mutual merging, as demonstrated in the following quote:

> Research in the 1990s emphasizes the way state law penetrates and restructures other normative orders through symbols and through direct coercion and, at the same time, the way nonstate normative orders resist and circumvent penetration or even capture and use the symbolic capital of state law ... Some research explores the way nonstate normative orders constitute state law. (Merry, 1988: 881)

This understanding of the relationship between the state and nonstate laws does not leave space for a third interpretation where the state does not adopt 'nonstate normative orders', but simply tolerates or ignores their existence.

THE SEMI-ILLEGALITY OF SQUATS

On its first floor, GiG has a complex facility containing a bar and club area, and a small eating place that is difficult to call a restaurant. The visitor first enters the bar area, then turns right and, after few steps up, enters the club area. There are few tables to sit around, a dancefloor area in front of the stage, and by passing the stage, one ends up in a small side room with a billiard table and a few tables and chairs. The furniture is old, clearly second-hand, or just picked up from the street and generally worn out. In the winter time, this part of the club is heated through a small metal oven that Germans call an

FIGURE 5.1. Ganz im Gegenteil (GiG). Photo by the author.

Allesbrenner and that is usually heated with round pieces of coal. This is also the reason why GiG is never warm during the winter months, because the oven is not powerful enough to heat the space – or, as one of my informants said, 'I'd rather not go to GiG in winter, you freeze your arse off there!' (Ich gehe ungerne zum GiG im Winter, Du frierst dir dort deinen Arsch ab!). In the club area, one sees a small door that hides the *Küche* (kitchen), as it is called. Except for one or two days a week, GiG also functions as a hangout for regulars who come there for a drink, to play cards or just to meet people. Over the years, people have formed friendship circles (in German *Stammtisch*) that meet in the club on a particular day. For example, a group of friends met in the club every Tuesday to play cards, whereas once a week (I think it was on Thursday) some women came for a *Frauenstammtisch* (regular women's table).

The kitchen opens late, no earlier than 9 PM, but it is nevertheless popular for its cheap and tasty food. The menu is usually not very long: as a rule, the 'restaurant' offers one fish, one meat and one vegetarian dish, except on the day when a vegan punk girl is cooking – her menu is vegan only. However, the dishes vary daily. The fish often depends on the daily catch of Pieps, a passionate amateur fisherman who loves to offer the customers freshly caught fish cooked in different ways. Meat dishes could be sausages or cooked meat. The only standard dish was the *Käseschnitzel*, a cheese schnitzel. The sides are usually either fries, baked or boiled potato, or in some cases noodles. Customers could eat their meals either around two or three tables in the eating area or take their meals to the tables in the concert area. The money earned in the restaurant went towards the common stock, as did everything earned by the concerts. The bar in the front room is usually run by volunteers, who liked the job and did not mind that they were paid a symbolic amount, only €10–15 a night. Each one of them played his or her favourite music and that drew customers for a specific night – Pyh, a skinhead, played usually harder punk and Oi!, while someone else would play *Deutschpunk*, or goth or hardcore.

On other floors was accommodation for people who lived in and ran the house, at the time of the research a total of six people. One was Pieps, the chef of the kitchen who had apparently invented the signature dish of GiG, a cheese schnitzel, basically fried cheese. Another was Pyro, the sound engineer for the concerts that were held in GiG. While Pieps and Pyro were veterans of the left-wing punk scene in Halle (see the Introduction), the rest were considerably younger, having started their punk career in the late 1990s. All six of these people were closely involved in the daily life of the house; they organized concerts, participated in renovation work when needed and kept the technical equipment intact and bar well supplied. These six people also collectively governed the house: they organized regular collective meetings or *Hausplenum* and all decisions were made through voting wherein decisions had to be unanimous, a traditional way of decision making in German squats. All six, except one person, were men in their late thirties or early forties. The singular woman was a girlfriend of Pieps and they lived together in a roomy apartment. Pyro also lived together with his girlfriend, who was not involved in the governance of the house, and they had a child together. Other people of the house, as far as I knew, were single or in short-term relationships.

When interviewing people about the history of GiG, I discovered that they had little knowledge of it. Most of my interviewees suggested I talk about it with Pyro, who had been living in GiG more or less since the beginning. It appeared that all the rest had moved into the house later, Pieps being the second-longest inhabitant. My interview with Pyro showed that he also had only a vague memory about the beginnings of the club. According to him and other sources, GiG started as a squat exploiting the transition era after German reunification with its fuzzy property relations. The building, being built during the GDR period, was not made the subject of a property restitution and was more or less abandoned by Halle's municipal council, so the punks made use of the situation and took possession. Later GiG's property claim reached a certain semi-legal status, but how and when remained unclear.

All the inhabitants and some regulars informed me that the club's status was unclear. However, in order to operate, it needed some legal recognition, which was why the cultural association with a limited liability, the e.V., was established. For instance, the legal status made it possible to purchase beverages and foodstuffs at the wholesalers Metro, which sells only to enterprises. The official status also enabled the GiG crew to organize concerts or football matches, since all such events in Germany require a permit from the municipality. On the other hand, at the time of my fieldwork, the question of who the building legally belonged to remained unsolved. Since the building was not made the subject of a property restitution and it was seemingly not in the interests of the municipality to remove the inhabitants and risk massive protests or street battles, the building was left alone. Moreover, judging from the constant so-called solidarity concerts, with the aim of collecting money to renovate GiG's roof or corridors, the socialist-era building was in bad shape and in need of serious investment to bring it up to modern living standards. Hence the remark of Pyro about the tolerated illegality – officially punks had little legal ground to inhabit the house, but the authorities allowed it.

FIGURE 5.2. Inside GiG. Photo by the author.

The cultural association did not pay any taxes, but did not receive any subsidies from the city either (the opposite was the case with many alternative clubs in West Germany). The condition of the building was rarely controlled by municipal officials, either for fire safety or for hygiene. The question is why? As Bernt explained to me: 'They [the municipality and police] know where we are and so they can always locate us. When they drive us away all these people here can go underground and we will be out of sight. I think it is more comfortable for them to leave us alone until anything serious happens.' His statement reflects the widespread belief in Germany – and not only among the 'radicals' – that the police tolerate to a certain extent right- and left-wing activities (be they demonstrations, concerts or housing projects) in order to maintain control over these groups.

Nevertheless, GiG did not exist in a legal vacuum, ignoring all existing official norms and laws. Most concerts in the club were registered with the municipality. As I was told, some concerts have been rescheduled because neighbours complained about the noise. So, live music was, as a rule, not played very late on workdays. The establishment of a cultural association with the purpose of supplying the bar with beverages and organizing concerts was mentioned above. It can be interpreted as the 'involuntary' cooperation with the state, as Negus (1999) discussed in the case of underground music and the music business, but I have never noticed that this was understood in this sense by punks from GiG. When it comes to concerts, Halle has a long history of organizing performances for extremely underground punk bands in the town's restaurants, commercial clubs and even in very bourgeois ice cream cafés.[2] To my mind, Pieps and others did not take it as an act of collaboration with the *Nazistaat*, but something that was needed to be done in order to keep the scene functioning. In order to demonstrate their oppositionism and spread their 'uncompromisingly radical anti-state message', they had to know certain laws or regulations and follow them. I am not sure whether the irony of the situation ever occurred to people in and around GiG: that in order to preserve their authenticity of being 'underground' and oppositional, GiG had to be legal to a certain extent. As Razzaz (1994) correctly notes in discussing informal and formal land use in Jordan, people are conscious of the law's function and this also impacts illegal behaviour. Since visiting shared music events and face-to-face contact with scene members is crucial for having a punk scene, GiG's observance of some laws enabled the scene to develop and be sustained to further the message of opposition to the state. I would even argue that Pieps and his colleagues did a lot to integrate Halle's punk scene into the local community. For example, GiG helped organize anti-fascist football matches in the summer of 2004 and 2005, which I visited. In itself, these events were nonpolitical youth-oriented leisure events where different football teams played their games on a few fields; barbecue and beer stands helped to create a good atmosphere and the only thing hinting at the punk background of the organizers was the music blasting out of the loudspeakers. These football matches were well attended by teenagers from different sports clubs and their parents; I felt no negative feelings from them. Although the purpose of the events was political – to promote an anti-fascist agenda and to 'show the presence' or being visible in the city – it was an ordinary working-class neighbourhood weekend event, something that E.P. Thompson (1964: Chapter 12.1) dedicated a whole chapter to. Here we encounter something that Geertz names 'polyglot discourse' (Merry, 1988: 887), where contradictory aims, strategies and narratives cross. It can be said that the punks in GiG as a whole did what is referred to as 'the dirty work of boundary maintenance' (Crowley, 1999: 155), i.e. drawing, through different symbolic activities, the boundary between 'us' and 'them', between people with left- and right-wing sympathies.

COMING TO TERMS WITH THE POLICE

'Cops in Halle are left wing, therefore they tolerate us and look through their fingers when we clash with Nazis', Pieps explained to me one day after a successful anti-fascist demonstration organized as a counter-demonstration for the analogous right-wing gathering. I have no further evidence for the left-wing sympathies of Halle's police force other than the countless anecdotes I heard from my punk informants, but the fact is that in Halle, a certain uneasy truce existed between punks and the police force. When I discussed this with Benke, he told me: 'During the last concert in GiG, the concert that was half the size of a festival, there stood a few *Mannschaftswagen* [personnel carrier] in the next street. Did you notice it? Cops were there but they did not interfere; they also did not provoke.'

As far as I could understand, the history of the political underground in the public space of Halle goes back to the *Wende* period. Clashes with police and between different political factions, which were typical of the period, had faded out by the end of the 1990s. This meant that older police officers and veteran punks had sufficient time to get to know each other. Especially when it comes to legal demonstrations, the organizers' side always had specific persons who registered the event and were also contact persons with the law enforcement institutions and the municipality. Pieps and Pyro, the leading people behind GiG, fell into this category. Over the years, certain police officers and punk activists had developed a mutual respect, but not necessarily a friendship. In most cases, both sides – the police and the organizers of demonstrations – were interested in avoiding conflicts and criminal incidents. Punk activists were keen to keep order in their ranks, controlling 'burners' who perhaps wanted to provoke the police, and keeping demonstrators from being arrested. The police officers, on their side, were interested in maintaining public order and not allowing street riots. Based on what I have heard and know about Pieps, he, in his very controlled and friendly way, was able to diplomatically calm down hotheads and solve problems with the police representatives. When talking to my informants, I discovered a certain degree of respect towards the police and a sense of them all being part of the same community. It was Pieps who told me that:

> Therefore they do not interfere when we organize anti-Nazi actions. Police themselves do not like Nazis. They turn a blind eye when we do something against the Nazis. Policemen are *Hallenser* [inhabitants of Halle] and this town has traditionally been left wing. Halle is a town of industry and the working class, therefore left-wing ideas have always been dominant here. (Pieps, 2006, interview)

As mentioned above, I do have my own doubts about all the arguments in this statement. There is no proof that the Halle police force have any sympathies for left-wing activism, nor is the town's industrial past any guarantee of leftist sentiments dominating in the population. In fact, Eastern Germany was associated throughout the 1990s with supporting xenophobic and nationalist right-wing groups and parties. The municipal and federal elections in 2017 demonstrated strong support for right-wing movements and organizations like Pegida (Patriotic Europeans Against the Islamization of the Occident – *Patriotische Europäer gegen die Islamisierung des Abendlandes* in German) or Alternative für Deutschland.

Nevertheless, it is beyond doubt that GiG punk regulars shared common views with other nonpunk people around them, got along with nonpunks and often worked together. Olli and many others were well-respected construction workers in town, while Pyh had a reputation as an IT specialist; tattoo artists who were also regulars knew different people outside the scene and many punk women worked in different service sectors. During the Christmas market time, several GiG regulars worked on the stall that smoked fish and sold sandwiches made of the freshly smoked fish. These people were often appreciated for their skills and trustworthiness. Punks themselves were not sealed off from the rest of society. For example, at the end of my fieldwork, an elderly man turned up at a *Stammtisch* that included Pyro. He was treated with respect and most of the time he sat quietly at the table sipping beer. I was told that he was a work colleague of Pyro, a lonely widower who Pyro invited to come to GiG for a beer. In a similar way, punks mixed with 'normal people' in Halle's two *Schwartzkneipe* or illegal bars.

Hoebel argues that 'underlying every culture is a body of basic postulates implicit in the world view of the members of the society in question. These are broadly generalized propositions as to the nature of things and what is qualitatively desirable and what is not' (1958: 225). German small towns and villages have a strong sense of community, local patriotism and identity. As Merry (1988: 871) states, it is often difficult to determine what the subgroup's rules are. In many cases, an overlap takes place on all sides. Local police forces are in many ways linked to local communities, and this is probably the reason why police forces from outside are used for controlling football matches, a game directly linked to local identity and community solidarity. Galantier distinguishes different levels of enforcing state laws: 'There are several levels of agencies, with "higher" agencies announcing (making, interpreting) rules and other 'lower' agencies assigned the responsibility of enforcing ... these rules' (1974: 96). What the discussion about legal pluralism misses about the relationship between the state law and folk law, traditional norms or local customs is that sometimes the state law not only adopts the 'folk law',[3] but in some cases simply tolerates its existence; this happens in Halle with the street-level policemen who decide to exercise their 'lower agencies' by not interfering in the affairs of certain punks. Here we come to the assertion made by Hooker (1975) that normative plurality exists because the state allows it. The uneasy tolerance of illegality is based – in the Foucauldian sense – on the state's role as the power holder that also is expressed in the formation and implementation of formal laws. Halle's police forces decided not to interfere in certain illegal or semi-illegal activities of local punks and in a sense legalized some of the punks' practices and politics. Without the consent of the police and municipal institutions, GiG and many other underground places in Halle would not have been able to exist. Both sides have reached what Mitchell defines as a 'norm consensus' that also inspired a 'norm directed behaviour' (1969: 285). The observations show that when punks kept their rebellion at bay, law enforcement agencies did not push for total obedience to the law.

CONCLUSION

Style-based subcultures tend to portray themselves as an oppositionist culture revolting against the state or the 'system'. This is a common feature of all such groups. Moreover, sometimes such a spirit of opposition is the only common nominator when we compare subcultural ideologies in general. In practice, there are different ways and strategies for opposition. While hippies attempted to withdraw from mainstream society by establishing communities (Feigelson, 1970; Miller, 1999; Rorabaugh, 2015), the Teddy Boys drew the boundary through demonstrative violence (Macilwee, 2015), rockers and bikers emphasized their freedom through motorbike riding (McDonald-Walker, 2000), skateboarders clash with the state over the use of public spaces

(Chiu, 2009; Drissel, 2013; Rundquist, 2007) and hip-hop breaks down traditional song structures and music-making technologies (Demers, 2003; Rose, 1989; Vaudhyanathan, 2001). In punk the confrontation was manifested not only through song texts, but also through political activities and squatting (Dunn, 2016). The research on subcultures has traditionally also taken the state and/or mainstream conflict with youth cultures as the basis for the phenomenon of subculture. This is very well demonstrated in the subcultural theory that defined the essence of subcultures through rebellion and class conflict (Hall and Jefferson, 1986). The whole myriad of research shows that the conflict indeed exists and is expressed through practices that can be categorized as shocking, destructive or rebellious. However, very often it does not require much effort to be provocative. In its earlier days, rock'n'roll music created shock through its infantile language (Appel, 2014), while later it was through its different ways of enjoying music like slam dancing (Tsitsos, 1999), ambitious language used to express rebellious ideas (McLeod, 2003) and, with the most obvious way to signal one's rebellion, through a distinctive style (Hebdige, 1979; Ibrahim, 2008; Jenkins, 1983). Under the surface, these and other forms of rebellion or self-distancing help to signal conflicts due to poverty, inequality, race and gender (Brill, 2008; Daugavietis and Lāce, 2011; Forman, 2002; Leblanc, 2001; Marciniak, 2015; Oosterbaan, 2009).

However, there, has been less research on how the subculture fits into the broader societal framework and is even sanctioned by it. Peter Wade demonstrates in the case of Afro-Colombian rap that the underground culture can have a dual ambivalent relationship with the mainstream culture and state authorities. As he shows, rap artists will draw a certain line in order to maintain their distinctive identity, but will simultaneously try to adapt into the hegemonic concept of culture to gain commercial success (Wade, 1999). Similar conflicts are also explicit in the electronic music and metal scene, where commercialization often leads to accusations of selling out, but also to certain compromises in style and music (Bryson, 1996; Gilbert, 2009; Hjelm, Kahn-Harris and LeVine, 2011; Murthy, 2007; Taylor, 2007; Ventsel and Araste, 2015; Wallach, Berger and Greene, 2011).

The approach of this chapter differs substantially from both ways of interpreting the relationship between the subculture and state. The main thesis of this chapter is that when a subculture wants to avoid open conflict, it is forced to exist within the limits set by the state. In certain cases, like the punk scene in Halle, these limits can be relatively broad, including even some aspect of illegality. As the data show, authorities accept and tolerate punks' activities when they do not go too far into criminality. When GiG activists and regulars keep to the basic norms, law enforcement turns a blind eye to other (and often minor) violations. One reason for this is that the tolerance makes the club and its regulars to some extent controllable and predictable.

On the other hand, the existence of GiG can be interpreted as an expression of a local and community solidarity that also includes a degree of mutual respect. This kind of sense of community is also depicted in Paul Willis' seminal book *Learning to Labour* (2000), where a certain trickster-like youth rebellion is actually part of local working-class community culture. This kind of cultural and social intermingling of different ages and social groups is also discussed by E.P. Thompson (1964), who analyses how common leisure, rituals and social networks create a working-class community's coherence and solidarity. This is what is also observable in Halle, where punks and 'normals' tend to communicate on different levels. Mitchell writes about the 'norm consensus' and 'norm directed behaviour' in urban settings (1969: 285). As was shown above, punks are far less 'outsiders' in Halle and are more connected to various 'other' people via different practices of work and leisure, not least because they share certain common norms. The manipulation of laws and regulations from the GiG side (e.g. registering as a limited company) and tolerance from the official side are a framework for such embeddedness.

Notes

1. The best examples of this rhetoric can be found in a series of Schlachtrufe BRD (Battle songs for Federal Republic Germany), issued in the 1990s and containing songs from the most important German punk bands of the era.
2. I owe a lot here to Kai, who on several sessions told me his post-*Wende* biography. He organized concerts for such notorious 1990s street punk bands as Beck's Pistols or OHL wherever he could facilitate a big crowd. As he told me: 'I had constantly more than 10,000 DM those days in my bank account. It was a wild trip but some bands drew huge audiences and I organized concerts on a regular basis. All the big [punk] bands played in Halle and in most cases I had absolutely no problems with finding a place for the gig!'
3. This is exactly how I read the following quote: 'Research in the 1980s has increasingly emphasized the dialectic, mutually constitutive relation between state law and other normative orders. I think this reflects a new awareness of the interconnectedness of social orders, of our vulnerability to structures of domination far outside our immediate worlds, and of the ways implicit and unrecognized systems of control are embedded in our day-to-day social lives' (Merry, 1988: 880).

CHAPTER

6

GENDER IN PUNK ROCK

> Olli: Every time I visit her, she has nothing to eat. The fridge is always empty.
> Irene: I never buy food for home. I always eat out. If Olli wants food he can buy it himself.

For as long as I can remember, gender issues like equality, masculinity and femininity have been a topic of discussion in the German punk scene. Most German fanzines I read regularly in the 1990s (*Skin Up, Ox, Plastic Bombs, Moloko*) tended to criticize machismo, sexism and the humiliation of women in the music scene and everyday life. However, gender roles are problematic to evaluate in the punk scene. The plurality of opinions is, among other things, caused by multiple fractions within the punk world. The ideology of gender equality is merged simultaneously with the idealization of promiscuous male toughness and sexualization of the female body, and criticism of both. For example, among some groups of the newer hardcore scene or very political left-wing punks, feminism is enthusiastically supported and practised in both word and deed. Gender in Germany is a hotly debated issue and is important on many levels. The first thing that springs to mind – and the most recognizable symbol of such gender equality is the use of gender-conscious language. While plural forms of nouns in German are based on the male form of the word, the gender-conscious plural is formed from the feminine form of a word. For instance, when the correct plural form of the word 'fascist' is Faschisten or the plural of the male gender of the word, the politically correct way of writing it is FaschistInnen, with a capital 'I', to symbolize both men and women.[1] When pronouncing it, the person should pause before the suffix – '-innen'.[2] In certain situations a person could be openly denunciated for not using this gender-conscious grammar and yet I have witnessed discussions about whether such a way of speaking is necessary at all.[3] The use of gender-conscious grammar also signals the political profile of a punk fanzine or speeches the singer makes between songs.

Another realm of potential conflict can be found in jokes or using certain terms that could be found offensive. In using such language, one runs the risk of being confronted with criticism, either by other people or authors of the fanzines. However, in many respects, such a linguistic fight for gender equality within the punk scene seems to remain on the surface and has very little to do with reshaping existing social norms and practices. Moreover, the politically correct language or publicly critical stance toward sexist jokes does not reflect the complexity of the attitudes and practices that can be encountered. A good example is the same politically correct grammar, for while it is used by some leftist groups within or outside of punk, it is greatly ridiculed by other groups. This, however, does not mean that people who do not speak the 'gender language' are necessarily sexist. The group at the centre of the research is interesting in this sense. They decline to use politically correct speech and have adopted the image of a 'prole' (*Proll* in German) group of the local scene, but in practice masculinity and femininity are played out not only in a conservative way, but also using different, often controversial strategies. These punks attempt to reform the existing mainstream (and middle-class) perceptions of gender concepts, but also to subvert politicized gender equality within the punk scene.

The first time I had such thoughts was in the mid-1990s, when I attended a concert of the popular German Oi! punk band Pöbel & Gesocks in Berlin. The lyrics of their songs are often about heavy alcohol consumption, but also about sex from a perspective that feminists would find misogynistic and offensive. Nevertheless, the first few rows of the audience were dominated by skinhead girls who sang along with obvious enthusiasm. The peak of the concert was when the band performed a cult song 'Bier, Bars und Bräute' ('Beer, Bars and Girls') and the singer unzipped his jeans and played with his genitals. The ardour of the audience reached a climax and loud screams filled the concert hall. The topic of many of Pöbel & Gesocks' songs is – diplomatically defined – the sexual exploitation of women. On their records, the lyrics of the female protagonists are sung by women or even a female choir. The question that arises is why do young punk girls not feel humiliated when singing in a studio the part of a woman who is supposed to perform oral sex on the singer of a band? Seemingly, the women in the audience who enthusiastically sing along to these songs do not feel humiliated. Therefore, in order to understand gender relations within the street punk scene, we have to accept the simultaneous existence of different concepts, practices, attitudes and approaches, and to ask whether they form a coherent subcultural world at all. This chapter attempts to offer a more nuanced view on the topic, arguing that subcultural gender is a two-sided interplay in which multiple masculinities and femininities, performed in different situations, cannot be separated.

PUNK FEMININITY

The revolutionary self-image of punk is that it supports gender equality. For example, it is argued that the safety pin, used to repair holes in clothes, was a symbol of women's liberation – punk girls did not need to fix their boyfriends' clothes (Lydon, 1993: 317). Of course, it remains unknown whether most early punks really saw it that way. On the one hand, academic studies and autobiographies suggest that female punk bands had to struggle for recognition and female members of the punk scene were targets of sexual harassment and bigotry (O'Meara, 2003: 299–313; see also Albertine, 2014; Leblanc, 2001: 286). On the other hand, young girls found a platform for rebellion in punk and an outlet for the reconfiguration of existing gender roles (Baker, 2009; McRobbie, 1993; McRobbie and Garber, 1993; Schilt, 2003). These views tend to ignore feminist political groups within the subculture, like the above-mentioned fanzines, who are advocating a gender-equal approach within the punk scene.

However, there is a gap in the academic literature on gender in subcultural studies, especially when analysing harder forms of rock music. Very often, scholars focus solely on masculinity, mentioning women only in passing (Haenfler, 2006; Williams, 2011b; Nayak, 2003; Nayak and Kehily, 2013; Pilkington et al., 2010), or discuss it in relation to music making and performing (Lähteenmaa, 1989). When women in the scene are discussed, this topic has two predominant approaches. From one perspective, the female side of the scene is viewed as an almost autonomous space (Leblanc, 2001; Schilt, 2003). In such cases, women subculturalists are depicted as having an almost escapist ideology, with the main goal of establishing a mono-gender alternative social or physical space within the scene. Another and more common view is to discuss femininity and women's position within the group as a reaction to the attitudes of their male counterparts. The argument that skinhead girls are seen by boys as sex objects (Möller, 1997: 115–38) or that women bikers have to 'survive the "trial of tedium"' to be recognized by men (McDonald-Walker, 2000) has a similar perspective – due to their subordinate status, the behaviour and position of women depends on what the men allow them to do (see also Fox, 1987; Leblanc, 2001; Willis, 1993). Both approaches are one-sided and ignore the complex nature of gender relations in subcultures.

Indeed, punk women struggle with their less equal status within the scene, which leaves them with less space for self-manifestation. In general, in open discussions, all the punk women I talked to sooner or later admitted that 'men have it easier' within the scene and that 'men can do things that women would not get away with'. Essentially, women are automatically not taken seriously in different life situations. For example, Caren, a singer and a guitarist of a Potsdam-based punk trio, told me: 'It is very easy to be branded as a girl-band. As a fact, you do not even need an all-girl line up, sometimes it is enough when there is only one girl in the band. The status of an all-girl band usually means that you are somehow inferior [*minderwertig*], it means that you cannot play so well, and that you do not have to know how to play.' Back in the 1990s, when I was writing for a Berlin-based skinzine *Skin Up*, a female friend of mine told me about one editor-in-chief, Drutchen, a skinhead woman: 'Do you think she has it easy? To be accepted as someone [a scene activist]? In that male-dominated [German skinhead] scene a woman has to do better and do more to be part of the scene's elite.' Drutchen was indeed very active – she was well connected, she knew most key record labels and bands in Europe, she wrote excellent articles and she found great writers for the fanzine. She also had a strong character and was able to 'take a stand' against all opponents and critics.

Street punk, a cornerstone of the microworld of the GiG scene, is a tough proletarian wing of punk with explicit and a serious 'hegemonic masculinity' (Connell, 1987, 1995) problem:

> Hegemonic masculinity can be defined as the configuration of gender practice which embodies the currently accepted answer to the problem of the legitimacy of patriarchy, which guarantees (or is taken to guarantee) the dominant position of men and the subordinate position of women. (Connell, 1995: 77)

In practice, this means that women should compete with men for their subcultural position in a situation where relatively few higher prestige positions are available and most of them are somehow associated with men. Musicians roles in punk are male-dominated and seen as masculine; only the playing of wind instruments in ska bands is where women could be seen in larger numbers (Farin and Seidel-Pielen, 2002). Moreover, even an untrained eye can see that women's roles in the punk scene are defined by the hegemonic masculinity or, as Connell puts it, masculinity is 'simultaneously a place in gender relations, the practices through which men and women engage that place in gender, and the effects of these practices on bodily experience, personality and culture' (1995: 71). The crews of bands or technical staff in clubs ('roadies') are usually all male because it is physically hard work. Women could be encountered more often as sound engineers or bar staff, whereas security is again male-dominated, and a few women do it only because in this occupation in Germany men do not have the right to search women. Schippers writes that men's 'legitimate' dominance over women is guaranteed when this is 'symbolically paired with a complementary and inferior quality attached to femininity' that 'provides a rationale for social practice more generally' (Schippers, 2007: 85–102).

Nevertheless, the more subordinated status of women within the punk scene does not exclude multiple paths to gain recognition. Apart from being a musician, a woman could be a concert promotor, a journalist, someone who organizes charity and solidarity events (e.g. *Volksküche*), working in the bar in an alternative pub or running an alternative music radio show on a local radio station. In any case, the position in a subcultural hierarchy is not only defined through the importance of her activity, but also by personal characteristics. Those few women I have personally met were powerful women ready to challenge their hidden subordinate status, using their vitality and strength to build their careers on the scene. However, the women who have reached higher positions, general recognition and are well known beyond their close circle are still a minority. Due to the fact that women, by and large, are probably not a minority within the punk scene, we can talk about a certain type of sexism. The best way to answer the question of whether there is a sex imbalance in the scene was given by Pieps: 'You are wrong. There are as much girls in the scene as boys. The thing is that girls usually do not hang out in pubs that often. But when there is an event, a gig, you see more or less the same number of girls as guys.' Indeed, after several years of being among GiG regulars, I can attest to the fact that many women stopped dropping into the pub after they 'grew up' or had children and 'proper jobs' (which will be discussed below), and yet continued visiting concerts relatively frequently.

Punk women are not a coherent group and there is no standard way of dressing as a female punk. Their style could be described as a 'practice of improvisation' (Butler, 2004: 1) varying from oversexy to undersexy. The former means wearing, for example, short miniskirts, leather jackets, heavy provocative make-up and combat boots, whereas the latter is in the direction of a more casual style – sneakers, hooded sweatshirts or faded-looking pullovers, skirts, jackets and jeans (this is discussed in more detail in Chapter 2). While men keep to more coherent personal styles, punk women are more playful and experimental. One person could dress for different occasions in different styles, from the more conservative new wave look (a modest skirt, a white button-down shirt and a narrow tie) to an intentionally dressed-down hardcore outfit (band T-shirt, baggy jeans and skate shoes). Many women often wore standard 'normal' clothes and their subcultural identity was frequently indicated only by modest small band buttons on a collar or their bag. Such avoidance of a strict dress code by punk women seems to confirm the

FIGURE 6.1. Girls in punk. Photo by the author.

argument of the post-subcultural theory scholars about the demise of a subculture with its fixed dress code (Muggleton, 2000: 198). However, nothing could be further from the truth. Experimenting with different styles is fully accepted in the punk scene and does not automatically mean being 'less' punk than someone with a fixed focus on one style. Lauraine Leblanc argued correctly that female punks use the punk subculture 'to resist the prescriptions of femininity' (2001: 219). Therefore, dressing down or overdressing both symbolize how punk girls 'subvert and challenge femininity, engaging in a reconstruction of its norms' (ibid.: 13). Simone de Beauvoir writes in her seminal book *The Second Sex* that sexuality cannot be controlled rationally because sexuality contains a certain 'dramatic aspect' (de Beauvoir, 1993: 61). Feminine punk sexuality makes use of what Schippers calls *pariah femininity* – oversexualized femininity, often associated with violence and other characteristics that demonstrate female agency (2007: 95). There is a rich variety of styles in the scene regarded as feminine and sexual, both by women and men. From a mainstream point of view, punk girls could seem 'ugly' or look like 'slags', and this is certainly an intentional provocation in order to stress the escapist attitude of punk. Wilkins (2004: 328–49) juxtaposes female sexuality within the goth scene with the more regulated female appearance in mainstream society and – drawing on Lees (1993) and Tolman (1996) – writes that in mainstream society, 'to avoid the potentially ruinous label, young women must constantly manage their self-presentations, shelving their own freedom and desires' (Wilkins, 2004: 331) or risk stigmatization as a 'slag'. German society is not dissimilar from US or British society, and I recall both my male and female friends and respondents telling me many times that: 'Halle is a conservative place where people stare at you when you look different.' While overplaying one's sexuality means contesting the dominant norms of 'good taste' – or 'proper femininity' according to Wilkins (2004), underplaying it also has a similar connotation. Discussing the practices of *chola* gangster girls in a San Francisco Bay Area high school, Norma Mendoza-Denton (2008) argues that wearing gang-associated clothes endows the girls with a power – they are feared. In her study of high school subcultures in Bay City High School in California, Mary Bucholtz (2011) shows that nerd girls who dress and behave asexually thereby address their lack of common ground with other subcultures in the schoolyard, but also with nonsubcultural youth. Judith Butler writes that 'gender proves to be performative, constituting the identity it is purported to be. In this sense, gender is always a doing' (1999: 33). Young punk women who openly challenge the perception of modesty or sexuality in adopting a certain image, simultaneously reproducing their outsider status to society and at the same time signalling their association with the punk scene.

In Chapter 2 I showed that the radicalism of a woman's outfit is determined by her courage and also by her life outside of the subculture. Psychobilly girl and hairdresser Wenke told me: 'I must pay attention to how I look. Some customers are very conservative, and my income depends on my reputation. Therefore, I wear jumpers that cover my tattoos.' When comparing pictures of Wenke when she drops into GiG to have a beer after work with how she dresses for weekend concerts, the difference is remarkable. The modest, and somewhat boring outfit, of a 'decent' hairdresser includes a grey jumper, corduroy trousers and a ponytail. Her weekend outfit usually means an open, slim 1950s-style fit dress exposing her tattoos.

Punk women of the GiG crew have turned the necessity to avoid the 'spectacular' subcultural style into a virtue by stressing that in such a way, they can work, earn money and be autonomous. Selina Todd argues that the main difference between working-class and middle-class women in the United Kington has always been that working-class women worked, whereas middle-class women tended to be housewives (2015: 209) and argues that 'the vital aspect of working-class "community" [is] work' (ibid.: 176). The tradition of the middle-class *Hausfrau* or housewife that was very common in West Germany did not exist in the GDR. However, the proletarian cult of self-sufficiency exists in Eastern Germany across the sex divide and therefore women also take pride in earning enough money to be financially autonomous, regardless of whether the income is legal or illegal. This is the point where necessity is turned into a virtue. There exists research showing that middle-class and working-class punk women dress differently. Interestingly, the results can be contradictory – namely, some studies show that unlike middle-class punk women, working-class punk women dress in a more conventional feminine way, whereas other research demonstrates the opposite. Kathryn Fox (1987: 349) found that middle-class punk women 'dressed in a more traditionally feminine manner, glorifying and exaggerating the glamor girl image reminiscent of the sixties', whereas working-class punk women 'identified with a more masculine, working class image, de-emphasizing their feminine attributes'. Leslie Roman shows that when working class punk girls preferred sexual attire then girls from the middle class background were distinguished by their 'purportedly ambisexual or unisex clothing' (1988: 176). Lauraine Leblanc adds that in her research, she has found 'no stylistic differences among punk girls that could be attributed to class differences' (2001: 141). In Halle, and in Germany in generally, a more visible and extreme visual style within the punk scene is usually associated with squatters, people participating in alternative culture centres, bohemian art projects and leftist communes. In Halle, such people were concentrated in a much younger scene around Reil 78 club. Very often, this fraction of punk has a significant share of university, especially art school students.[4] In Germany, many such people come from relatively wealthy homes where parents can afford to send their children regular money to rent a flat and cover their everyday needs. While I never really noticed any enmity between the regulars of Halle's different alternative club nights, a dislike of the 'normal' students of *Mittelschicht* was not unusual. For example, when I suggested to Wenke that we should go to a soul night in the town's most prominent student club, she looked at me with dismay, saying: 'Du kriegst mich nie in einen Studentenclub!' (You will never get me into the student club!). One of the funniest examples is when I decided to go for a drink with Irene, who was the girlfriend of Olli. We landed in a café that housed, at that time, an art auction of local artists. At some point, we decided to withdraw to the smoking room and when the door closed behind us, Irene sighed: 'Did you see these hippies? Did you notice how they are dressed? Totally without any taste!' She then went into a monologue where she ridiculed the outfits of the people in the main room. It was obvious that she disliked them all, dismissing them as 'hippies', a popular disparaging expression in the street punk scene to criticize everything middle class or akin to the typical university student.

When looking at women among GiG regular guests then, with one exception, none of them had a university education. Instead, they went through a vocational school or state-funded retraining courses where they learned to be waitresses, shop attendants, hairdressers or bakery workers, and some of them had no formal professional education at all. These women were well aware of the gap between them and the more affluent *Mittelschicht*, and also acknowledged their affiliation with the working class (see more on social mobility, the education gap and hidden class in Chapter 3). I recall a chat with Wenke when I asked here who her closest friends were, and her response was: 'Halt Arbeiter' (Just working class).

The participation in a subculture gave women the option not only to ignore the dominant perceptions of femininity – or 'hegemonic femininity' as Bucholtz (1999: 123) calls it – in German society, but also to rebel against the gender roles of working-class women in particular. The style of working-class girls in Germany is, as in many other European countries, oversexualized and flamboyant. This is a style associated with cocktail bars, disco culture and expensive techno clubs. This style is in constant flux, but certain elements like expensive heavy jewellery, skintight clothes and long dyed hair seem to remain unchanged. Such women are often referred to by 'scene girls' as *Bierdermädchen*, an expression that is difficult to translate. *Biederlich* as an adjective means 'petit bourgeois' in German, but *Bierdermädchen* or *biederliche* girl means a Victoria Beckham-esque flashiness, which is controversial from the point of view of generally accepted good taste. Coming back to the subcultural style, it offers a great variety of possibilities to express one's identity through clothes and accessories while avoiding an expression of mainstream sexiness and femininity. This issue has been discussed in more detail in Chapter 2, but style offers a possibility to address one's belongingness and sexuality through almost invisible details. Since the dawn of the Teddy Girls of the 1950s followed by the mod girls of the 1960s, a disposable income offered working-class subcultural girls and women a means to decide about their appearance (Macilwee, 2015: 113; McRobbie and Garber, 1993: 185). This is also the beginning of a controversial status that McRobbie and Garber (ibid.: 182) call the 'relative subordination of girls'. On the one hand, financial independence meant and means control over one's life and style, while on the other hand it still means acknowledging the dominance of masculine or even patriarchal social norms within the group. This all puts women from a subculture in a position where they resist the mainstream notion of a 'good decent girl' and the subcultural solidarity offers them the social space to do it, but simultaneously they are confronted with a social pressure from the male side of a subculture.

In general, belonging to a punk subculture helps women to meaningfully 'cross boundaries' where unconventional behaviour and style can be channelled into a creative music making, as Viv Albertine shows in the case of the all-girl band The Slits (Albertine, 2014: 162–63). In this sense, it is hard not to agree with Stacy Thompson, who writes that punk is 'a threat and liberation' (2004: 5). Challenging the dominant concept of femininity is, of course, one part of the subcultural identity, but this should not be seen as the purpose for dressing 'differently'. In the inward-looking world of a subculture, a message sent to fellow subculturalists is as important as provoking the mainstream. Some studies show that in harder styles of punk, like hardcore, women do not participate in the mosh pit on an equal basis with men due to the physically aggressive way of punching and elbowing in front of the stage (Haefner, 2004; Willis, 1993, Williams, 2011b). In the concerts held in the clubs in Halle, such voluntary segregation was not apparent. This is partly explained by the more melodic music performed in such clubs. Ska, melodic punk rock, street punk and folk punk are less aggressive than hardcore, and so is the dancing associated with these. In a similar way, there was no clear gender difference when it came to alcohol consumption: some women drank heavily, others more modestly. Being drunk at a concert was nothing they could be condemned for. Social identities in the subculture are not bound to the degree of alcohol consumption, as the trend tends to be in the mainstream societies of most European countries (see McDonald, 1994b). A relaxed attitude to alcohol consumption reflects the egalitarian nature of a subcultural atmosphere and – like the sexual egalitarianism in goth clubs noted by Wilkins – 'obfuscates the broader landscape of gender inequality' (2004: 329). In the clubs in Halle, where men's attitudes to their female counterparts are usually respectful, there exists a sense of solidarity, and any kind of sexual harassment is not tolerated. Moreover, a man should never take advantage of the intoxication of a woman. Because drinking is a standard part of clubbing, accepting a drink or being drunk should not be interpreted as a signal from a woman to a man. 'I have the feeling that when I behave in a nasty way to some girl, I get all the guys on my neck', I was told by Stephan, a skinhead in his mid-thirties. In the German street punk scene, women are usually regarded as being 'part of the gang' and protecting your female friends is the duty of every man, which is, no doubt, a hegemonic masculine role, but also a demonstration of subcultural solidarity.[5] This gives them a sense of security and indeed 'our' women tend to be protected from harassment, at least at public events like concerts. On the other hand, such egalitarian solidarity creates an illusory gender equality with its hidden hierarchies that to a large extent remain unvoiced and unquestioned (cf. Wilkins, 2004). Nevertheless, I recall hearing claims that a rock-based subculture is the highest form of emancipation a girl can have in a subcultural world, and these claims were usually related to the notion that in the rock, punk or metal scenes, the women can behave more in a way that in other circumstances would be inappropriate.

It has been argued that women's participation in subcultures is rather passive and they often withdraw and create their own 'bedroom cultures' (McRobbie and Garber, 1993: 177–88; Schilt, 2003), but according to my observations, this was not the case in Halle. Another argument is that women in subcultures are invisible or play a secondary role (McRobbie and Garber, 1993). As I have shown in Chapter 4, in an economic sense women are indeed secondary within the scene, being able to contribute much less to the reciprocal networks. This position is also vaguely reflected in the social culture of GiG, where an important aspect of communication is chatting about work or negotiating future jobs. When this happens – and it is quite frequent –women at the table or the bar counter usually seem quite excluded from the conversation. On the other hand, when the discussion involves a more common ground like music, films, local news or gossip, there is no difference in the participation of the sexes.

However, one aspect where many of my female informants felt discriminated against was in terms of sexual freedom, where 'it is more allowable for men than for women'. Promiscuous behaviour was more often condemned in the case of women, and not only by men. A remark made by one psychobilly woman when our conversation turned to F., a rebellious punk woman who had a reputation for constantly changing her partners, was not unusual in this respect. 'She has had them all', she said, hinting that F. had slept with most men on the GiG circuit, an unrealistic assumption in any sense. The close-knit nature of the GiG crew means that most people were aware of other people's dating or break-up stories. Therefore, many women kept it secret when they were simultaneously dating different men. Perhaps because I had a certain outsider status, in private conversations some women confessed to me that they were dating more than one man and sometimes even married men. 'I have my own sexual needs [*Bedürfnisse*]', said one punk woman. However, it seems that a promiscuous sex life means having multiple partners who did not belong to the GiG group. In this way, such relationships could be kept secret and the partner could be dropped without the public drama of partnerships ending within the group.

Nevertheless, extraordinarily promiscuous behaviour was an exception and according to my observations, most people around me were in traditional long-term relationships. Yet, the nature of such relationships was controversial, as demonstrated by the quotes given at the beginning of the chapter. In the relationships, two different views on gender roles were often apparent. The independence of punk girls in terms of deciding how to live their own lives conflicted more often than not with the more conservative and traditional views on relationships with men. Women in punk circles are simultaneously subordinated and bend themselves to traditional gender roles, especially when it comes to motherhood. On the other hand, they rebel against dominant German *bürgerliche* (petite bourgeoisie) gender roles through dress, alcohol consumption, relative sexual freedom and sometimes even violent behaviour.

STREET PUNK MASCULINITY

Self-discipline and controlling one's drives is a symbol of masculinity that leans on the proletarian understanding of toughness and credibility. Probably the respondents of this study are lucky – unlike the working-class Geordies in the studies undertaken by Nayak (2003; 2006: 813–31), they have not been confronted by a sudden decrease in traditional working-class jobs on the scale of that seen in the former industrial towns in England, with the ensuing high levels of unemployment. The crisis of masculinity due to the shift from 'learning to labour' to 'learning to serve' has little relevance in the case of the 'tough guys' from GiG who are mainly engaged in 'real work' (cf. Nayak and Kehily, 2013). With few exceptions, most of them earn their main or partial income from manual jobs like construction work, cooking, the distribution of food and clothes by a charity or working as roadies. The engagement with physical jobs is ritualistically confirmed after work in GiG, when one of the beloved topics is discussing the hardship of the latest working day or cursing supervisors for their stupidity. As explained below, when several studies of the tougher edge of punk relate masculinity with the idealization of an aesthetically worked-out male body, the street punks of Halle do not correspond to that approach. Therefore, it can be argued that the focus of masculinity has shifted from a body cult to one of self-control and self-reliance. Valuing people not according to their appearance and style helps to maintain the belief that 'the family' is an egalitarian group, based on solidarity, where a relatively small man could be relied upon in spite of his body type.

The above-mentioned vocal discussions about the working day were also a ritualistic confirmation of masculinity. As Judith Butler wrote: 'There is no gender identity behind the expressions of gender; that identity is performatively constituted by the very "expressions" that are said to be its results' (2004: 33). The narratives of a working day were directly related to the working-class origins of the people present, but also reflected and reinforced their masculinity. I understood it better once I had listened to hours of stories about carrying heavy sacks on the construction site or constantly repeating stories about how underpaid –'almost for free' – such work was. The working man's masculinity in such narratives is juxtaposed with the 'soft masculinity' (Heath, 2003) of their superiors, middle class or 'students and hippies' as these people tend to be referred to. Demonstrating how everything is linked to masculinity is well illuminated by a quote from Olli. After being forced to listen to his complaints about rich engineers, whom he stated drive fancy cars but do not know anything about building, he finished by tapping me on my shoulder: 'But at the end of a day we get their girls!' Butler argues correctly that sex and concepts of gender are inseparable (2004). Later on, I will show how this link can produce controversies, how sexual prowess is present in discussions in male-only company, and when men start to boast about their sexual conquests at open-air festivals.

It is impossible to argue that the GiG take on punk contains one coherent concept of masculinity, femininity, sexuality or gender relations. When an observer goes to GiG on a regular night, they see different ways of dressing and behaviour. Men usually preferred clothing that emphasized their masculinity. The mixture of different styles could be called 'street style' with a certain skinhead and punk touch (this is discussed in further detail in Chapter 2). The preferred look was the 'clean and neat' outfit or loose-fitting jackets, a plain or band T-shirt or polo shirt, or button-down shirts of different brands, and baggy trousers or Levi's 501 jeans. Bright (especially neon) colours are unusual for men and women alike, as in Germany these are associated with techno, hipster or student culture. The footwear of choice is usually trainers and skate shoes from certain brands, or Dr. Martens boots. It is important that most of the details could be associated with particular punk, hardcore, skinhead or hooligan styles. Muscular bodies and dirty jokes demonstrate that these men are mostly engaged in hard physical labour and are 'tough guys', *Arbeiter* or working-class men. One's hairstyle is an important element of the look, so both men and women pay great attention to this. Although the regular GiG crowd contained few men with long hair – usually in a ponytail or dreadlocks – most sported shorter hair or no hair at all. From a shaved head to a crew cut or rockabilly quiffs, everything was present and – as a rule – in superb condition. Beards, in general, are not very popular; most men are always more or less clean-shaven, but a few had sideburns. This style fits in well with the globally popular proletarian masculine mode of dressing. However, among friends and GiG regulars, there were men who differed in their appearance, such as Matthias, a beloved and highly regarded member of the GiG crew. He was relatively small and slim, wore his hair long due to a preference for metal music and did not convey a tough impression at all. He was rather androgynous and softly spoken.

Punk masculinity in subculture studies is often interpreted as being a form of communication with the dominant society (i.e. sending out certain signals of rebellion) or embodying subcultural fantasies. This is true to some extent, but sometimes the communication between subculturalists from both sexes is more important. Studies have shown how influential friends and peer groups are performing masculine feats because 'friends are the point of reference' (Trell and von Hoven, 2014: 317-–36). Butler (1999) states that gender is enacted at specific social sites and so are certain roles that men enact within the scene. These roles, as a rule, are related to personal qualities such as toughness, reliability, loyalty and honour.

The street punk or Oi! music, which draws punks and skinheads similar to those who visit GiG, is a masculine music style when it comes to its per-

FIGURE 6.2. Rituals of masculinity. Photo by the author.

formance. As is usual in most other genres of punk, street punk is a male-dominated music scene; women are rarely in bands[6] and are the minority in the audience. This music is usually performed in small and medium-sized clubs, hence the familial and relatively relaxed atmosphere of concerts. The egalitarian nature of the genre is stressed through the interaction between musicians and the audience; often, people from the audience climb onto the stage to sing along with the chorus. What makes street punk distinct from many other genres of punk is its emphasis on the masculine performance aspect of the concerts. Sooner or later, several men from the audience take off their shirts and one can see lots of bare-chested men on the stage or in the front rows of the crowd. In small smoke-filled clubs, sweaty bodies rubbing against each other, a plethora of tattoos and an aggressive but nevertheless carefully practised pogoing, which creates a specific feeling of brotherhood or 'one gang' as it is referred to in many songs.[7]

Street punk shows are the quintessence of what the scene claims to be. Masculine closeness and solidarity is symbolized through various rituals, starting with how a group of friends arrives to the venue, buys beer and then cheers loudly before taking a first sip. It is common to arrive in groups of four to six men 'because it makes the impression of a gang', as I heard it put in my Berlin days. Friends greet each other loudly and with hugs. The presentation of male punks and skinheads is – as a rule – as self-confident and 'tough'. This does not necessarily mean the way they dress, but a certain body language and the aura that surrounds them.[8] The masculinity in question is complicated. While the fans of hardcore music are notorious for their athletic bodies and preoccupation with bodybuilding, there is hardly a body ideal when it comes to street punk. Looking at the male customers of GiG, it is impossible to find an example of the dominant model of a 'good-looking' physique. Pumped-up bodies are sometimes present, but more often beer bellies are in evidence. While most men prefer a shaved head or short hair, I have never observed any enmity towards those men who wear dreadlocks or have long hair. For example, Olli is a sturdy tall man who dresses in a stereotypical 'punk rock way', and one his best friends is the relatively small, skinny metal fan Matthias (mentioned above), who wears his hair long.

In the academic literature on punk and its derivatives, the body cult is mainly associated with hardcore (especially straight edge) and the right wing. These groups pay attention to body image, and regular training is associated with self-control and discipline (Pilkington, 2010: 187–209; Pilkington et al., 2010; cf. Haefner, 2007; Willis, 1993: 365–83).

The GiG crew understands self-control differently. One part of my ethnographic fieldwork was conducted on construction sites helping Olli with his tasks and making observations about the economic practices of my respondents. We usually got up early, around 7 AM, and drove to the site. On the way, we had our first coffee at one of the small kiosks that can be found in any German town. Without breakfast, we worked until lunchtime. While I then expected some food, Olli had other plans. We hastily drank a few cups of coffee, smoked some cigarettes and returned to work. We kept on until the end of the working day, then went to eat either at home or on the way home in a takeaway. I learned very quickly that Olli and his comrades do not like to be reminded about food during working hours. On one of my first days, I heard how an older worker explained to a young apprentice the working ethos: 'You finish your work. I mean, you finish your task, not your work day. If it takes longer, you do it as long as it is needed. Then you go to eat.' There were of course exceptions. On a few occasions, we had a lunch break, especially when we worked in the villages around Halle. We took an hour to walk to a local butcher who also made food, bought some soup or sausages, had a cup of coffee and returned after we were finished. It might be that Olli decided to have a lunch break because he – like most Germans – highly appreciates the food offered by traditional village butchers. On the other hand, I recall how he firmly refused to eat when I helped him renovate a private home and the landlady offered us sandwiches. On another occasion, when Olli took a three-day break from drinking due to a drunken weekend, I heard him explaining his temporary abstinence by stating: 'I have everything under control!'

Referring back to the beginning of this section, physical toughness is acted out at concerts where masculinity is very much on display. In the words of the music sociologist Frith (1996: 157): 'Music, like identity, is both performance and story, describes the social in the individual and the individual in the social, the mind in the body and the body in the mind.' Energetically pogoing to lyrics about the working-class struggle, the harshness of street life or eternal brotherhood relates the 'troublesome body' of a working-class man (Nayak, 2003, 2006) to a respective ideology-laden text and gives a certain rebellious edge to the dancing. The body exposure and contact in street punk pogo is simultaneously aggressive and carefully choreographed. Pogoing can mean an occasional elbow in one's face, but usually this is avoided because people on the dancefloor make sure that others do not get hurt. A person who loses his balance and falls down is usually dragged to his feet by bystanders because there is a risk of being stomped on by heavy Dr Marten boots. During stage diving, people from the audience helpfully form a human pillow to catch the person who jumps from the stage. In concordance with the song texts, these small symbols of camaraderie tie together the self-proclaimed 'otherness' of the East German working class, showing their masculine group solidarity, in opposition to the hippies' soft music and calm ways of enjoying it (see also Büsser, 2007: 29).

Another aspect of street punk masculinity is a certain tongue-in-cheek homosociality. Physical contact between men is relatively usual at and outside of concerts.[9] When meeting each other, men greet with demonstrative hugs. In half-naked pogoing, guys grab one another's arms, heads or shoulders. At first glance, this seems to be a contradiction, but only initially. The German street punk scene is not especially homophobic, but certain forms of behaviour like holding hands is regarded as unmasculine or even effeminate. In European culture, male homosociality has not always being associated with homosexuality and, in fact, this transformation is very recent (Wilkie, 2010: 127). Nevertheless, sexuality – or denial of it – seems to be important here in our case. Some studies on skinheads have documented certain erotic undertones in male physical contact and the exposure of nakedness (Pilkington et al., 2010; Möller, 1997: 115–38), but I discovered no sign of it among people during my studies. Homosociality, as an expression of camaraderie, is regarded here as a masculine, and nonerotic, form of communication. I did not hear any crude jokes about homosexuality to help distance the actors from homosexuals and to define their practices as heterosexual (cf. Trell and von Hoven (2014) regarding men's dancing and Pilkington et al. (2010) for Russian skinhead homosocial friendship practices). Hugging and other forms of physical contact instead send the signal 'You have nothing to be afraid of, I am not homosexual!' and its anti-erotic nature could be associated with German or more generally West European ways of understanding male body contact.[10]

Nayak and Kehily define gender practices as a lived process that 'is "summoned into life" under [the] weight of particular historical conditions, how it is discursively struggled over, repudiated or enacted' (2013: 5). Demonstrative physical contact among the punks researched for this book is a provocative challenge of dominant attitudes in German society, where physical closeness among heterosexual men is rather limited. Its nonsexual nature nevertheless goes back to the ethos of certain heavily physical and masculine working-class occupations like industrial workers, miners or the military, which all have a strong legacy in Halle, and is probably linked to life situations where men have to rely on each other without paying attention to any 'shameful' connotation. In any case, when I mentioned the popularity of specific homosocial practices to my informants, I received either a surprised stare or the response: 'It is just friends!'[11]

The general acceptance of masculinity as a practice and spiritual quality not bound to particular body ideals is nowhere more noticeable than during drinking sessions and aggressive behaviour. Heavy alcohol consumption is widespread among Halle's punks, notwithstanding their allegiance to different crews, clubs and bars. In the academic and nonacademic literature, the embeddedness of alcohol among street punks is often connected to a proletarian bravado or even to what Martin Büsser calls 'regressive stereotypes of the proletariat' (2007: 31) and, indeed, alcohol consumption offers a huge variety of strategies to express one's masculinity. In contrast to many other countries, different sorts of drinks in Germany are only vaguely related to social identity (cf. Nayak, 2003: Introduction; Shapin, 2012; Haine, 2006). It could be argued that wine is more of a middle-class drink, but beer is popular among all social groups; the difference is in the excessiveness of consumption. According to my experience, heroic drinking stories are an important part of German punk folklore. Alcohol-related adventures pop up when people tell stories from the festivals, a recent concert or their last night out. When looking at pictures of open-air concerts, collective holidays or a spontaneous pub visit in my own archive, the common features of these photos are jolly grins and raised beer bottles or cans. Consuming alcohol is a natural part of relaxing in German punk circuits, with the exception of some groups like the straight edge crowd. The stories often involve descriptions of falling over, consuming enormous amounts of alcohol, ending up in fights or just having a very vague memory of what happened in the last few hours of the party. Cultivation of the 'regressive stereotypes' is probably also one reason why beer and strong liquor like Kümmerling, Jägermeister and Moskovskaya vodka is immensely popular among punks.[12] Drinking could be a rebellious act in certain circumstances (Dragadze, 1994: 145–52; Toren, 1997: 153–74), where participants push the acceptable limits in the mainstream. When discussing alcohol consumption in Andean communities, Harvey states: 'Given that drinking is a social affair, the style of drinking is extremely important' (1997: 209–34). Here we again can return to the beginning of the section. When people arrive at the concert, one of the first things they do is to buy beer, bang beer glasses together and greet each other with demonstratively loud cheers. This is a ritualistic way of signalling the presence of a 'gang' in the venue. In between, one of the lads buys a round of schnapps – small bottles of hard liquor like Kümmerling – which are emptied in one gulp. Such social drinking is very common among the German working class, especially mixing beer with shots of hard liquor. Sometimes it seems that for punks in Germany, almost any kind of socializing includes drinking. For example, the role of alcohol in communication was also emphasized by Olli when he explained why he was having his 'business talks' in clubs: 'When "normal" people want to discuss business, they meet to have a cup of coffee, we meet for a beer.' In punk circuits, drinking is a method of creating and cementing social ties; this is especially the case for men, but is also not unusual among women. Therefore, it is no wonder that this practice is also generally accepted by both sexes.

Another – and logical – expression of masculinity is aggression and violence. It is wrong to argue that violent behaviour is frequent among the people who were the subjects of my study. However, fighting occurs and is not that unusual. One of my first personal encounters with violence among Halle's punks was at a birthday party I was invited to in 2002. One of the visitors was a stout, overweight skinhead with a provocative attitude. At some point, his jokes crossed a line for another visitor, who was also a skinhead, a fight broke out and the first skinhead was thrown out. Punks and skinheads around GiG could be characterized not as violent, but as constantly ready for violence. Skinheads in this context are considered, as a rule, more aggressive than punks. A readiness for aggressiveness was named as the first indicator when I asked during my interviews what the difference was between punks and skinheads:

> Me: Is there any difference between punks and skinheads?
>
> Berndt: Mmmm, I think they are pretty much the same. Skinheads are more prone to violence, they are more aggressive. (Field notes, 2006)

The common understanding is that a man should stand up for himself when necessary, whereas the 'necessity' is defined spontaneously. 'I went to Bauernclub last week', Olli told me once. 'When I was in the toilet then some guy came up to me and said, "You guys think you are so cool". I punched him twice in face, but the whole evening was ruined.' This incident is illuminating in many respects. Olli is definitely a man who follows the rule that 'I will not allow anyone to tell me what to do' (Ich lass mir nichts sagen!), but he does not enjoy violent situations.[13] Nevertheless, in certain situations he feels like he has to use physical force. Of course, some members of the scene were more violent, like Pyh, a skinhead who was described to me as a 'burner' (*Brenner*), a football term for an impulsive and aggressive person. Indeed, he happened to be involved in violent situations relatively often. One day he recommended a Turkish kebab house in the city centre to me, adding: 'Unfortunately I cannot go there for a while.' When I asked him for some clarification as to why, he told me: 'Not that long ago I passed the place during the night. The Turk came out and said something about me being a Nazi. I stopped and told him to fuck off. We had a little argument and he touched me in the face [i.e. hit me in the face]. So I hit him back and he fell down. Other Turks ran out with their kebab knives and I had to run away before they cut me into pieces.' Pyh was definitely not a racist; indeed, he gained some fame in the local press in 2010 when he protected a small group of refugees in a night tram from harassment by local neo-Nazis and ended up in a fist fight with four of them. The classic study by Dunning et al. on football hooligans shows that the acceptance of aggression is higher among the working classes, where young people confront the violent behaviour of others at an early age and grow up with 'a more positive attitude towards aggressive behaviour' (1988: 209). The authors also add that 'fighting in its various forms can be exciting, and that too, can be enjoyable' (ibid.: 192). Indeed, some people, like Pyh, enjoy fighting and therefore constantly get in trouble. The important point is that in most cases, such violent behaviour is not condemned. As is mentioned in the studies referenced in Chapter 7, deviancy and criminal behaviour indicate that the reason to behave violently is more often related to seeking recognition among friends and one's close social environment. I would add that a peer group's approval of violence makes it easier to start a fight.

For an environment where violence is relatively common, a few regulations work as a 'code of honour' (*Ehrenkode*). There are certain rules that make one's behaviour in a violent conflict 'honest', but these are difficult to define. Some rules are out of the question, e.g. a man should not hit a woman, someone lying on the ground should not be hit, and a group of men should not attack a lone person without good reason. All other scenarios are a matter of debate. For example, one skinhead girl told me during my Berlin years 'Nazis are not included in the code of honour', which means that even those few existing rules do not apply for 'outsiders' or 'enemies'. The rest is debatable and often creates controversy. An event that was typical of the scene was when during a party, one very drunk man pressed a burning cigarette into the forehead of another guest. The perpetrator woke up next morning without any memory of what he had done. The incident caused some controversial feelings among their friends. Some condemned the incident. Another position was summed up by Ian, who used to be a violent skinhead in his younger days: 'This is the thing with street punk. We sing about violence and pretend we like it. Then when we are confronted with it, people start moaning.'

To conclude this section, the masculinity in the GiG street punk ethos is firmly related to a certain readiness to answer or initiate violence to demonstrate loyalty, solidarity or 'pride' (*Stolz*), as well as self-control and economic independence, while it is less closely linked to the physical qualities of the body or one's outlook.

Many examples from the discussions I had during the fieldwork confirm that women also share these views. The approval of violence by women in the street punk and hardcore scene is an interesting topic and shows a salient dominance of the working-class 'tough guy' ethos. There are researchers who argue that on the working-class side of punk, girls support masculine behaviour and often adopt it (Roman, 1988). Punks are not alone here. Teddy Girls not only favoured aggressive guys as boyfriends, but also used to fight themselves (Macilwee, 2015: 117–19), the Mexican criminal Cholo subculture in the United States contains aggressive and criminal girls, *chola* (Mendoza-Denton, 2008), and some of the Russian neo-Nazi skinhead gangs in the northern Russian town Vorkuta had female gang leaders (Pilkington et al., 2010). In common with those working-class women in England who approve of violence more than their peers in other classes (Dunning et al., 1988: 197), punk women in Halle had a positive attitude to certain expressions of aggression. This moral support creates an atmosphere where men can have a feeling of being under pressure to 'strike back', as was the case with me at a concert in GiG. Some young guy turned over the metal furnace that was used to heat GiG during the winter. It fell on my boot, which was quite painful. When, because of the pain, I said a few harsh words to the proprietor, a girl next to me asked: 'Why didn't you knock him out?' For a second I had the feeling that I should do it, but then I regained control over my emotions.

GENDER IN RELATIONSHIPS

Punk femininity and masculinity in its multiple forms should not be seen as worlds separated from each other. GiG and all the concerts I have studied were attended by men and women, both young and old. Apart from hanging around in bars or concerts, people of both sexes met in the summer around the barbecue or to drink beer in the parks. As was mentioned above, long-lasting relationships were not uncommon on the punk scene, although these relationships were not always stable.

I recall when at the end of the 1990s, while living in Berlin, I read a youth magazine where different young people from East and West Berlin were asked to explain whether relationships in the 'East' and 'West' were different. One constantly repeated argument was that young people in the 'East' were more eager to move in together, whereas *Wessies* maintained their apartments and had a visiting relationship. Among punks in Halle who were in a relationship, moving together into one flat was a common practice. Simultaneously, of course, there were couples who kept their individual apartments. The 'doing gender' (West and Zimmerman, 1987: 125–51) in these households – as hinted at in the epigraph at the beginning of the chapter – were rather controversial. On many occasions, I observed that on the one hand, the women attempted to maintain their independence, whereas the men on the other hand tried to force them into a more traditional role. The relative equality of the punk scene affects the attitudes of the women, but contradicts the more conservative patriarchal working-class stance of many men when it comes to relationships. The questioning of the 'masculine hegemony' led to conflicts and break-ups; in one case, the woman moved out to find her own apartment. Simultaneously, men claim more freedom for themselves. 'Olli wants to have me around, but then he just disappears for several days and does not call me', lamented his girlfriend Irene.

Subcultural partnerships often start because people meet in a subculture-related environment – concerts, scene bars or clubs – but very soon become similar to the 'mainstream' with a subcultural edge. The double standards considering promiscuity are not specific to a subculture, and nor are conflicts over money, as I have witnessed with many couples more generally. When I rented a room in Olli's flat, I often had to listen to disputes between Olli and his then-girlfriend Sandra, in which the main issue was money. For instance, Sandra regularly failed to pay her share of the rent. I recall one of these disputes when Olli raised his voice, pointing at the corner of the living room table: 'I have told you many times that every fifth day of the month the money should be put here!' The next time Sandra came home from work, she put – without saying anything – several bank notes there.

Another case of conflict was when Sandra failed to renew her driving licence because on the last day she decided to go shopping with her friends and faced a €1,000 fine. She went to stores selling underground clothing or looking for accessories that could be combined with her rock'n'roll style like key chains or badges with cherries. Here two things merge: Olli truly despises the rock'n'roll subculture and regarded spending money on rock'n'roll insignia as stupid and a waste. On the other hand, he was annoyed that Sandra regularly failed to fulfil her financial commitments to him.

Logically, many dating relationships progressed into family life, a civil partnership or a registered marriage. Couples with children are usual in the punk scene in Halle and outside of it. Studies on ageing in the subcultures seldom analyse the marriages and family lives of subculturalists. Davis (2012: 105–18) discusses 'growing up' and 'giving up' among US punk musicians. The focus is very symptomatic of such literature, where the author thematizes whether musicians are able to combine musicianship and family life. Haenfler dedicates two-and-a-half pages to 'parenting' in subcultures and concludes that subcultural parents can, but do not have to 'pass subcultural capital to their children' (2014: 153) via sharing knowledge, record collections or taking children to concerts and dance parties.

Both Davis and Haenfler conclude that this form of 'ageing' means that the subculturalist must combine the 'normal' world with the subcultural lifestyle, and that in certain circumstances, it can cause tensions. It sounds plausible that being a member of an actively touring band can raise alarming issues, both in the family and in the band. However, musicians are a minority in the punk scene in Germany, where many 'ageing' punks successfully combine family life and their subcultural pursuits. At the end of the 1990s, a friend of mine, a skinhead named Ian from Berlin, got married. His wedding ceremony had two parts – an ordinary blessing of state officials and a subsequent party in a punk club. In the first part, only a few friends from his band attended (one of them as the best man), whereas no 'normal' relatives came to the club.

A punk couple – married or not – are generally well accepted by their relatives and the scene. It is not unusual to sit in GiG and be shown pictures of children of members of the scene. I have also attended family events where grandparents sit at one table with their tattooed children and grandchildren. I recall when I met Pyh on a street in Halle with his partner and their newborn son in the pushchair. He stopped me and, full of pride, showed me his son and introduced the child's mother. Henrietta L. Moore's (2012: 151–71) reading of Butler's gender performativity theory stresses the 'actuality of ambiguity and multiplicity in the way gender is enacted and subjectivities are formed' (ibid.: 155). A family with children is confirmation of the dominance of heterosexual normativity, embedded in the salience of the working-class ethos. My anecdotal experience shows that in Berlin, there is often discussion about whether having children is *spiessig* (petit bourgeois) or not, but among punks in Halle, successful families are treated with respect. On the one hand, this confirms the assumption that subcultures ceased to be purely *youth resistance* (cf. Haenfler, 2014: 151). On the other hand, scene habitus cannot be disconnected from the social background and environment (see O'Connor, 2008). Similar to the punks in Mexico, in Halle 'punk subculture is selectively accepted ... according to what makes sense for their situation' (O'Connor, 2002: 225–36). Punk parents combine the subculture and family life by attending concerts and festivals, and playing in bands. The compromises they make are approved – for example, not going to a concert when no one can babysit the child. Being a parent also means being self-sufficient and responsible, features related to the street punk ethos (Chapter 4, but rooted in a local working-class worldview. Therefore, having a family is rarely seen as a problem.[14]

Partnerships in the street punk style involve a constant manoeuvring between different and contradicting perceptions of how to shape the relationship. On the one hand, women who are part of the scene gladly sing along to songs that radical left-wing feminists classify as sexist and humiliating, debunking both radical left-wing views on gender order and a petit bourgeois understanding of good behaviour. On the other hand, the relationships are shaped by the dominance of masculinity with a strong touch of patriarchy. Simultaneously, both men and women reject the feminist gender order of more radical left-wing punk as too politically correct and limiting. The banning of some Oi! bands because of their alleged sexism in such clubs was a constant source of jokes. To put the quote 'The real question is what is the logic of relationship?' (Ortner, 1996: 108) in the context of this study, a partnership was a (sometimes uneasy) combination of a subcultural lifestyle with the traditional working-class gender order and hierarchies.

Notes

1. It seems like the current trend is to use * instead of the capital 'I', so the new correct form of the gender-conscious writing is Mieter*innen or Gründer*innen (see, for example, https://www.berlin.de/rbmskzl/regierender-buergermeister/michael-mueller/interviews/2016/artikel.708035.php (retrieved 9 December 2019)).
2. I recall seeing the gender-equal form of the word 'fascists' in one fanzine discussing political views of the controversial German punk band OHL. I admit that I was surprised to discover such a respect for female fascists in a left-oriented journal.
3. A body of academic work studies how language use stresses gender distinctions in popular culture. For example, Anna Feigenbaum writes that 'adjectival gender markers and gender binaries also work to support an authentic/inauthentic dichotomy that devalues women. This type of distinction often precedes a non-gender specific noun, such as, "the *girl* rocker" or "a *chick* singer". These markings are usually employed only when women are being referred to. One does not often come across "the *male* rocker", just "the rocker". Similarly, female fans will be identified as, for example, "the overwhelmingly *female* audience".' She goes on to argue that: 'This either treats the fans as an anomaly or stresses their gender in a way which marks them as outside of the "real" rock community' (Feigenbaum, 2005: 37–57). Simon Frith and Jon Savage argue that linguistic distinction shows how 'some sectors of [the popular audience] are seen as more significant than others' (Frith and Savage, 1997: 15). Judith Butler writes that: 'Central to ... these views, however, is the notion

that sex appears within hegemonic language as a *substance,* as, metaphysically speaking, a self-identical being' (Butler, 1999: 25–26). For Luce Irigaray (1985), grammar itself supports a model of gender as a binary relation. I agree with McCallum (1996: 77–99) in that in such interpretations, we should also look at the nature of the language where the meaning of certain words and grammatical particularities can be language-specific.

4. Some research indicates that class differences are felt in the US-American punk scene (Fox, 1987; Lamy and Levin, 1985; Torrez, 2012: 131–32). Buszek (2012: 147–48), for example, describes the Riot Grrrl movement as a rebellion of feminist female art school and university students. In Germany in the 1990s, I recall no enmity within the punk scene expressed in terms of class, but a different understanding of lifestyle indicated this sentiment very well. The working-class cult of self-sufficiency (Jones, 2011; Todd, 2015) was expressed in the expensive clothing and footwear of skinheads and street punks, as well as the habit of having their *Stammtisch* in relatively expensive pubs. Moreover, popular ska and punk/Oi! festivals (like the first Holidays in the Sun Festival in Berlin in 2000) were expensive. This relatively expensive lifestyle was criticized by squatter punks as 'commercial', whereas squatters were often described by my skinhead friends as 'dirty' and 'unwashed'.
5. The gang-like nature of skinhead/punk groups is not very well studied but it is, nevertheless, illuminated in the subculturalists' literature. Steve Goodman (1995) describes it in his book *England Belongs to Me* and it is very well illuminated in Gavin Watson's photo book *Skins & Punks* (2008).
6. There are some classic and newer street punk bands with female singers like Vice Squad or Deadline, and a few all-girl bands have made international career, like the Japanese Thug Murders or American Devochkas. Part of the reason why these bands have been successful is without doubt the fact that they have one or more attractive female members.
7. There are plenty of songs about solidarity in punk, but the best ones for me are 'Saturday's Heroes' by The Business, 'Never Alone' by Dropkick Murphys and of course the anthem 'If the Kids Are United' by Sham 69.
8. I recall an illuminating case from the late 1990s. I had organized a private event in a Berlin gay squat basement party room, where I invited fellow students from the university, but also my usual skinhead friends. One of my female classmates arrived slightly later. I was DJing and saw her coming through the dancing crowd. She beckoned to me, smiled and then she saw a smallish skinhead sitting by the wall. I also noticed how the smile froze on her face. Later she confessed to me: 'When I came in and saw him sitting by the wall ... I was afraid just because of how he looked' (see also the Introduction to Gavin Watson's seminal photo book *Skins* (2001)), which starts with the story how a former American hippie met his first skinheads in London in the late 1960s. He states: 'Nevertheless, I knew instinctively that these were not the sort of nice people I'd come to England looking for' (Polhemus, 2001: 6).
9. Hugs in greeting are demonstrated in many street punk videos. See 'Ghost & Ghettos' by The Loaded, 'Shipping Out to Boston' by Dropkick Murphys or 'Cultus Interruptus' by Toxpack.
10. I have observed an uneasiness connected with similar practices in Estonia and Russia.
11. Similar casual, nonsexual bodily contacts between the sexes are also common both in GiG and among German youth and young adults in general. In practice, this

means hugging and kissing as a greeting or goodbye among people who belong to the same group of friends. According to my observation, the bodily contact goes no further, as can be observed in Spain or Greece.

12. This attitude is very well expressed in a famous song of Cock Spaerrer, 'We Know How to Live', where beer is juxtaposed with 'fancy French wines' and the weekend is described as a time for vast amounts of beer and sex.
13. Olli is nevertheless someone who likes to display his masculinity and he is not the only one in the local punk scene. This is very well illuminated in a story he told me, where at one concert, he met a former girlfriend who was there with her boyfriend. When Olli chatted very familiarly with the women, the boyfriend 'grimaced' (Hat Fresse gezogen!). When I asked what happened next, Olli answered: 'What could he do, he was twenty centimetres shorter than me' (field notes, 13 October 2010).
14. The academic research on 'ageing' in punk and especially family life is indeed extremely scarce. My own anecdotal experience shows that in some countries like Estonia and Russia, family tends to mean 'growing out' of punk and 'becoming normal', at least in terms of dress style, but in some other countries like Germany, the United kingdom and the United States, people continue to dress and behave recognizably in a punky way. Since I have very little experience with older punks from Western Germany, I cannot say whether there are differences between East and West when it comes to establishing a family. At least in Berlin, I cannot recognize remarkable differences between Eastern and Western Germans.

CHAPTER

7

PUNK ROCK TERRITORY

The Construction of Enemies

Me: Why do you hate Nazis?
Bert: Because Nazis hate us!

The subcultural world is full of inter- and intra-subcultural conflicts, enmities and antipathies. It is hardly an exaggeration to claim that there are very few subcultures that are tolerant of all other groups and who do not juxtapose themselves in relation to other groups. From a superficial skimming of fanzines or subcultural websites, one frequently comes across the biting criticism addressed at other subcultures in terms of their music, masculinity/femininity, politics, social or economic status and style. Quite often, such enmities have not remained purely verbal, but have manifested themselves in physical clashes. Some of these conflicts have been immortalized in films, such as the British subculture classic *Quadrophenia* with its depiction of mods vs. rockers, or the antipathy between punks and skinheads in the German film *Oi! Warning*. However, there is a much broader variety of alliances and warring traditions than the small number of mainstream films has ever been able to show. For example, international skinhead and punk folklore has a rich tradition of stories about the skinhead–punk conflicts or their alliances against right-wing factions. The early skinheads were proud of their skirmishes with bikers, especially the Hells Angels (Marshall, 1993). Some hardcore fans are well known for their dislike of hip-hop fans and 'long hair' metalheads (Büsser, 2007; Haefner, 2007).[1] Metal fans often dislike techno fans, regarding them disdainfully as those who listen to inhuman music![2] Most of the subcultures mentioned above despise hippies and historically have attacked them as a soft target. Also well known is the street punk and skinhead warped perception of the goths as a semi-feminine and degenerate subculture.

These conflicts and 'heroic' fight narratives are seldom reflected in the academic literature. Such articles, which are few in number, tend to ignore the complexity within intra-subcultural feuds, reducing them to one or two nominators. A famous sociological work by Stanley Cohen, *Folk Devils and Moral Panics* (1972), is an analysis of a moral panic and presents the media representation of the clashes between mods and rockers, yet it does not go into an in-depth analysis of the real events and causes of the subcultural enmities. Phil Cohen often uses the term 'subcultural conflict' but understands it as a conflict between working class youth and mainstream society (P. Cohen, 1972). In such cases, the position of the dominant society is mostly seen in terms of power relations, and only recently have works appeared that focus on the violence and victimization of subcultures (e.g. Garland and Hodkinson, 2014). In addition, there are several works where authors discuss a subculture's opposition to the state as an enemy, but do not go into such nuances as why punks loathe hippies (e.g. Crossly, 2008; Krokovay, 1985; Lamy and Levin, 1985; Moore, 2007). Similarly, when the topic of right-wing skinhead violence against (allegedly) left-wing punks in Germany or the United States is raised, there is scant material on the reasons and dynamics for such feuds, and it is dismissed as just another aspect of the right-wing/neo-Nazi aggression towards racial, ethnic or other minorities (Dennis and Laporte, 2011; Hamm, 1995; Moore, 1993). Such a simplified perspective overlooks the complicated identity conflicts between right-wing adherents and punks, based on different perceptions of aesthetics, music, lifestyle and masculinity. However, some notable exceptions include: a coauthored monograph on Russian right-wing skins where local punk–skinhead conflicts are briefly mentioned (Pilkington et al., 2010); the classic of skinhead studies, *The Lads in Action* by David Moore (1994), which discusses fights between English skinheads and Australian locals; a section on the uneasy alliance and feuds between Czech skinheads and punks in the collected volume *Fight Back: Punk, Politics and Resistance* (Novotná and Heřmanský, 2014); and an analysis of the subcultural space in a Californian school in *White Kids* (Bucholtz, 2011). The last monograph grapples with subcultural identities and space in a schoolyard, but it reveals nothing about the cause of the animosity that is realized as possible physical fights inside or outside of the school.

This brings us to another topic of this chapter: the territorial claims of subcultures. Bucholtz (2011) analyses schoolyard territorialities of various youth groups at a Californian school and relates these directly to communication patterns, subcultural values and the stylistic preferences of pupils. The territorial affiliation of subcultures is a familiar topic in the academic literature and beyond, often with a special focus on such concrete spaces as dance halls and clubs (Böse, 2005; Cressey, 2008; Muggleton, 2005; Stanley-Niaah, 2004; Salasuo and Seppälä, 2004; Thornton, 1996). For example, one of the earliest and now classic studies on subcultures, *Street Corner Society* by William F. Whyte (1998), looks at racketeering youth in the context of the street and neighbourhood. Territorial ambitions of hip-hop gangs and their rules are mentioned by academics (Ogg and Upshal, 1999) and portrayed in numerous films. There are even music style-based subcultures that are related to particular territories, such as the dubstep connection to East London (Gilbert, 2009). However, the subcultural space is often viewed as a relationship and/or conflict with the dominant mainstream culture. The reason is probably because subcultural territorial ambitions seem to violate the 'government sanctioned frame of space and imagination' (Rundquist, 2007: 180). This aspect is well illuminated by studies on skaters who tend to use urban spaces for their own interest, in this way exercising a 'transgressive activity that challenges the regulations imposed on urban space' (Chiu, 2009: 26). In such situations, the streets become a 'stage for performance' where subcultures 'colonise' the space (Drissel, 2013: 125). Confrontations between the various subcultures and the dominant society, and between official planning and perceptions of the public, indeed contain elements of a power struggle where the subculture spares no effort to create and maintain its urban space (Bahrova, 2008; Drissel, 2011; McGrellis, 2005, Muršić, 2009). While skinhead ambitions to be associated with a certain district or town are acknowledged by academic circles (Brake, 1985; Clarke et al., 1976; Farin, 2001; Muños and Marin, 2006, Yong and Craig, 1997), the academic reading of punk mostly focuses on aspects of style or politics. Even promising articles on punks' territoriality tend to focus on muggings in front of favoured stores and only briefly mention intra-subcultural rivalries on space (Kennedy and Baron, 1993).

While scholars tend to ignore such hostilities, subcultural 'insider' literature and the 'scene' media is more engaged with these topics. Skinhead skirmishes with bikers and 'greasers', but also with mods and punks are covered in the iconic skinhead book *Spirit of '69* by George Marshall (1993). Right-wing skinhead and punk conflicts are frequently described in German, British and American literature (O'Hara, 1995; Smith, 2006; Westhusen, 2005b). Football team-related as well as subcultural rivalries in punk and ska concerts at the end of the 1970s are the stuff of British folklore (Mader, 1996; Marshall, 1990). In her autobiography, Pauline Black – the singer in Two Tone ska group The Selecter – mentions the competing identities of skinheads, hippies and rockers in a small English town during the 1960s (Black,

2011). From autobiographical and documentary writing on the 1970s punk scene, clashes between ageing Teddy Boys and skinheads were already common during the genesis of the punk movement (Bushell, 2010; Lydon, 1993; Savage, 1991). Martin Büsser argues in his book about the German punk and hardcore scene that the audience's behaviour attending German hardcore concerts acted as a deliberate contrast to the hippies' events, with their emphasis on peace and the power of meditation (Büsser, 2007: 28–29). The subcultural pulp fiction of 'cult' literature often tends to exploit this same topic, as if confirming the identity of a group under the radar (Allen, 1994; Goodman, 1995). Moreover, several German punk rock fanzines reflect subcultural antipathies by giving the authors an opportunity to express their scorn for a broad category of people, usually described as 'hippies' or 'proles'. In many cases, feuds are related to territorial ambitions where different subcultures compete for the same space. By reviewing the different forms of literature, it becomes obvious that juxtaposition plays an important role in subcultural practices and ideology, not only as depicted in the mainstream but also across a broad spectrum of subcultures.

Interestingly, when I was trying to conceptualize subcultural feuds and territorial acclaims, I found theoretical support and inspiration more often when reviewing (mainly sociological) literature on delinquent groups. In this segment of social science literature, 'subculture' is directly related to 'deviant' behaviour, often in the form of gang-related criminal activity. However, subcultural feuds are not to be confused with the significant tradition in sociology of studying delinquent youth, gangs and crime, popularized in the mainstream media through TV documentaries such as *Ross Kemp on Gangs* (see also Kemp, 2007). In general, gang violence has much more of an economic background than conflicts between the style-based groups, which are to a lesser degree engaged with racketeering or drug dealing. This does not exclude the importance of style and common identity for delinquent youth in cultural criminology (McCulloch and McNeill, 2007; Moran, 2007); however, deviancy scholars tend to see this aspect as relatively marginal in their analysis of crime, delinquency and violence (Bloch and Niederhoffer, 1958; Hughes and Rowe, 2007; James, 2007; Lister et al., 2001). This is interesting because some research shows the prevalence of style forming the identity of violent and criminal youth groups. Appearance and music help these groups to draw a clear border between them and other criminal and noncriminal actors in their environment, as is apparent for the Neds in Scotland (Young, 2013), Chavs in England (Martin, 2009) and black Tsotsi (Glaser, 2000) or white Ducktails (Mooney, 1998, 2005) in South Africa.

What the literature on sociology and (far too rarely) anthropology on delinquent youth, gangs and violent groups helps us to understand is that these groups are not necessarily fully excluded from mainstream society and often share or reflect its values, ideologies and social norms. The seminal work by William Whyte on Italian street gangs in late 1930s Boston describes the career path of young men from racketeering street gangs to respectable community officials (Whyte, 1998). It is not much different in the Republic of Georgia, where the criminal youth was later able to make a career as an official in the ministry (Koehler, 2000). The trick is that the interpretation of what is 'violent' or just 'rough' also often differs for the 'average' person compared to how the state sees it (Fournier, 2013). Such a differing valuation of the 'bad' and 'good' violence makes it possible for the acceptance of violent behaviour in certain circumstances (see Nayak, 2003).

The social environment plays a significant role by shaping individual norms for accepting deviant behaviour and joining deviant groups. The research shows that joining gangs is more often 'conventional peer grouping' than driven by economic interests (Swaner and White, 2010: 14). For young people in gangs, personal reputation is what motivates them to be engaged in the gang and not direct economic profit, which is usually spent without any great consideration (Mullins, 2006; Yablonsky, 1962). Simon Harding uses Bourdieu (1985) to argue that the 'environment forms the physical, psychological, socio-cultural and emotional landscape which is the social field of the urban street gang' (Harding, 2012: 196). In short, the actions of gangsters are directed by the habitus and oriented towards achieving reputation and status.

IDEOLOGY

While most of the above-mentioned works go into *how* these enmities are manifested, they do not explain the causes behind them. It is not an easy task to determine why specific subcultures dislike or even hate each other so passionately. The mainstream media often reduce Nazi-skinhead vs. punk conflicts in Germany to a right-wing vs. left-wing battle, so politically motivated hatred still remains largely unexamined by journalists. However, looking at how journalists and academics portray right-wing supporters globally, a common denominator that is emphasized is the lack of interest in any sophisticated political ideologies by the average right-wing foot soldier (Drahtzieher, 1996; Hamm, 1995; Kimmel, 2007; Yong and Craig, 1997). Several works demonstrate that the attempt of right-wing activists to give 'the right extremist Thing' (Shoshan, 2014) a political dimension is rather unsuccessful and the right-wing 'emotional collectives' are often just how the right-wing leaders depict their movement for outsiders (Virchow, 2007). The youth associate themselves with the right wing for reasons such as the 'shock value' of the media image (Deicke, 2007), 'disintegration of the social fabric', especially working class erosion and migration (Shoshan, 2014: 155, 156, 167). It might seem to be an exaggeration and, indeed, right-wing apologists often accuse the media and scholars of a biased approach. However, having met numerous right-wing foot soldiers, I am not surprised by this portrayal. It is simply the case that many (especially young) right-wingers are not bothered about the precise clarity and logical structure of the political views they are supposed to support. In many cases, young right-wing supporters simply find a cause wherein to express their bravado (cf. Kimmel, 2007); they are seeking thrills and land on the right-wing side often due to their personal relations with some extremist groups (e.g. Virchow, 2007: 158). This is confirmed by my encounters with former neo-Nazis. One man, who was an active West German right-wing skinhead in the 1980s, explained his motives for a 'ruck', echoing a popular racist undercurrent and 'yellow' press mentality: 'We were young and wanted to get rid of our aggression. Dark skinned foreigners are an easy target for this. First of all, they are easy to spot in a crowd. And also you do not need to find any excuse to attack them.'

On the other hand, militant left wingers rarely demonstrate any substantial political education based on different Marxist, Leninist, Trotskyist or Anarchist schools of thought. There exists next to no research on the left-wing side of the political spectrum in contemporary urban life. The semi-autobiographical work by deceased left-winger Dave Hann on anti-fascist militancy in the United Kingdom indicates that left-wing violence was more class-based and related to solidarity than any clear political ideas (Hann, 2013). Online, one can find national and international militant left-wing websites that refer to themselves as Marxist, Trotskyist or Anarchist, but there is very little proof that all the followers of these movements are committed to the ideological cause.[3]

In Halle, as mentioned in the Introduction and Chapter 2 there are at least three distinct circles based on three different clubs. While the so-called 'old lefties' in VL and the 'young and politically correct' in Reilstrasse occasionally showed some interest in communist, anarchist or socialist theory, the 'proles' in GiG were ignorant of any official or elaborated ideology. In my interviews, only one informant out of the GiG regulars explained his antipathy towards the right-wing based on ideas of tolerance and human rights; all the other informants drew on the history of physical conflicts and a traditional mutual hatred. British punk has historically been sceptical towards any political party, including parties with a socialist or communist orientation (Worley, 2012). During all the discussions on German punk culture with my informants, this is something that East German street punks have in common with their British 'ancestors'. It was difficult, if not impossible, to establish or locate any specific sympathies to a political party. Gregor Gysi, the leader of the German Left Party, enjoyed some approval and respect from a few of the punks in Halle, but this was due more to his role in (East) German politics as an articulate and intelligent critic of the parties in power.[4] In our discussions, some people in GiG expressed their sympathy for some leaders of the local, and quite small, grassroots leftist association in the town and region. However, the main reason was that people had known these leaders personally for years and helped or supported them when possible; a clearly defined ideology did not play a significant role in these friendships and activities. On the other hand, GiG regulars openly joked about the small communist group renting rooms on the club's ground floor. 'We should kick out the communists and make a rehearsal room in their office', said a punk musician who worked occasionally in GiG as a bar tender. As I understood it, the only interest in keeping the communists in the house was that the money they paid was needed to cover the club's electricity bills. Moreover, the GiG circle distanced themselves from politically oriented punk groups in the town, deriding them as 'politically correct' or 'hippie-punks'. This all shows that there must exist more important grounds for the right-wing vs. left-wing enmity in the city.

PLACING PUNK TERRITORY AND SUBCULTURAL CONFLICT IN A CONTEXT OF ENMITY

In Halle, left-wing vs. right-wing enmities are directly linked to territorial claims from both sides. Theoretically, it is possible to take a city map and mark the supposedly 'right' or 'left' districts on it. In this informal territorial division, from the punk perspective the inner city and some neighbouring districts are 'theirs', whereas the concrete apartment building districts, built during the GDR period (Halle-Neustadt and Südstadt), are considered to be 'Nazi'. However, this does not mean there is a total subcultural segregation. Despite the claims of the punks, 'Nazis' did not seem convinced of the applicability of this territorial regulation. In the old town of the inner city, there exist several bars and pubs with the reputation for being right-wing hooligan hangouts. GiG, located a short walk from the Marktplatz central square, is not far away from a discotheque called Flower Power, a notorious right-wing hooligan hangout. Everybody who wanted to go from the city centre to GiG, or the other way round, had to pass the aforementioned discotheque. Opposite the discotheque is a takeaway that serves as a stopover for punks and hooligans who tend to enjoy a beer or some food before going up the hill to GiG or over the road to Flower Power. Therefore, the street in front of Flower Power is a well-known location for clashes between punks and the disco's regulars. A short distance through the city centre is the cinema and club called La Bim. Nearby is a small bar, the King's Cross, with a reputation for hosting late-night hooligan drinking parties. Nevertheless, the city centre of Halle is still considered to be a relatively safe area for immigrants, punks, bohemians and hippies, contrary to the outskirts of the city, which are considered a no-go area for anybody 'who looks different'.

In January 2011, Pieps, a promoter of GiG, took me to an African bar in Halle's old town. We were watching a mediocre and heavily stoned reggae band jamming with some African drummers when Pieps said: 'Without us, this place would not have been here!' He was referring to our discussion about the legendary Red Bombers,[5] a left-wing skinhead gang of which he was a member in the 1990s. The Red Bombers received their name from the red flight jackets they usually wore and Pieps' anecdote made it clear that in order to understand the subcultural landscape in Halle, the history of the 1990s should not be left out.

Pilkington and Johnson (2003) argue that 'national histories' are important in order to understand subcultures, which tend to develop their own forms of Anglo-American youth cultures. It is generally acknowledged that the politicization of subcultures in the GDR occurred in the mid-1980s as skinheads became increasingly affiliated with right-wing ideas and distanced themselves from their former punk friends. Simultaneously, in the GDR, small groups of extremely radical neo-Nazis appeared whose political views were influenced chiefly by Western German neo-Nazi groups (Furian and Becker, 2012; Hasselbach, 2001). These political rivalries culminated in a notorious attack by West and East German right-wing skinheads on a punk concert in the East Berlin Zionskirche in October 1987 (Fenemore, 2007: 277), an event that is today considered a landmark in GDR punk history. After German reunification, East German punks, right-wing skinheads and other youth cultures experienced turbulent times. The former state control disappeared and in many respects the new state was not able to control society and the space. In the subcultural world, this led to several unoccupied buildings being taken over by squatters and turned into clubs and bars, a process I would call the 'politics of place and identity' (Tucker, 2002: Chapter 8). It was not only left-wingers who squatted; in several East German cities there were also right-wing squats (Hasselbach, 2001). Margaret Kohn claims that: 'Political spaces facilitate change by creating a distinctive place to develop new identities and social, symbolic, and experimental dimensions of space. Transformative politics comes from separating, juxtaposing, and recombining these dimensions' (2004: 3–4). These spaces are important for identity building and are in Germany usually called *Freiräume* (see also Chapter 3 and 5).

Indeed, around these early squats, alternative pubs and clubs, people gathered with distinctive political and subcultural identities on both sides of the left–right divide and these identities were often confirmed through violent actions. The everyday of these politicized squats and clubs consisted of frequent attacks on each other's premises throughout the 1990s.

It is interesting that the period that for many former GDR citizens is retrospectively seen as an era of disaster lives on in the memories of Halle's punks as a kind of 'golden era' when 'everything was possible'. The growth of various subcultural groups also meant the 'territorialization' of the city's space. As in other East German cities, the frontline was allegedly formed according to left–right-wing divisions: punks, left-wing skinheads, hip-hoppers, ravers, etc. on one side and right-wing skinheads, neo-Nazis, football hooligans, etc. on the other. According to my informants' memories of the period after the collapse of the GDR, in Halle it was an era of intensive clashes, attacks on each other's clubs, the defending of squats and sporadic street violence. In the 1990s, Halle was not so clearly divided and the clubs and bars were established randomly in whatever empty building was available. The squatting was accompanied with intensive political street life: political demonstrations with counterdemonstrations, solidarity festivals or picketing happened frequently. On both sides of the political spectrum, there appeared militant groups – like the Red Bombers – whose main goal was to fight the other side. This period was pivotal for cementing the feeling of a collective, the 'scene', and later the establishment of Halle's subcultural political geography. The history provides the 'narrative of continuity' (Neill, 2001), which justifies the territorial claims of GiG punk rockers and helps to explain the exceptional coherence of the local underground scene. Even today, several of my informants explain their friendships by stating 'We were together in the anti-fascist front in the 1990s', addressing the symbolic meaning and the impact of a violent and turbulent era. For the older generation of Halle punks, this collective past is even more important than any subcultural affiliation. In the last fifteen to twenty years, several people, who were part of the local punk scene, have turned to hip-hop, blues or techno and no longer see themselves as punks. However, the friendship between former 'brothers-in-arms' has not faded. Nowadays, the scene in Halle is subculturally significantly more mixed than in Berlin or Leipzig, especially at the older end of the scene, and it is not unusual to see punks at underground raves or hip-hoppers at punk concerts.

Subcultural rivalry and its geographical segmentation in Halle cannot be reduced to only politics or subculture. The masculinity, attitudes and violence of working-class subcultures is mostly rooted in the habitus of the working class, simply brought to another level (Clarke et al., 1976; Pilkington et al., 2010; Willis, 2000). It is a product of certain historical developments and following a closer look, it is possible to trace it back to the aggressive male culture of the GDR. Apart from the masculine bravado, East German proletarian culture contains an attempt to challenge the state's control of the social space; these 'tactics to dominate the street' (de Certeau, 1988: 113) were later exported to the 'street oriented youth culture' (Harding, 2012: 202). Most of my older informants came from villages outside of Halle and love to talk about the village fights from their youth. One constant theme discussed were the clashes between men from different villages who met in the weekend discos of the area. According to the interviews, some of these battles were extremely violent, resulting in serious injuries and sometimes even deaths:

> I cannot fight. I do not fight as any normal person. I try to kill. When I was younger, around seventeen or eighteen, in our village disco a few guys beat somebody from the neighbouring village to death. They smashed his head with iron bars and then pissed on the corpse. Of course, they were drunk and were jailed later. This is where I grew up! (O., Field diary, 20 November 2012)

Of course, one should not take all such stories at face value, but nevertheless these fights were usually a show of male bravado carried out under the excuse of defending the 'village honour'. While occasional fist-fights took place in villages throughout the GDR era and afterwards, at the weekend 'city disco' fights, all local conflicts were forgotten and punks, metal fans, rockers and 'normals' ganged together to fight men from another village. For example, in the mid-1980s, the villages south of Halle (like Gutenberg) were notorious for this kind of regional rivalry and in some cases people were even killed. This sort of 'justified violence' is no different from how criminal gangs behave (Mullins, 2006; Swaner and White, 2010) and it must again be mentioned that street punks talk about these fights with pride.

As historical research shows, it was not only Halle or the surrounding villages that were prone to violent behaviour; street gangs, 'street culture' and 'street knowledge' for solving conflicts through physical violence was a general problem in the GDR (Fenemore, 2007: 86–87, 119–25). The historian Mark Fenemore argues that the violent and delinquent behaviour of (especially young) men in the GDR was due to multiple reasons. In the GDR, as a proletarian state, working-class virtues like toughness were highly valued at the state level. It was an honour, not a stigma, to be a worker. In this way, support for proletarian values and militarism gave birth to a masculine popular culture of territorial street gangs (ibid.: 121–23). As a rule, the GDR leadership did not condemn violence in general, only violence exercised by the 'wrong groups', behaviour that was not 'officially directed, channelled and controlled'. As such, there was a paramilitary wing of the GDR youth organization FDJ – Ordnungsgruppen – who would police and were entitled to 'sort out the gangs', especially criminals and rockers; in other words, they could fight local informal gangs to 'maintain the law and order' (ibid.:

FIGURE 7.1. Playing pool inside GiG. Photo by the author

125). The practice of answering 'deviant' violence with sanctioned violence and applying 'good' violence to control 'bad' youth was not unusual in socialist countries (see also the film *Stilyagi,* based on real-life events and the historical research of Gleb Tsipursky, 2012). Notwithstanding the moralizing rhetoric of state officials, male aggression was encouraged through such practices as sanctioned paramilitary organizations for school pupils, military training classes as part of the school curriculum and numerous war films.[6]

DEFENDING THE TERRITORY

Such machismo and thuggish behaviour did not diminish following the collapse of the GDR. The surrounding villages and also Halle's former proletarian districts remained places where a male stranger should be careful and 'know people' in order to be safe. In the summer of 2007, a punk girl who lived in a village some 20 kilometres outside of Halle was brutally beaten and her apartment was smashed up. Various rumours surfaced on the Halle punk scene. Some argued that this had happened because she had a Kurdish boyfriend; others claimed that she did not want to lend money to some village boys – actually her former schoolmates – who planned to buy cocaine. A different dimension to the incident was provided by one of Halle's older punks who told me: 'I cannot do anything [to help her], this village is beyond the line where my word counts.' As it turned out, most punks of village origin maintained their network and loyalties to their home village, and when required provided or found support in or for the village. The existence of these links became apparent to me when I was invited to a village disco. 'You are with me, no one will touch you' was usually the first thing I heard when entering the premises. The second move was usually to introduce me to my host's friends with the request 'to keep an eye on him, he is a stranger, you know'. I must admit that I did not particularly enjoy most of these parties, under the suspicious stares of those locals who took a dislike to me.

The experience at the village disco got me thinking about the political nature of the case described at the beginning of this section. Probably there was a degree of xenophobia involved, and the Kurdish origin of the girl's boyfriend made her vulnerable to harassment. However, there is little doubt that any 'outsider' is not easily accepted in such village communities and their girlfriends could be targets for intimidation. On the other hand, this event demonstrates the perception of solidarity exported from the village culture into Halle's subcultural world. It seems that village-based informal networks have been infused with the existing subcultural networks and one person can simultaneously perform several roles in these combined networks without any hesitation. A small-town punk is thus able to switch between the role of a member of the extended village community and back. My informant was willing to 'sort out' a conflict because 'one of us' was targeted, but his informal network did not reach the village where the aforementioned girl lived. In itself, this was a typical strategy for local East German village communities when people attempt to settle conflicts without involving the police, instead relying on informal local networks and their personal reputation.

In the GiG crowd, the concepts of the gang, toughness and home turf became fused with the subcultural identity. The area around GiG is a 'contested site' where 'space' is constantly 'created' (Stanley-Niaah, 2004: 357) through the presence of music, people, posters and graffiti. This was a particular area experienced by the majority of regulars; a territory belonging to the club and 'keeping it *Nazi-frei*' was a matter of constant concern. In December 2010, rumours circulated that in a cheap bar a few streets away from GiG, young 'Nazi-kids' were regularly hanging out. I happened to be in GiG when the issue was being discussed. One person suggested: 'We should go there and show our presence.' And it was not only the distinctive 'Nazis' who fall under the radar; I witnessed a case when a young drunken teenager received a beating because he smashed beer bottles on the street. Another informant, who did the beating, explained to me: 'I live here and walk my dogs in these streets. How can I walk my dogs when these idiots break bottles? And then people in the district think that we did it!' In this sense, the notion of home turf in GiG is no different from the concept in hip-hop culture, where a gang feels a responsibility to punish people who violate their 'rules' and dominance of an area (Ogg and Upshal, 1999; Rose, 1994; Zips and Kämpfer, 2001).

As a rule, such a perception of regulating space through violence was not particularly gender-specific. Research on crime committed by young women shows that the female sex can have similar attitudes to their male counterparts in relation to crime, but are engaged in different forms of crime (Moran, 2007; Shepherd et al., 2013). Basically, research on the Halle punk scene confirms that social norms are overwhelmingly shared independent of sex; punk women supported male aggression and nurtured a similar emotional affiliation to the territory as their male counterparts. As argued by the researchers of the English riots in 2011, 'the limited spaces available to young people to meet can mean that public spaces are now even more important' (Kelly and Gill, 2012: 229). Governance of the public space gives a sense of solidarity to both girls and boys (ibid.: 225) and this was no different in Halle. In discussions about the strategies for 'showing our presence', girls approved of these acts and made their own suggestions like: 'You should maybe let us go in first. In the case there is a brawl, you can turn up and take them out!'

Pilkington and Johnson (2003: 271) write about Russian subcultural youth who 'reach out to global cultural music, styles and affiliations to differentiate themselves from "others" at home'. A punk posture in Halle did not start the violence, but helped to channel and justify it. It became more visible during anti-fascist militant actions that took place a few times a year. Some of the GiG regulars were engaged in the local wing of a militant anti-fascist movement ANTI-FA and participated eagerly in what was called 'counter-action' (*Gegenaktion*) in reaction to signs of 'fascist activities'. In most cases these 'activities' were the legal marches of right-wing parties, often happening outside the city centre and in more distant districts of Halle. For such a counter-action, a group of GiG regulars mobilized themselves and joined with people from other anti-fascist groups. An informant confided in me that he usually served in such undertakings as a scout. His task was to sit on a bench, dressed in an old tracksuit and baseball cap, with a cheap beer in his hand, disguised as an unemployed 'prole', and then inform the others via mobile phone about the 'enemy's' movements. Depending on the earlier announced route of the right-wing demonstration, ANTI-FA planned its attacks. People were divided into groups, supplied with a city map and moved as independent units in the locality trying either to hunt for single right-wing supporters or to collectively attack the whole demonstration. The 'action' was planned so that attackers could retreat quickly and without being caught by the police when their mission was accomplished. When I asked what the aim was behind these attacks, I received the reply: 'We show them that we hold the city!'

Even in these highly militant actions, some of the girls not only approved but also actively participated. This is not unusual in the violent skinhead scene, where women participate in fights like men or even lead the group (on the subject of the role of skinhead girls as gang leaders and their participation in occassional aggression, see Marshall (1993); Pilkington et al. (2010)). I do not have any evidence that in Halle, punk girls were active planners of militant anti-fascist actions, but some punk girls were definitely participating in the conflicts not as 'victims' or 'protectors', as Johnson describes the role of black women in the 1943 race riots in England (Johnson, 2002: 255). 'I cannot go anymore to the anti-fascist rallies' a 26-year-old punk girl confessed to me in 2010. 'I was quite into fighting already. But I just cannot stand aside! When I see those bastards, I lose my mind and run through the police chain to attack them!'

CONCLUSION

Studies on criminal behaviour indicate that the reason why people get involved in illegal activities is often thrill-seeking (Burt and Simons, 2013). From my own observations, the adrenaline rush pushes people into fights, especially in the skinhead faction of the local scene. Locally, skinheads had the image of being more violent than punks. Some very notorious skinheads of Halle got into fights with anyone, paying little attention to politics. When I arrived in Halle in the autumn of 2011, I was told that Pyh, one of the most notorious skinheads, had made media headlines when he defended an African asylum seeker in a tram and ended up in a fist-fight with three alleged neo-Nazis. When I met Pyh myself, he did not want to go into the story in much detail, but instead told me about his recent conflicts with the owners of a Turkish takeaway. Behind his back, Pyh was locally classified as a *Brenner* (burner), a term for an impulsive and aggressive person. However, his nature of 'aggro'[7] was widely approved of by the local scene as meaningful behaviour. Pyh acted according to the rules of the habitus of his 'social field', demonstrating masculinity and loyalty through his behaviour when necessary.

The German sociologist Ralf Bohnsack argues that violence in some (East) German youth cultures is caused by the lack of warmth and communication in the families where young people grew up (Bohnsack, 1997). Among my informants were people who had a dysfunctional relationship with their parents, but also a substantial number who, like US punks, had especially caring parents (O'Connor, 2008: 54, 56, 64). I tend to believe that their attitude to violence was affected by the tradition of masculinity and group actions, which were adopted from the GDR village and urban 'thug' tradition. In urban spaces, the youth are often called trouble-makers (Banks et al., 2000; Bianchini, 1995; Hollands, 2002; Lovatt and O'Connor, 1995) and the territorial perception of right-wing and left-wing groups in Halle was a direct challenge to the state control of the cityscape because rival groups saw certain districts as belonging not to the state, but to them.

Chaney writes that lifestyle sites are spaces that actors can appropriate and control (1996: 91–92). He limits this to the clubs, but these lifestyle sites can in practice be much larger territories, covering several districts. Therefore, my friend Pieps was so proud about the existence of an African music bar because it symbolized the control of Halle's inner city by 'us' and the defeat of 'Nazis' through the existence of a black music venue. In a narrower sense the area around GiG and in a larger sense most of the inner city was a territory to be defended from 'others' who were suburban Nazis. Simultaneously this was also a 'sartorial resistance to hegemony' (Tucker, 2008: 119) or a negation of the state's right of dominance. The subcultural rivalries in Halle create an alternative mode for reading the city map, a space divided among conflicting subcultures largely ignoring the existence of the police or the city council. This informal division of the urban space and defending one's turf was ideologically supported by a mix of working-class bravado and machismo, the punk concept of 'loyalty', 'crew' and 'fighting back', and a flirtation with left-wing ideology.

Notes

1. Listen to the speeches of the Agnostic Front singer Rodger Miret in the concert recording of *Working Class Heroes* (2002, I Scream Records split with Discipline), where he advises fans not to buy hip-hop records because 'they do not buy our records'.
2. Personal discussion with Lii Araste, who has conducted fieldwork on the Estonian metal scene since 2003, 12 November 2013.
3. A good example of such ideological ignorance is the short-lived Berlin chapter of RASH (Red and Anarchist Skinheads), which was established in the first half of the 1990s. This was a time of extreme political polarization. In order to organize skinhead concerts in militant left-wing punk clubs, RASH served as an alibi against the accusation of right-wing sympathies of bands and the audience.
4. In the late 1990s, Gregor Gysi was very popular with a range of people who held different views. The reason for this was his 'earthy' nature. He was more or less the only top politician who spoke deliberately in the Berlin dialect instead of received German, although the Berlin dialect was associated with a lower social stratum. Si-

multaneously, he was known as smart, educated and as having an interest in classical music. Gysi's style of discussion was self-confident, but nevertheless respectful to his opponent or discussion partner. He also did not appear to live a glamorous lifestyle, as did many other politicians of his rank, but always wore modest suits with ties that usually did not match the colour of his suit. His popularity was and is also based on the fact that he was supporting the East German cause, demanding equal pensions and salaries for all regions of Germany.

5. 'Bomber' or 'Bomberjacke' is the German word for the American military pilots' flight jacket worn in different colours by skinheads internationally.
6. I feel tempted to add my own experience of such voluntary law enforcement groups. As a teenage punk in Tallinn, Soviet Estonia, I had numerous encounters with these young volunteers – usually pupils of older school classes. In the mid-1980s, Soviet *militsiia* (police) patrolled by night accompanied with two to four such volunteers. This obviously had a practical purpose because one task for the police was to arrest underage youth who were on the street after 10–11 PM, bring them to the police station, inform their parents and order them to come and pick up their children. When we tried to run away, the volunteers were usually faster than the adult policemen and were more efficient in catching us up.
7. This is an abbreviation from the English term 'aggravation' (but some people argue that it comes from 'aggression') and was adapted from the British street punk slang via records.

CONCLUSION

> Me: What is the difference between punks and skinheads?
> Pyh: There is no big difference, skinheads are just more aggressive.

Academically, punk is probably the most studied youth subculture, and skinheads also enjoy a certain popularity as an object of research. This popularity can be traced back to several important concepts like style or homology, first defined through punk by Dick Hebdige and others in the late 1970s and early 1980s (Hebdige, 1979; Hall and Jefferson, 1986). Another reason could also be that there are many scholars who in one way or another feel an attachment to punk (and its derivatives or splinter groups) and therefore choose to study these subcultures (see, for example, O'Connor, 1990: 27–41; 2002: 225–36; 2004: 175–95; 2008; Haefner, 2004: 406– 36; 2007; Willis, 1993: 365–83; Pilkington, 2010: 187–209; 2014: 71–87, Dines et al., 2017; Furness, 2012a). Can we say we already know everything about punk and can the field of study be considered to have been exhausted? No, there seems to be plenty of unstudied possibilities to write about punk.

I must admit that I am critical of several sociological and culture studies concepts and debates situated around youth subcultures as a research topic. Maybe the first disagreement with the post-subcultural theory school is about whether we can speak about the subcultures at all, i.e. groups with a distinct identity having a homological relationship to the look and style. This book shows that subcultures exist. In Germany, in different groups, people use different words to describe themselves – skinheads prefer to speak about *Kult* (cult), while punks use the terms *Subkultur* or *Szene*. They both see themselves as a group with a distinctive identity opposed to the 'mainstream', which they used to call *Normalos*. The question I want to explore in this book is why people need a subcultural identity. The homology certainly exists, but is lived out in a less straightforward way compared to how this concept is interpreted. I recall my first interview in this research project when my interviewee said: 'From all the music I listen to punk makes up probably only 10 per cent.' When I later went through his record collection, I discovered that there were only punk records. The problem that hinders generalization is that people who consider themselves punks are not immediately distinguishable; they listen to different music genres and have different lifestyles. Most of them have a concept of what is punk for them, but the problem is a simultaneous existence of multiple interpretations of 'What is punk?' This is also the case with the 'boundaries' between the punks and skinheads. People have different ways of dressing and different music tastes, but they nevertheless tend to know which side of the line they are on. Modern punk is still (as was shown in Chapter 2) an innovative combination of different clothes and footwear, which are not that spectacular or shocking, but the semiotics of reading details is needed in order to identify people. People who are interested in music are, as a rule, interested in different styles of music and constantly look for new music. Nevertheless, there is a certain regularity to this – for example, in Germany, one can see often skinheads at psychobilly concerts, old-school hardcore fans at reggae gigs, and new-school hardcore fans also being into hip-hop and metal. For example, hip-hop and sound-system dancehall reggae have always been closely connected (Toop, 1992: 351; Demers, 2003: 41–56; Ogg and Upshal, 1999). In a real life, it does not mean the erasure of boundaries between subcultural identities, but rather an overlapping in musical tastes. When looking back into the history of subcultures, it is not a new phenomenon – for example, the early British punks liked reggae music and spent their time in gay disco clubs. This tendency, despite its solid history, has been left unstudied and does not seem to be that compelling to academics.

Another misleading concept from the critics of subculture theory is that subcultures have ceased to be face-to-face communities because they use the internet and rely on telecommunication. There is an abundance of research that shows how subcultures have moved to the internet and have stopped being physical communities (e.g. Bennet, 2004; Magnet, 2007; Williams, 2006). However, the reality is that at the core of a subculture, there remains a physical and face-to-face community where interpersonal communication and meeting at concerts hold the group together. Punks in this research use the internet and all the available gadgets to stay in contact with people far away, and these are the tools utilized to keep in touch and organize the concerts for touring bands. To some extent, the internet has replaced fanzines and the postal service, but otherwise I have noticed very little difference compared to what I experienced in the 1990s – people met each other regularly in bars, visited concerts together and travelled together to other cities

FIGURE 8.1. Quiet moment. Photo by the author.

to see famous 'big bands' like American band Slapshot, The Exploited from Scotland or 1960s Jamaican ska artists. Being together and doing 'subcultural things' is of the highest importance in keeping the scene alive. The national scenes differ hugely compared to the global level in terms of the way they are structured, the politics nurtured and the tensions between different punk microscenes and so on. One reason for the existence of national and regional scenes is that most subcultural styles in general, and punk in particular, are still based on face-to-face communication. Of course, the advent of the internet and new communication technologies have also had an impact on the world of subcultures. Subculturalists were quick to adapt and use them for their own means – mainly in order to communicate with each other and spread music.

Throughout this book, I have demonstrated that class as an identity can be part of subcultural life. In Eastern Germany, class is the factor that binds the punk, hardcore and skinhead subculture to the national setting. The punk scene (and related scenes of Halle) proves that social and economic dynamics are mirrored in the subcultural world. Paradoxically, the subculture that is opposed to the state reflects changes in national politics. The rhetoric surrounding the precariat and 'unemployed parasites' causes social alienation among the unemployed or underemployed working-class people, who turn to an alternative: subversive subcultures. German society has become increasingly individualistic, where the dominant view is that one's success is linked to a correct *Lebensphilosophie*. I have shown in Chapters 2–4 that behind this, there is a lack of equal access to education, a decrease in the importance of blue-collar jobs, and the neoliberal nature of the politics of privatization in the economy of the GDR after the *Wende*. There are many features of working-class culture – bravado, aggressiveness, idealizing of alcohol consumption, self-sufficiency, autonomy, collectivism, macho culture and local patriotism – that correspond to the elements of a subcultural lifestyle and are used as tools to shock mainstream society. Many of these attributes can be politicized and given an ideological aura of resistance. It is intriguing the way that punk can be an umbrella for controversial views, and presents this mixture as a coherent ideology of *punk rock*. Simultaneously, the *Szene* becomes a substitute society for people of the Unterklasse, where their values are honoured and become the central social normative behaviour for the group.

In a rigid and hierarchical German society with very limited social mobility, the *Szene* becomes an oasis where one can earn respect and a social position that is not available outside of the subculture. This, I believe, is one very important element in the attractiveness of the underground subculture. The periodically expressed negative views of the 'parasitical' working class (see the citations to Thilo Sarrazin (2010) in Chapter 3) address the lack of respect shown to an entire social group and stir up a counterreaction through the provocation and cultivation of the position of outsiders. This is also the reason why the socially mixed scene around GiG has become, in the words of Pieps, more for the *Arbeiter*. Punk has become a language for one social group to express their identity. Therefore, the concept of the 'supermarket of styles' as an analytical tool should be broadened and there should be more discussion as to why people choose certain styles and how this choice is linked to the culture of their immediate peer group. People bring their tastes, norms and values with them into the *Szene*; these become modified to a certain extent, but my research shows that the transformation is not particularly radical. This is also the reason why subcultures are in a state of constant flux and national scenes differ from each other – each new generation contributes its views and values, while older members provide a counterweight by keeping their views and practices intact as much as possible.

Today it is very misleading to equate subcultures with youth cultures. When looking at the 'classical' subcultures discussed in the sociological writing of subcultures – Teddy Boys, modernists, rockers, punks, rastas or skinheads – they all still exist and still include a healthy number of people who joined their ranks when the style first appeared. These people combine a subcultural lifestyle, look and ideology with a life in mainstream society, in some instances hiding their subcultural identity, while at other times displaying it openly. I know of cases where the concept of youth culture has excluded such people or even whole scenes from any academic research. These various forms of identity building through adaptation to the adult citizens' lifeworld combine maintaining different social and cultural practices and tastes, and deserve to be examined in more depth. In Chapter 6, discussing gender roles in punk, I showed how a family life is not a contradiction in punk, but that people have problems in combining a 'proper' working life and children with their subcultural activities and remaining a 'real punk'. Obviously, getting older within a subculture forces people to make compromises, yet on the other hand, there exists no directive that adopting features of the 'average' lifestyle would harm one's 'street credibility'. In reality, such ageing causes fewer conflicts than a researcher would expect and in real life seldom contradicts subcultural ideologies.

While organizing my field material into a structured academic book, I realized that it is not sufficient to rely solely on the theories used in the analysis of subcultures, youth cultures and pop cultures. I frequently discovered concepts and theories developed and used in other disciplines to be far more useful. Social studies of crime and economics, anthropology and legal studies enabled me to discuss the informality of the punk economy. And even economic theories have influenced my analysis, all of which I hope has contributed to a broader and more comprehensive approach.

REFERENCES

Albertine, V. 2014. *Clothes, Music, Boys: A Memoir.* London: Faber & Faber.

Alexander, C.E. 2000. *The Asian Gang: Ethnicity, Identity, Masculinity.* New York: Berg.

Allen, R. 1994. *Skinhead.* Dunoon: S.T. Publishing.

Allott, A., and G.R. Woodman (eds). 1985. *People's Law and State Law: The Bellagio Papers.* Dordrecht: Foris.

Ammann, J. 1987. *Who's Been Sleeping in My Brain? Interviews Post Punk.* Frankfurt am Main: edition suhrkamp.

Anderson, D. 2007. 'Mobile Archidecture and Social Life: The Case of the Conical Skin Lodge in the Putoran Plateau', in V. Vate and S. Beyeries (eds), *Les Civilisations du renne d'cier et d'aujourd'hui. Approches ethnohistoriques, archeologiques et anthropologiques.* Antibes: Editions APDCA, pp. 43–64.

Appadurai, A. 1990. 'Topographies of the Self: Praise and Emotion in Hindu India', in C.A. Lutz and L. Abu-Lughod (eds), *Language and the Politics of Emotion.* Cambridge Cambridge University Press, pp. 92–112.

Appel, N. 2014. '"Ga, Ga, Ooh-La-La": The Childlike Use of Language in Pop-Rock Music', *Popular Music* 33(1): 91–108.

Ashwin, S., and T. Lytkina. 2004. 'Men in Crisis in Russia: The Role of Domestic Marginalization', *Gender & Society* 18(2): 189–206.

Attali, J. 1985. *Noise: The Political Economy of Music.* Manchester: Manchester University Press.

Back, L. 2000. 'Voices of Hate, Sounds of Hybridity: Black Music and the Complexities of Racism', *Black Music Research Journal* 20(2): 127–49.

———. 2013. *New Ethnicities and Urban Cult.* New York: Routledge.

Bahrova, V. 2008. 'Postsocialist Punk Identity: From Dissidents to Workers', in I.W. Schröder and A. Vonderau (eds), *Changing Economies and Changing Identities in Postsocialist Eastern Europe.* Halle (Saale): LIT Verlag, pp. 155–170.

Baker, S.L. 2009. 'Pop in(to) the Bedroom: Popular Music in Pre-teen Girls' Bedroom Culture', *European Journal of Cultural Studies* 7(1): 75–93.

Balandier, G. 1970. *Political Anthropology.* Harmondsworth: Penguin.

Balibar, E. 1991. 'Class Racism', in E. Balibar and I. Wallerstein (eds), *Race, Nation, Class: Ambigous Identities.* London: Verso, pp. 204–216.

Banks, M., et al. 2000. 'Risk and Trust in the Cultural Industries', *Geoforum* 31(4): 453–464.
Barrow, S., and P. Dalton. 1997. *Reggae: The Rough Guide: The Definitive Guide to Jamaican Music, from Ska through Roots to Ragga.* New York: Penguin.
Baulch, E. 2002. 'Creating a Scene: Balinese Punk's Beginnings', *International Journal of Cultural Studies* 5(2): 153–77.
Bennett, A. 1999. 'Subcultures or Neo-tribes? Rethinking the Relationship between Youth, Style and Musical Taste', *Sociology* 33(3): 599–617.
———. 2001. '"Plug in and Play!": UK "Indie-Guitar" Culture', in A. Bennet and K. Dawe (eds), *Guitar Cultures.* Oxford: Berg, pp. 45–62.
———. 2006. 'Punk's Not Dead: The Continuing Significance of Punk Rock for an Older Generation of Fans', *Sociology* 40(219): 219–35.
———. 2011. 'The Post-subcultural Turn: Some Reflections 10 Years On', *Journal of Youth Studies* 14(5): 493–506.
Bennet, T. (ed.). 2004. *After Subculture: Critical Studies in Contemporary Youth Culture.* Basingstoke: Palgrave Macmillan.
Benwell, B., and E. Stokoe. 2006. *Discourse and Identity.* Edinburgh: Edinburgh University Press.
Berdahl, D. 1999. *Where the World Ended: Re-unification and Identity in the German Borderland.* Berkeley: University of California Press.
———. 2011. *On the Social Life of Postsocialism: Memory, Consumption, Germany.* Bloomington: Indiana University Press.
Berdahl, D., M. Bunzl and M. Lampland. 2000. *Altering States: Ethnographies of Transition in Eastern Europe and the Former Soviet Union.* Ann Arbor: University of Michigan Press.
Beyer, J. 2015. 'Customizations of Law: Courts of Elders (Aksakal Courts) in Rural and Urban Kyrgyzstan', *PoLAR: Political and Legal Anthropology Review* 38(1): 53–71.
———. 2016. *The Force of Custom: Law and the Ordering of Everyday Life in Kyrgyzstan.* Pittsburgh: University of Pittsburgh Press.
Bianchini, F. 1995. 'Night Cultures, Night Economies', *Planning Practice & Research* 10(2): 121–126.
Bird-David, N.H. 1995. 'Hunter-Gatherers and Other People: A Re-examination', in T. Ingold, D. Riches and J. Woodburn (eds), *Hunters and Gartherers: History, Evolution and Social Change.* Oxford: Berg, pp. 17–31.
Black, P. 2011. *Black by Design.* London: Serpent's Tail.
Blackman, S. 2005. 'Youth Subcultural Theory: A Critical Engagement with the Concept, Its Origins and Politics, from the Chicago School to Postmodernism', *Journal of Youth Studies* 8(1): 1–20.
Bloch, A., and A. Niederhoffer. 1958. *The Gang: A Study in Adolescent Behaviour.* New York: Philosophical Library.
Bohlman, P., M. 2003. 'Music and Culture: Historiographies of Disjuncture', in M. Clayton, T. Herbert and R. Middleton (eds), *The Cultural Study of Music: A Critical Introduction.* New York: Routledge, pp. 45–56.
Böhmer, R. 2005. *Der Geist des Kapitalismus und Aufbau Ost.* Dresden: Thelem.
Bohnsack, R. 1997. 'Adoleszenz, Aktionismus und die Emergenz von Milieus. Eine Ethnographie von Hooligan-Gruppen und Rockbands', *Zeitschrift für Sozialisationsforschung und Erziehungssoziologie* 17(11): 3–18.
Borneman, J. 2000. *Belonging in the Two Berlins: Kinsgip, State, Nation.* Cambridge: Cambridge University Press.

Bottà, G. 2014. 'Lo spirito continua: Torino and the Collettivo Punx Anarchici', in M. Worley (ed.), *Fight Back: Punk, Politics and Resistance.* Manchester: Manchester University Press, pp. 155–69.
Bourdieu, P. 1977. *Outline of a Theory of Practice.* Cambridge: Cambridge University Press.
———. 1984. *Distinction: A Social Critique of the Judgment of Taste.* Cambridge, MA: Harvard University Press.
———. 1985. 'The Genesis of the Concept of the Concepts of Habitus and Field', *Sociocriticism* 2(1): 11–24.
Boyer, D., and A. Yurchak. 2010. 'American Stiob: Or, What Late-Socialist Aesthetics of Parody Reveal about Contemporary Political Culture in the West', *Current Anthropology* 25(2): 179–221.
Böse, M. 2005. 'Difference and Exclusion at Work in the Club Culture Economy', *International Journal of Cultural Studies* 8(4): 427–444.
Brandtstädter, S. 2003. 'The Moral Economy of Kinship and Property in Southern China', in C. Hann and "Property Relations" Group (eds), *The Postsocialist Agrarian Question: Property Relations and the Rural Condition.* Münster: LIT Verlag, pp. 419–440.
Brake, M. 1985. *Comparative Youth Culture: The Sociology of Youth Cultures and Youth Subcultures in America, Britain, and Canada.* London: Routledge & Kegan Paul.
Brigg, D. 2012a. *Crack Cocaine Users: High Society and Low Life in South London.* London: Routledge.
Brigg, D. (ed.). 2012b. *The English Riots of 2011: A Summer of Discontent.* Sherfield Gables: Waterside Press.
Brill, D. 2008. *Goth Culture: Gender, Sexuality and Style.* Oxford: Berg.
Bryson, B. 1996. '"Anything But Heavy Metal": Symbolic Exclusion and Musical Dislikes', *American Sociological Review* 61(5): 884–99.
Bucholtz, M. 1999. '"Why Be Normal?" Language and Identity Practices in a Community of Nerd Girls', *Language in Society* 28(2): 203–223.
———. 2011. *White Kids: Language, Race and Styles of Youth Identity.* Cambridge: Cambridge University Press.
Butler, J. 1999. *Gender Trouble: Feminism and the Subversion of Identity.* New York: Routledge.
———. 2004. *Undoing Gender.* New York: Routledge.
Büsser, M. 2007. *If the Kids Are United: Von Punk zu Hardcore und zurück.* Mainz: Ventil Verlag.
Cañas Bottos, L. 2008. *Old Colony Mennonites in Argentina and Bolivia: Nation Making, Religious Conflict and Imagination of the Future.* Leiden: Brill.
Carlin, W., and C. Mayer. 1995. 'The Treuhandanstalt: Privatization by State and Market', in O. Blanchard, K. Froot and J. Sachs (eds), *Transition in Eastern Europe,* vol. 2. Chicago: University of Chicago Press, pp. 189–214.
Cartledge, F. 1999. 'Distress to Impress? Local Punk Fashion and Commodity Exchange', in R. Sabin (ed.), *Punk Rock: So What?* New York: Routledge, pp. 143–153.
Castells, M. 2000. 'Materials for an Exploratory Theory of the Network Society', *British Journal of Sociology* 71(1): 5–24.
Chaney, D. 1996. *Lifestyles.* London: Routledge.
Chang, K.-C. 2011. 'A Path to Understanding Guanxi in China's Transitional Economy: Variations on Network Behavior', *Sociological Theory* 29(4): 315–339.
Castillo, G. 2008. 'East as True West: Redeeming Burgeois Culture, from Socialist Realism to Ostalgie', *Kritika: Explorations in Russian and Eurasian History* 9(4): 747–68.

Chase, E., and R. Walker. 2013. 'The Co-construction of Shame in the Context of Poverty: Beyond a Threat to the Social Bond', *Sociology* 47(4): 739–754.

Cheal, D. 1996. 'Moral Economy', in A.E. Komter, *The Gift: An Interdisciplinary Perspective*. Amsterdam: Amsterdam University Press, pp. 81–94.

Chiba, M. 1985. 'The Channel of Official Law to Unofficial Law in Japan', in A. Allott and G.R. Woodman (eds), *People's Law and State Law: The Bellagio Papers*. Dordrecht: Foris Publ., pp. 207–216.

Chiu, C. 2009. 'Contestation and Conformity: Street and Park Skateboarding in New York City Public Space', *Space and Culture* 12(1): 25–42.

Clark, D. 2003. 'The Death and Life of Punk, the Last Subculture', in D. Muggleton and R. Weinzierl (eds), *The Post-subcultures Reader*. Oxford: Berg, pp. 223–36.

Clarke, J., et al. 1976. 'Subcultures, Cultures, and Class', in S. Hall and T. Jefferson (eds), *Resistance Through Rituals: Youth Subculture in Post-war Britain*. London: Routledge, pp. 9–74.

Clarke, S. 1992. 'Privatization and the Development of Capitalism in Russia', *New Left Review* 196(1): 3–27.

Cohen, A.K. 1955. *Delinquent Boys: The Culture of the Gang*. Glencoe: Free Press.

Cohen, P. 1972. *Sub-cultural Conflict and Working Class Community. Working Papers in Cultural Studies*. Vol. 2. Birmingham: Centre for Contemporary Cultural Studies, University of Birmingham.

Cohen, S. 1972. *Folk Devils and Moral Panics*. Oxford: MacGibbon & Kee.

Comaroff, J., and J. Comaroff. 2000. 'Millenial Capitalism: First Thoughts on a Second Coming', *Public Culture* 12(1): 291–343.

Connell, R.W. 1987. *Gender and Power: Society, the Person and Sexual Politics*. Cambridge: Polity.

———. 1995. *Masculinities*. Cambridge: Polity Press.

Connell, J., and C. Gibson. 2003. *Sound Tracks: Popular Music, Identity and Place*. New York: Routledge.

Cressey, P.G. [1932] 2008. *Taxi-Dance Hall: A Sociological Study in Commercialized Recreation and City Life*. Chicago: University of Chicago Press.

Cross, R. 2010. '"There Is No Authority But Yourself": The Individual and the Collective in British Anarcho-punk', *Music and Politics* 4(2): 1–20.

Crossly, N. 2008. 'Pretty Connected: The Social Network of the Early UK Punk Movement', *Theory Culture Society* 25(6): 89–116.

Crowley, J. 1999. 'The Politics of Belonging: Some Theoretical Considerations', in A. Geddes and A. Favell (eds), *The Politics of Belonging: Migrants and Minorities in Contemporary Europe*. Aldershot: Ashgate, pp. 15–41.

Currid-Halkett, E. 2018. *The Sum of Small Things: A Theory of the Aspirational Class*. Princeton: Princeton University Press.

Daugavietis, J., and I. Lāce. 2011. 'Subcultural Tastes in Latvia 2002–2010: The Content of Style', *Studies of Transition States and Societies* 3(2): 42–56.

Davidson, E. 2010. *We Never Learn: The Gunk Punk Underground, 1988–2001*. New York: Backbeat Books.

Davis, J.R. 2012. 'Punk, Ageing and the Expectations of Adult Life', in A. Bennet and P. Hodkinson (eds), *Ageing and Youth Cultures: Music, Style and Identity*. New York: Berg, pp. 105–18.

de Beauvoir, S. 1993. *The Second Sex*. London: David Campbell.

de Certeau, M. 1988. *The Practice of Everyday Life*. Berkley: University of California Press.

De Garzia, V. (ed.). 1996. *The Sex of Things: Gender and Consumption in Historical Perspective.* Berkeley: University of California Press.

Dedman, T. 2011. 'Agency in UK Hip-Hop and Grime Youth Subcultures: Peripherals and Purists', *Journal of Youth Studies* 14(5): 507–22.

Deicke, W. 2007. 'Resistance and Commercialisation in "Distasteful Movements": Right-Wing Politics and Youth Culture in East Germany', in W. Deicke and P. Hodkinson (eds.), *Youth Cultures: Scenes, Subcultures and Tribes.* New York: Routledge, pp. 93–110.

Demers, J. 2003. 'Sampling the 1970s in Hip-Hop', *Popular Music* 22(1): 41–56.

Dennis, M. 2000. 'Perceptions of GDR Society and Its Transformation: East German Identity Ten Years after Unity', in C. Flockton, E. Kolinsky and R. Pritchard (eds), *The New Germany in the East.* London: Frank Cass, pp. 87–105.

Dennis, M., and E. Kolinsky. 2004. 'United and Divided: Germany since 1990: An Introduction', in M. Dennis and E. Kolinsky (eds), *United and Divided: Germany since 1990.* New York: Berghahn Books, pp. 1–16.

Dennis, M., and N. Laporte. 2011. *State and Minorities in Communist East Germany.* New York: Berghahn Books.

DeSoto, H. 2000. 'Crossing Western Boundaries: How East Berlin Women Observed Women Researchers from West after Socialism, 1991–1992', in H. Desoto and N. Dudwick (eds), *Fieldwork Dialemmas: Anthropologists in Postsocialist States.* Madison: University of Wisconsin Press, pp. 73–99.

Dewe, B., and A. Scherr. 1995. 'Jugendkulturen, Lebenskonstruktionen und soziale Deutungsmuster', in F. Ferchhoff, U. Sander and R. Vollbrecht (eds), *Jugendkulturen – Faszination und Ambivalenz. Einblicke in jugendliche Lebenswelten.* Weinheim: Juventa, pp. 133–145.

Dines, M., A.G. Gordon and P. Guerra. 2017. *The Punk Reader: The Research Transmission from the Local to the Global.* Chicago: University of Chicago Press.

Domdey, K.H. 1998. 'Privatisation in the New Bundesländer: A Critical Assessment of Treuhand', in T. Lange and J.R. Shackleton (eds), *The Political Economy of German Unification.* New York: Berghahn Books, pp. 44–54.

Drahtzieher. 1996. *Drahtzieher im braunen Netz. Ein aktueller Überblick über den Neonazi-Undergrund in Deutschland und Österreich.* Hamburg: Konkret Literatur Verlag.

Dragadze, T. 1994. 'Gender, Ethnicity and Alcohol in the Former Soviet Union', in M. McDonald (ed.), *Gender, Drink and Drugs.* Oxford: Berg, pp. 145–52.

Drissel, D. 2011. 'Anarchist Punks Resisting Gentrification: Countercultural Contestations of Space in the New Berlin', *International Journal of the Humanities* 8(10): 19–44.

———. 2013. 'Skateboarding Spaces of Youth in Belfast: Negotiating Boundaries, Transforming Identities', *Spaces and Flows: An International Journal of Urban and Extraurban Studies* 2(4): 115–37.

'Dropkick Murphys'. 2000. *Over the Edge*, 96–98.

Dunn, K. 2016. *Global Punk: Resistance and Rebellion in Everyday Life.* New York: Bloomsbury.

Dunning, E., P. Murphy and J. Williams. 1988. *The Roots of Football Hooliganism: An Historical and Sociological Study.* London: Routledge & Kegan Paul.

EE. 1995. *Eesti Entsüklopeedia*]. Tallinn: Eesti Entsüklopeediakirjastus.

Eidson, J. 2003. 'Heritage and Inheritance in Small Business Families of Postsocialist East Germany: Two Case Studies from Leipzig's Southern Region', in H. Grandits and P.

Heady (eds), *Distinct Inheritances: Property, Family and Community in a Changing Europe.* Münster: LIT Verlag, pp. 347–70.

Eidson, J., and G. Milligan. 2003. 'Cooperative Entrepreneurs? Collectivisation and Privatisation of Agriculture in Two East German Regions', in C. Hann and 'Property Relations' Group (eds), *The Postsocialist Agrarian Question: Property Relations and the Rural Condition.* Münster: LIT Verlag, pp. 47–92.

ENE. 1975. *Eesti Nõukogude Ents*üklopeedia. Tallinn: Valgus.

Engler, W. 1999. *Die Ostdeutschen. Kunde von einem verlorenen Land.* Berlin: Aufbau-Verlag.

Evan, W.M. 1963. 'Non-contractual Relations in Business: A Preliminary Study: Comment', *American Sociological Review* 28(1): 67–69.

Farin, K. 1996. *Die dritte Halbzeit: Fußballfans und Hooligans.* Berlin: BasisDruck GmbH.

——— (ed.). 2001. *Die Skins. Mythos und Realität*, Berlin: Verlag Thomas Tilsner.

Farin, K., and E. Seidel-Pielen. 2002. *Skinheads.* Munich: C.H. Beck Verlag.

Feigelson, N. 1970. *The Underground Revolution: Hippies, Yippies, and Others.* New York: Funk & Wagnalls.

Feigenbaum, A. 2005. '"Some Guy Designed This Room I'm Standing in": Marking Gender in Press Coverage of Ani Difranco', *Popular Music* 24(1): 37–57.

Fenemore. 2007. *Sex, Thugs and Rock'n'Roll: Teenage Rebels in Cold-War East Germany* New York: Berghahn Books.

Fischer, A., et al. 2000. *Jugend 2000. 13. Shell Jugendstudie.* Opladen: Leske+Budrich.

Flockton, C. 2004. 'Financing German Unity: Challenges, Methods and Longer-Term Consequences', in M. Dennis and E. Kolinsky (eds), *United and Divided: Germany since 1990.* New York: Berghahn Books, pp. 36–54.

Forman, M. 2002. *The 'Hood Comes First: Race, Space and Place in Rap and Hip-Hop.* Middletown: Wesleyan University Press.

Foster, H. (ed.). 1983. *The Anti-aesthetic: Essays on Postmodern Culture.* Port Townsend, MA: Bay Press.

Fournier, L.S. 2013. 'Violence and Roughness in Traditional Games and Sports: The Case of Folk Football (England and Scotland)', *Folklore: Electronic Journal of Folklore* 54: 39–50.

Fox, K.J. 1987. 'Real Punks and Pretenders: The Social Organisation of a Counterculture', *Journal of Contemporary Ethnography* 16(3): 344–370.

Friedman, S., and D. Laurison. 2019. *The Class Ceiling: Why It Pays to Be Privileged.* Bristol: Policy Press.

Frith, S. 1983. *Sound Effects: Youth, Leisure and the Politics of Rock 'n' Roll.* London: Routledge.

———. 1996. *Performing Rites: On the Value of Popular Music.* Cambridge, MA: Harvard University Press.

Frith, S., and J. Savage. 1997. 'Pearls and Swine: Intellectuals and the Mass Media', in S. Redhead (ed.), *The Clubcultures Reader: Readings in Popular Cultural Studies.* Oxford: Blackwell, pp. 7–17.

Furian, G., and N. Becker. 2012. *'Auch im Osten trägt man Westen': Punks in der DDR – und was aus ihnen geworden ist.* Berlin: Archiv der Jugendkulturen Verlag KG.

Furness, Z. 2012a. 'Attempted Education and Righteous Accusations: An Introduction to Punkademics', in Z. Furness (ed.), *Punkademics: The Basement Show in the Ivory Tower.* Wivenhoe: Minor Compositions, pp. 5–24.

———. 2012b. *Punkademics: The Basement Show in the Ivory Tower.* Wivenhoe: Minor Compositions.

Galantier, M. 1974. 'Why the "Haves" Come out Ahead: Speculations on the Limits of Legal Change', *Law & Society Review* 9(1): 95–160.
Galenza, R., and H. Havemeister (eds). 2005. *Wir wollen immer artig sein...: Punk, New Wave, HipHop, Independent-Szene in der DDR 1980–1990*. Berlin: Schwarzkopf & Schwarzkopf.
Galvin, K.-L. 2001. 'Schneider Revisited: Sharing and Ratification in the Construction of Kinship', in L. Stone (ed.), *New Directions in Anthropological Kinship*. Lanham: Rowman & Littlefield Publishers, Inc, pp. 109–124.
Garland, J., and P. Hodkinson. 2014. 'F**king Freak! What the Hell Do You Think You Look Like? Experiences of Targeted Victimization among Goths and Developing Notions of Hate Crime', *British Journal of Criminology* 54(4): 613–31.
Gelder, K. (ed.). 1997. *The Subcultures Reader*. New York: Routledge.
———. 2007. *Subcultures: Cultural Histories and Social Practice*. New York: Routledge.
Gibbon, M.J., K.S. Mack and B.A. Shingleton. 1995. *Dimensions of German Unification: Economic, Social, and Legal Analyses*. San Francisco: Westwiew Press.
Giddens, A. 2006. *Sociology*. 5th edn. Cambridge: Polity Press.
Gilbert, J. 2009. 'The Hardcore Continuum? A Report of "The Hardcore Continuum?" Symposium Held at the University of East London, April 29th 2009', *Dancecult: Journal of Electronic Dance Music* 1(1) 118–22.
Gilroy, P. 2002. *There Ain't No Black in the Union Jack*. New York: Routledge.
Glaser, C. 2000. *Bo-Tsotsi: The Youth Gangs of Soweto, 1935–1976*. Cape Town: David Phillip Publishers.
Godelier, M. 1975. 'Modes of Production, Kinship, and Demographic Structures', in M. Bloch (ed.), *Marxist Analyses and Social Anthropology*. London: Malaby Press, pp. 3–28.
Golte, J., and A. Norma. 1987. *Los Caballos de Troya de los invasores: estrategias campesinas en la conquista de la Lima.*Lima: Institiudo de Estudios Peruanos.
Goodman, S. 1995. *England Belongs to Me*. Dunoon, Argyll: Low Life.
Goody, E.N. 1973. *Context of Kinship: An Essay in the Family Sociology of the Gonja of Northern Ghana*. Cambridge: Cambridge University Press.
Gorbachev, M. 1987. *Perestroika: New Thinking for Our Country and the World*. New York: Harper & Row Publishers.
———. 1993. *Gody trudnykh reshenii. Izbrannoe. 1985–1992 gg.* Moskva: Al'fa print.
———. 1995. *Soiuz mozhno bylo sokhranit'*. Moskva: Aprel'-1985.
Gordon, A. 2012. 'Building Record Studios Whilst Bradford Burned: DIY Punk Ethics in a Field of Force', in Z. Furness (ed.), *Punkacademics: The Basement Show in the Ivory Tower*. Wivenhoe: Minor Compositions, pp. 105–24.
Gorsuch, A.E., and D.P. Koenker. 2013. 'Introduction: The Socialist 1960s in Global Perspective', in A.E. Gorsuch and D.P. Koenker (eds), *The Socialist Sixties: Crossing Borders in the Second World*. Bloomington: Indiana University Press, pp. 1–24.
Griffiths, A. 2002. 'Legal Pluralism', in R. Banakar and M. Travers (eds), *An Introduction to Law and Social Theory*. Oxford: Hart Publishing, pp. 289–310.
Gudeman, S. 2008. *Economy's Tensions: The Dialectics of Community and Market*. New York: Berghahn Books.
Gullestad, M. 2002. 'Invisible Fences: Egalitarianism, Nationalism and Racism', *Man, New Series* 8(1): 45–63.
Haenfler, R. 2004. 'Rethinking Subcultural Resistance: Core Values of the Straight Edge Movement', *Journal of Contemporary Ethnography* 33(4): 406–36.

———. 2007. *Straight Edge: Clean-Living Youth, Hardcore Punk, and Social Change.* New Brunswick, NJ: Rutgers University Press.
———. 2014. *Subcultures: The Basics.* London: Routledge.
Haine, W.S. 2006. 'Drink, Sociability, and Social Class in France, 1789–1945: The Emergence of a Proletarian Public Sphere', in M.P. Holt (ed.), *Alcohol: A Social and Cultural History*. Oxford: Berg, pp. 121–144.
Hall, S., and T. Jefferson (eds). 1986. *Resisitance through Rituals: Youth Subcultures in Post-War Britain.* London: Hutchinson.
Hamm, M.S. 1995. 'Hammer of the Gods Revisited: Neo-Nazi Skinheads, Domestic Terrorism, and the Rise of the New Protest Music', in J. Farrell and C.R. Sanders (eds), *Cultural Criminology.* Boston: Northeastern, pp. 190–212.
Hann, D. 2013. *Physical Resistance: A Hundred Years of Anti-Fascism.* London: Zero Books.
Hannerz, E. 2015. *Performing Punk.* New York: Palgrave Macmillian.
Harding, S. 2012. 'Street Government: The Role of the Urban Street Gang in the London Riots', in D. Brigg (ed.), *The English Riots of 2011: A Summer of Discontent.* Sherfield Gables: Watershed Press, pp. 193–213.
Harvey, P. 1997. 'Gender, Community and Confrontation: Power Relations in Drunkenness in Ocongate (Southern Peru)', in M. McDonald (ed.), *Gender, Drink and Drugs.* Oxford: Berg, pp. 209–34.
Hasselbach, I. 2001. *Die Abrechnung. Ein Neonazi steigt aus.* Berlin: AtV.
Heath, M. 2003. 'Soft-Boiled Masculinity: Renegotiating Gender and Racial Ideologies in the Promise Keepers Movement', *Gender & Society* 17(3): 423–444.
Hebdige, D. 1979. *Subculture: The Meaning of Style.* New York: Methuen.
———. 1987. *Cut'N'Mix: Culture, Identity and Carribean Music.* New York: Routledge.
Henry, T. 1989. *Break All Rules! Punk Rock and the Making of a Style.* Ann Arbor, MI: UMI Research Press.
Hesmondhalgh, D. 2005. 'Subcultures, Scenes or Tribes? None of the Above', *Journal of Youth Studies* 8(1): 21–40.
Hjelm, T., K. Kahn-Harris and M. LeVine. 2011. 'Heavy Metal as Controversy and Counterculture', *Popular Music History* 6(1–2): 5–18.
Hodkinson, P. 2011. 'Ageing in a Spectacular "Youth Culture": Continuity, Change and Community amongst Older Goths', *British Journal of Sociology* 62(2): 262–82.
Hoebel, E.A. 1958. 'Authority in Primitive Societies', in C.P. Friedrich (ed.), *Authority.* Cambridge, MA: Harvard University Press, pp. 222–34.
Hollands, R. 2002. 'Divisions in the Dark: Youth Cultures, Transitions and Segmented Consumption Spaces in the Night-Time Economy', *Journal of Youth Studies* 5(2): 153–171.
Hooker, M.B. 1975. *Legal Pluralism: An Introduction to Colonial and Neo-colonial Laws.* Oxford: Clarendon Press.
Horschig, M. 2005. 'In der DDR hat es nie Punks gegeben', in R. Galenza and H. Havemeister (eds), *Wir wollen immer artig sein ...: Punk, New Wave, HipHop, Independent-Szene in der DDR 1980–1990.* Berlin: Schwarzkopf & Schwarzkopf, pp. 30–70.
Hughes, G., and M. Rowe. 2007. 'Neighbourhood Policing and Community Safety: Researching the Instabilities of the Local Governance of Crime, Disorder and Security in Contemporary UK', *Criminology and Criminal Justice* 7(4): 317–46.
Humphrey, C. 2001. 'Inequality and Exclusion: A Russian Case Study of Emotion in Politics', *Anthropological Theory* 1(3): 331–353.

Hurrelmann, K. 2012. *Lebensphase Jugend: Eine Einführung in die sozialwissenschaftliche Jugendforschung (Grundlagentexte Soziologie).* Berlin: Beltz Juventa.

Ibrahim, A. 2008. 'The New Flâneur: Subaltern Cultural Studies, African Youth in Canada and the Semiology of In-betweenness', *Cultural Studies* 22(2): 234–53.

Irigaray, L. 1985. *This Sex Which Is Not One.* Ithaca, NY: Cornell University Press.

Jahn. 2006. 'Kolumne', *Trust* 121(3): 6.

James, Z. 2007. 'Policing Marginal Spaces: Controlling Gypsies and Travellers', *Criminology and Criminal Justice* 7(4): 367–89.

Jenkins, R. 1983. *Lads, Citizens and Ordinary Kids: Working-Class Youth Life-Styles in Belfast.* London: Routledge & Kegan Paul.

Johnson, C. 2002. 'The Dilemmas of Ethnic Privilege: A Comparison of Constructions of "British", "English" and "Anglo-Celtic" Identity in Contemporary British and Australian Political Discourse', *Ethnicities* 2(2): 163–188.

Jones, O. 2011. *Chavs: The Demonization of the Working Class.* London: Verso Books.

Jones, S. 1988. *Black Culture, White Youth: The Reggae Tradition from JA to UK.* London: Macmillian Education.

Jugendstudie. 2010. *Shell Jugendstudie 2010.* Opladen: Leske + Budrich.

Kahn-Harris, K. 2004. 'Unspectacular Subculture? Transgression and Mundanity in the Global Extreme Metal Scene', in A. Bennet and K. Kahn-Harris (eds), *After Subculture: Critical Studies in Contemporary Youth Culture.* Basingstoke: Palgrave Macmillan, pp. 107–18.

Kelly, L., and A.K. Gill. 2012. 'Reading the Riots through Gender: A Feminist Reflection on England's 2011 Riots', in D. Brigg (ed.), *The English Riots of 2011: A Summer of Discontent.* Sherfield Gables: Watershed Press, pp. 214–235.

Kemp, R. 2007. *Gangs: My Close Calls with the Hardest Men on the Streets, from Rio to Moscow.* London: Penguin Books.

Kennedy, L.W., and S.W. Baron. 1993. 'Routine Activities and a Subculture of Violence: A Study of Violence on the Street', *Journal of Research in Crime and Deliquency* 30(1): 88–112.

Kimmel, M. 2007. 'Racism as Adolescent Male Rite of Passage: Ex-Nazis in Scandinavia', *Journal of a Contemporary Etnography* 36(2): 202–218.

Kitwana, B. 2005. *Why White Kids Love Hip Hop: Wankstars, Wiggers, Wannabies, and the Reality of Race in America.* New York: Basic Books.

Koch, K. 1999. 'The Impact of German Unification on the German Industrial Relations System', in C. Flockton and E. Kolinsky (eds), *Recasting East Germany: Social Transformation after the GDR.* London: Frank Cass, pp. 52–68.

Koehler, J. 2000. *Die Zeit der Jungs: Zur Organisation von Gewalt und der Austragung von Konflikten in Georgien.* Münster: LIT.

Kohn, M. 2004. *Brave New Neighborhoods: The Privatization of Public Space.* New York, NY: Routledge.

Kohtz, A., et al. 2012. *'Auch im Osten trägt man Westen': Punks in der DDR – und was aus ihnen geworden ist.* Berlin: Archiv der Jugendkulturen Verlag KG.

Kollmorgen, R. 2005. *Ostdeutschland. Beobachtungen einer Übergangs- und Teilgesellschaft.* Berlin: VS Verlag.

Krokovay, Z. 1985. 'Politics & Punk', *Index on Censorship* 14(2): 17–21.

Laing, D. 2015. *One Chord Wonders: Power and Meaning in Punk Rock.* Oakland, CA: PM Press.

Lamy, P., and J. Levin. 1985. 'Punk and Middle-Class Values: A Content Analysis', *Youth & Society* 17(2): 157–170.
Lange, T., and G. Pugh. 1998. 'The Treuhand: A Positive Account', in T. Lange and J.R. Shackleton (eds), *The Political Economy of German Unification*. New York: Berghahn Books, pp. 56–71.
Lange, T., and J.R. Shackleton. 1998. 'Germany in Transition: An Introduction', in T. Lange and J.R. Shackleton (eds), *The Political Economy of German Unification*. New York: Berghahn Books, pp. 1–13.
Lawrence, J. 2000. 'Review Article: The British Sense of Class', *Journal of Contemporary History* 35(2): 307–18.
Leacock, E. 1954. *The Montagnais 'Hunting Territory' and the Fur Trade*. Menasha, WI: American Anthropological Association.
Leblanc, L. 2001. *Pretty in Punk: Girls' Gender Resistance in a Boys' Subculture*. New Brunswick, NJ: Rutgers University Press.
Lees, S. 1993. *Sugar and Spice: Sexuality and Adolescent Girls*. London: Penguin.
Leidecker, G., D. Kirchhöfer and P. Güttler (eds). 1991. *Ich weiss nicht ob ich froh sein soll*. Stuttgart: J.B. Metzlersche Verlagsbuchhandlung.
Lenz, K. 1995. 'Lebenswege durch Jugendphase. Ein Ost-West-Vergleich', in F. Ferchhoff, U. Sander and R. Vollbrecht (eds), *Jugendkulturen – Faszination und Ambivalenz. Einblicke in jugendliche Lebenswelten*. Weinheim: Juventa, pp. 146–160.
Letts, D. 2008. *Culture Clash: Dread Meets Punk Rockers*. London: SAF Publishing.
Lévi-Strauss, C. 1966. *The Savage Mind*. Chicago: University of Chicago Press.
———. 1969. *The Elementary Structures of Kinship*. London: Eyre & Spottiswoode.
Lewis, O. 1975. 'The Culture of Poverty', in J. Friedl and N.J. Chrisman (eds), *City Ways: A Selective Reader in Urban Anthropology*. New York: Harper and Row, pp. 391–401.
Lister, S., P. Hadfield, D. Hobbs and S. Winlow. 2001. 'Accounting for Bouncers: Occupational Licensing as a Mechanism for Regulation', *Criminology and Criminal Justice* 1(4): 363–84.
Lohman, K. 2017. *The Connected Lives of Dutch Punk: Contesting Subcultural Boundaries*. Basingstoke: Palgrave Macmillan.
Lohman, K., and M. Worley. 2018. 'Bloody Revolutions, Fascist Dreams, Anarchy and Peace: Crass, Rondos and the Politics of Punk, 1977–84', *Britain and the World* 11(1): 51–74.
Lotman, J. 1999. *Semiosfäärist*. Tallinn: Vagabund.
Lovatt, A., and J. O'Connor. 1995. 'Cities and the Night-time Economy', *Planning Practice & Research* 10(2): 127–134.
Lowney, K.S. 1995. 'Teenage Satanism as Oppositional Youth Culture', *Journal of Contemporary Etnography* 23(4): 453–484.
Luegner, A. 2005/2006. 'Randy: You Can't Keep A Good Band Down ...', *Slam* 23: 104–5.
Luvaas, B. 2009. 'Dislocating Sounds: The Deterritorialization of Indonesian Indie Pop', *Cultural Anthropology* 24(2): 246–79.
Lähteenmaa, J. 1989. *Tytöt & Rock*. Helsinki: Kansalaiskasvatuksen Keskus r.y.
Löfving, S., H. Moksnes and L. Rudebeck (eds). 2005. *Peopled Economies: Conversations with Stephen Gudeman*. Uppsala: Uppsala University.
Lydon, J. 1993. *Rotten: No Irish, No Blacks, No Dogs*. London: Hodder & Stoughton.
Macaulay, S. 1963. 'Non-contractual Relations in Business: A Preliminary Study', *American Sociological Review* 28(1): 55–67.

Macilwee, M. 2015. *The Teddy Bow Wars: The Youth Cult That Shocker Britain.* Croydon: Milo Books.

Mader, M. 1996. *Oi! The Book.* Vol. 1. Berlin: I.P. Verlag.

———. 1999. *New York City Hardcore.* Berlin: I.P. Verlag.

Magnet, S. 2007. 'Feminist Sexualities, Race and the Internet: An Investigation of Suicidegirls.Com', *New Media and Society* 9(4): 577–602.

Maira, S.M. 2002. *Desis in the House: Indian American Youth Culture in New York City.* Philadelphia: Temple University Press.

Manderscheid, K. 2006. 'Sozialräumliche Grenzgebiete: Unsichtbare Zäune und gegenkulturelle Räume – Eine empirische exploration der räumlichen dimension sozialer Ungleichheit', *Sozialer Sinn* 7(2): 273–99.

Marciniak, M. 2015. *Transnational Punk Communities in Poland: From Nihilism to Nothing outside Punk.* Lanham, MD: Lexington Books.

Marcus, G. 1989. *Lipstick Traces: A Secret History of the Twentieth Century.* London: Faber & Faber.

Mareth, C., and R. Schneider. 1999. *Haare auf Krawall: Jugendkulturen in Leipzig von 1980 bis 1991.* Leipzig: Connewitzer Verlagsbuchhandlung.

Marshall, G. 1990. *The Two Tone Story.* Glasgow: Zoot Publishing.

———. 1993. *Spirit of '69.* Dunoon: S.T. Publishing.

Martin, G. 2009. 'Subculture, Style, Chavs and Consumer Capitalism: Towards a Critical Cultural Criminology of Youth', *Crime Media Culture* 5(2): 123–45.

Maurice, C. 1998. 'U.K. Subs', *Wahrshauer,* 22–23.

McCallum, E.L. 1996. 'Technologies of Truth and the Function of Gender in Foucault', in S.J. Hekman (ed.), *Feminist Interpretations of Michel Foucault.* University Park, PA: Penn State Press, pp. 77–99.

McCulloch, T., and F. McNeill. 2007. 'Consumer Society, Commodification and Offender Management', *Criminology and Criminal Justice* 7(3): 223–42.

McDonald, M. (ed.). 1994a. *Gender, Drink and Drugs.* Oxford: Berg.

———. 1994b. 'Introduction: A Social-Anthropological View of Gender, Drink and Drugs', in M. McDonald (ed.), *Gender, Drink and Drugs.* Oxford: Berg, pp. 1–32.

McDonald-Walker, S. 2000. *Bikers: Culture, Politics and Power.* Oxford: Berg.

McGrellis, S. 2005. 'Pushing the Boundaries in Northern Ireland: Young People, Violence, and Sectarianism', *Contemporary Politics* 11(1): 53–71.

McIllwain, J.S. 1999. 'Organized Crime: A Social Network Approach', *Crime, Law and Social Change* 32(4): 301–23.

McLeod, K. 2003. 'Space Oddities: Aliens, Futurism And Meaning in Popular Music', *Popular Music* 22(3): 337–55.

McNeill, L., and G. McCain. 1996. *Please Kill Me: The Uncensored Oral History of Punk.* London: Abacus.

McRobbie, A. 1980. 'Settling Accounts with Subcultures: A Feminist Critique', in S. Frith and A. Goodwin (eds), *On Record: Rock Pop and the Written Word.* London: Routledge, pp. 66–80.

———. 1993. 'Shut up and Dance: Youth Culture and Changing Modes of Femininity', *Young* 113–31.

McRobbie, A., and J. Garber. 1993. 'Girls and Subcultures', in S. Hall and T. Jefferson (eds), *Resistance through Rituals: Youth Subcultures in Post-War Britain.* New York: Routledge, pp. 177–88.

Meagher, K. 2006. 'Social Capital, Social Liabilities, and Political Capital: Social Networks and Informal Manufacturing in Nigeria', *African Affairs* 105(421): 553–582.
Mendoza-Denton, N. 2008. *Homegirls: Language and Cultural Practice among Latina Youth Gangs.* Malden, MA: Blackwell.
Merry, S.E. 1988. 'Legal Pluralism', *Law & Society Review* 22(5): 869–96.
Middleton, J., and R. Beebe. 2002. 'The Racial Politics of Hybridity and "Neo-eclecticism" in Contemporary Popular Music', *Popular Music* 21(2): 159–72.
Miller, T. 1999. *The 60s Communes: Hippies and Beyond.* New York: Syracuse Univeersity Press.
Mitchell, J.C. (ed.). 1969. *Social Networks in Urban Situations,* Manchester: Manchester University Press.
———. 1974. 'Social Networks', *Annual Review of Anthropology* 3: 279–99.
Mohr, T. 2018. *Burning Down the Haus: Punk Rock, Revolution, and the Fall of the Berlin Wall.* New York: Hachette Algonquin Books.
Mooney, K. 1998. '"Ducktails, Flick-Knives and Pugnancy": Subcultural and Hegemonic Masculinities in South Africa', *Journal of Southern African Studies* 24(4): 753–74.
———. 2005. 'Identities in the Ducktail Youth Subculture in Post-World-War-Two South Africa', *Journal of Youth Studies* 8(1): 41–57.
Moore, D. 1994. *The Lads in Action: Social Process in an Urban Youth Culture.* Aldershot: Arena.
Moore, H.L. 2012. 'Whatever Happened to Women and Men? Gender and Other Crises in Anthropology', in H.L. Moore (ed.), *Anthropological Theory Today.* Cambridge: Polity Press, pp. 151–71.
Moore, J.B. 1993. *Skinheads Shaved for Battle: A Cultural History of American Skinheads.* Madison, WI: University of Wisconsin Press.
Moore, R. 2004. 'Postmodernism and Punk Subculture: Cultures of Authenticity and Deconstruction', *Communication Review* 7(3): 305–27.
———. 2007. 'Friends Don't Let Friends Listen to Corporate Rock: Punk as a Field of Cultural Production', *Journal of Contemporary Ethnography* 36(4): 438–74.
Moore, S.F. 1973. 'Law and Social Change: The Semi-autonomous Social Field as an Appropriate Subject of Study', *Law & Society Review* 7(4): 719–46.
Moore, W.E. 1963. 'But Some Are More Equal Than Others', *American Sociological Review* 28(1): 13–18.
Moran, L.J. 2007. '"Invisible Minorities": Challenging Community and Neighbourhood Models of Policing', *Criminology and Criminal Justice* 7(4): 417–41.
Morris, J. 2016. *Everyday Post-socialism: Working-Class Communities in the Russian Margins.* London: Palgrave Macmillan.
———. 2018. 'Automobile Masculinities and Neoliberal Production Regimes among Russian Blue-Collar Men', in C. Walker and S. Roberts (eds), *Masculinity, Labour and Neoliberalism: Global Perspectives.* London: Palgrave Macmillan, pp. 171–93.
Morrison, C., and G. Schwartz. 2003. 'Managing the Labour Collective: Wage Systems in the Russian Industrial Enterprise', *Europe-Asia Studies* 55(4): 553–74.
Muggleton, D. (ed.). 2000. *Inside Subculture.* Oxford: Berg.
Muggleton, D. 2005. 'From Classlessness to Clubculture: A Genealogy of Post-war British Youth Cultural Analysis', *Young* 13(2): 205–219.
Muggleton, D., and R. Weinzierl (eds). 2003. *The Post-subcultures Reader.* Oxford: Berg.

Mullaney, J.L. 2007. 'Unity Admirable But Not Necessarily Needed: Going Rates and Gender Boundaries in the Straight Edge Hardcore Music Scene', *Gender & Society* 21(3): 384–408.

Mullins, C.W. 2006. *Holding Your Square.* Cullompton: Willan Publishing.

Muños, G., and M. Marín. 2006. 'Music Is the Connection: Youth Cultures in Colombia', in P. Nilan and C. Feixa (eds), *Global Youth? Hybrid Identities, Plural Worlds.* New York: Routledge, pp. 130–148.

Muršić, R. 2009. 'Punk Anthropology: From a Study of a Local Slovene Alternative Rock Scene towards Partisan Scholarship', in L. Kürti and P. Skalník (eds), *Postsocialist Europe: Anthropological Perspectives from Home.* New York: Berghahn Books, pp. 188–206.

Murthy, D. 2007. 'A South Asian American Diasporic Aesthetic Community? Ethnicity and New York City's "Asian Electronic Music" Scene', *Ethnicities* 7(2): 225–47.

Möller, K. 1997. 'Hässlich, kahl und hundsgemein. Männlichkeits- und Weiblichkeitsinszenierungen in der Skinheadszene', in K. Farin (ed.), *Die Skins: Mythos und Realität.* Bad Tölz: Verlag Thomas Tilsner, pp. 115–38.

Nayak, A. 2003. *Race, Place and Globalization.* Oxford: Berg.

———. 2006. 'Displaced Masculinities: Chavs, Youth and Class in the Post-industrial City', *Sociology* 40(5): 813–31.

Nayak, A., and M.J. Kehily. 2013. *Gender, Youth and Culture: Global Masculinities and Feminities.* New York: Palgrave Macmillan.

Needs, K. 2005. *Joe Strummer and the Legend of The Clash.* London: Plexus Publishing.

Negus, K. 1996. *Popular Music in Theory: An Introduction.* Cambridge: Polity Press.

———. 1999. *Music Genres and Corporate Cultures.* New York: Routledge.

Nehring, N. 2007. '"Everyone's Given up and Just Wants to Go Dancing": From Punk to Rave in the Thatcher Era', *Popular Music and Society* 30(1): 1–18.

Neill, W.J.V. 2001. 'Memory, Spatial Planning and the Construction of Cultural Identity in Belfast and Berlin – an Overview', in W.J.V. Neill and H.-U. Schwedler (eds), *Urban Planning and Cultural Inclusion: Lessons from Belfast and Berlin.* Basingstoke: Palgrave Macmillan, pp. 3–23.

Nellis, J.R. 2007. 'Privatization in Developing Countries: A Summary Assessment', *SAIS Review* 27(2): 3–29.

Neubert, E. 2008. *Unsere Revolution. Die Geschichte der jahre 1989/1990.* München, Zürich: Piper.

Novotná, H., and M. Heřmanský. 2014. 'Shared Enemies, Shared Friends: The Relational Character of Subcultural Ideology in the Case of Czech Punks and Skinheads', in Subcultures Network (ed.), *Fight Back: Punk, Politics and Resistance.* Manchester: Manchester University Press, pp. 170–185.

NZO. 2006. 'I Got My Power', *Trust* 121: 2.

Nuttall, M. 1992. *Arctic Homeland: Kinship, Community and Development in Northwest Greenland.* Toronto: University of Toronto Press.

O'Brien, K., and L. Li. 2006. *Rightful Resistance in Rural China.* Cambridge: Cambridge University Press.

O'Connor, A. 1990. 'Culture and Communication', in J. Downing, A. Mohammadi and A. Sreberny-Mohammadi (eds), *Questioning the Media: A Critical Introduction.* London: Sage, pp. 27–41.

———. 2002. 'Local Scenes and Dangerous Crossroads: Punk and Theories of Cultural Hybridity', *Popular Music* 21(2): 225–36.

———. 2004. 'Punk and Globalization: Spain and Mexico', *International Journal of Cultural Studies* 7(2): 175–95.
———. 2008. *Punk Record Labels and the Struggle for Authonomy: The Emergence of DIY.* Lanham, MD: Lexington Books.
———. 2016. 'Towards a Field Theory of Punk', *Punk and Post-Punk* 5(1): 67–81.
O'Hara, C. 1995. *The Philosophy of Punk: More than Noise!* San Francisco: AK Press.
O'Meara, C. 2003. 'The Raincoats: Breaking Down Punk Rock's Masculinities', *Popular Music* 22(3): 299–313.
Ogg, A., and D. Upshal. 1999. *The Hip Hop Years: A History of Rap.* London: Channel 4 Books/Macmillan.
Oosterbaan, M. 2009. 'Sonic Supremacy: Sound, Space and Charisma in a Favela in Rio de Janeiro', *Critique of Anthropology* 29(1): 81–104.
Ortner, S.B. 1996. *Making Gender: The Politics and Erotics of Culture.* Boston: Beacon Press.
Panter, H. 2007. *Ska'd for Life: A Personal Journey with The Specials.* London: Pan Books.
Partington, A. 2014. 'Class, Clothes, and Co-creativity', *Clothing Cultures* 1(1): 7–21.
Peacock, E.A. 2012. 'The Authentic Village and the Modern City: The Space-Time of Class Identities in Urban Western Ukraine', *Anthropology of East Europe Review* 30(1): 214–236.
Peteri, G. 2008. 'The Occident within – or the Drive for Exceptionalism and Modernity', *Kritika: Explorations in Russian and Eurasian History* 9(4): 929–37.
Petridis, A. 2010. 'Misunderstood or Hateful? Oi!s Rise and Fall', *The Guardian*, 18 March.
Pickel, A. 1997. 'The Jump-Started Economy and the Ready-Made State: A Theoretical Reconsideration of the East German Case', *Comparative Political Studies* 30(2): 211–41.
Piketty, T. 2014. 'Capital in the Twenty-First Century'. Harvard: Harvard University Press.
Pilkington, H. 1994. *Russia's Youth and Its Culture: A Nation's Constructors and Constructed.* London: Routledge.
———. 1999. 'Reconfiguring "the West"', in H. Pilkington et al. (eds), *Looking West? Cultural Globalization and Russian Youth Cultures.* University Park, PA: Penn State Press, pp. 165–200.
———. 2010. 'No Longer "On Parade": Style and the Performance of Skinhead in the Russian Far North', *Russian Review* 187–209.
———. 2014. '"My Whole Life Is Here": Tracing Journeys through "Skinhead"', in D. Buckingham, S. Bragg and M.J. Kehily (eds), *Youth Cultutŕes in the Age of Global Media.* New York: Palgrave Macmillan, pp. 71–87.
Pilkington, H., and R. Johnson. 2003. 'Peripheral Youth: Relations of Identity and Power in Global/Local Context', *European Journal of Cultural Studies* 6(3): 259–283.
Pilkington, H., E. Omel'chenko and A. Garifzianova (eds). 2010. *Russia's Skinheads: Exploring and Rethinking Subcultural Lives.* New York: Routledge.
PISA. 2006. *PISA 2006: Science Competencies for Tomorrow's World: Volume 1: Analysis*, Paris: OECD Publishing.
Polhemus, T. 1997. 'In the Supermarket of Style', in S. Redhead, D. Wynne and J. O'Connor (eds), *The Clubcultures Reader: Readings in Popular Cultural Studies.* Malden, MA: Wiley-Blackwell, pp. 130–33
———. 2001. 'Introduction', in G. Watson, *Skins.* Chicago, Illinois: Olmstead Press., pp. 6–8.

Pospisil, L. 1973. 'E. Adamson Hoebel and the Anthropology of Law', *Law & Society Review* 537–59.

Potter, R.A. 1995. *Spectacular Vernaculars: Hip-Hop and the Politics of Postmodernism.* New York: State University of New York Press.

Price, R. 2002. *First-Time: The Historical Vision of an African American People.* Chicago: University of Chicago Press.

Pritchard, R.M.O. 2004. 'Challenges of Participation in German Higher Education: An East-West Comparison', in M. Dennis and E. Kolinsky (eds), *United and Divided: Germany since 1990.* New York: Berghahn Books, pp. 110–22.

Rapport, E. 2014. 'Hearing Punk as Blues', *Popular Music* 33(1): 39–67.

Razzaz, O.M. 1994. 'Contestation and Mutual Adjustment: The Process of Controlling Land in Yajouz, Jordan', *Law & Society Review* 28(1): 7–40.

Rethmann, P. 2009. 'Post-Communist Ironies in an East German Hotel', *Anthropology Today* 25(1): 21–23.

Reynolds, S. 2005. *Rip It up and Start Again: Postpunk 1978–1984.* London: Faber & Faber.

———. 2011. *Retromania: Pop Culture's Addiction to Its Own Past.* London: Faber and Faber.

Roesler, J. 1994. 'Privatisation in Eastern Germany: Experience with the Treuhand', *Europe-Asia Studies* 46(3): 505–17.

Roman, L.G. 1988. 'Intimacy, Labor, and Class: Ideologies of Femine Sexuality in the Punk Slam Dance', in L.G. Roman and L.K. Christian-Smith (eds), *Becoming Feminine: Politics of Popular Culture.* London: Falmer Press Ltd, pp. 143–84.

Root, R.A. 2005. 'Fashioning Independence: Gender, Dress, and Social Space in Postcolonial Argentina', in R.A. Root (ed.), *The Latin American Fashion Reader.* Oxford: Berg, pp. 31–43.

Rorabaugh, W.J. 2015. *American Hippies.* Cambridge: Cambridge University Press.

Rose, T. 1989. 'Orality and Technology: Rap Music and Afro-American Cultural Resistance', *Popular Music and Society* 13(4): 35–44.

———. 1992. 'Black Texts/Black Contexts', in G. Dent (ed.), *Black Popular Culture.* Seattle: Bay Press: 223–27.

———. 1994. *Black Noise: Rap Music and Black Culture in Contemporary America.* Middletown, CT: Wesleyan University Press.

Rundquist, R. 2007. 'Street Skateboarding and the Government Stamp of Approval', in A. Greenberg (ed.), *Youth Subcultures: Exploring Underground America.* New York: Pearson Longman, pp. 171–89.

Sabin, R. (ed.). 1999. *Punk Rock: So What?,* Milton Park, NY: Routledge.

Sahlins, M. 1972. *Stone Age Economics.* Frome: Tavistock Publications.

Salasuo, M., and P. Seppälä. 2004. 'Drug Use within the Finnish Club Culture as Marks of Distinction', *Contemporary Drug Problems* 31(2): 213–229.

Sandler. 1997. 'The Lurkers. 20. Dienstjubiläum + 1', *Skin Up* 43: 21–23.

Sarabia, D., and T.E. Shriver. 2004. 'Maintaining Collective Identity in a Hostile Environment: Confronting Negative Public Perception and Factional Divisions within the Skinhead Subculture', *Sociological Spectrum* 24(3): 267–94.

Sarrazin, T. 2010. *Deutscland schafft sich ab. Wie wir unseres Land aufs Spiel setzen.* Berlin: DVA.

Savage, J. 1991. *England's Dreaming.* London: Faber & Faber.

Schiermer, B. 2014. 'Late-Modern Hipsters: New Tendencies in Popular Culture', *Acta Sociologica* 57(2): 167–181.
Schilt, K. 2003. '"I'll Resist with Every Inch and Every Breath": Girls and Zine Making as a Form of Resistance', *Youth Society* 35: 71–97).
Schippers, M. 2007. 'Recovering the Feminine Other: Masculinity, Femininity, and Gender Hegemony', *Theory and Society* 36(1): 85–102.
Schubarth, W., and K. Speck. 2010. 'Zwischen Annäherung umd Spaltung – soziale Probleme ostdeutscher Jugendlicher im Ost-West-Vergleich', in M. Busch, J. Jeskow and R. Stutz (eds), *Zwischen Prekarisierung und Protest. Die Lebenslangen und dGenerationsbilder von Jugendlichen in Ost und West.* Bielefeld: transcript, pp. 155–174.
Schwarz, D. 1997. 'Oi: Music, Politics and Violence', in D. Schwarz (ed.), *Listening Subjects:Music, Psychoanalysis, Culture.* Durham, NC: Duke University Press, pp. 100–32.
Schweitzer, P.P. (ed.). 2000. *Dividends of Kinship.* New York: Routledge.
Scott, J.C. 1976. *The Moral Economy of the Peasant: Rebellion and Subsistence in Southeast Asia.* New Haven: Yale University Press.
———. 1985. *Weapons of the Weak: Everyday Forms of Peasant Resistance.* Yale: Yake University Press.
———. 2014. *Two Cheers for Anarchism: Six Easy Pieces on Autonomy, Dignity, and Meaningful Work and Play.* Princeton: Princeton University Press.
Selfhout, M.H.W., et al. 2008. 'Heavy Metal and Hip-Hop Style Preferences and Externalizing Problem Behavior: A Two-Wave Longitudinal Study', *Youth & Society* 29(4): 435–452.
Seliger, B. 2001. 'Cherries, Anyone? Part Four: Experiences with Privatisation and Restructuring'. http://www.ce-review.org/01/4/seliger4.html. Retrieved 7 July 2012.
Shaffer, R. 2013. 'The Soundtrack of Neo-Fascism: Youth and Music in the National Front', *Patterns of Prejudice* 47(4–5): 458–482.
Shafir, G. 1998. 'Introduction: The Evolving Tradition of Citizenship', in G. Shafir (ed.), *The Citizenship Debates.* Minneapolis: University of Minnesota Press, pp. 1–28.
Shapin, S. 2012. 'The Tastes of Wine: Towards a Cultural History', *Wineworld: New Essays on Wine, Taste, Philosophy and Aesthetics* 51(3): 49–94.
Shepherd, S.M., S. Luebbers and M. Dolan. 2013. 'Gender and Ethnicity in Juvenile Risk Assessment', *Criminal Justice and Behavior* 40(4): 388–408.
Shildrick, T., and R. MacDonald. 2006. 'In Defence of Subculture: Young People, Leisure and Social Divisions', *Journal of Youth Studies* 9(2): 125–40.
Shoshan, N. 2014. 'Managing Hate: Political Delinquency and Affective Governance in Germany', *Cultural Anthropology* 29(1): 150–172.
Siegmund, U. 1997. *Was Privatization in Eastern Germany a Special Case? Some Lessons from the Treuhand.* Davidson Institute Working Paper Series.
Simich, L. 2003. 'Negotiating Boundaries of Refugee Resettlement: A Study of Settlement Patterns and Social Support', *Canadian Review of Sociology and Anthropology* 40(5): 575–91.
Simpson, P.A. 2004. 'Germany and Its Discontents: Die Skeptiker's Punk Corrective', *Journal of Popular Culture* 34(3): 129–40.
Sklar, M., and M. DeLong. 2012. 'Punk Dress in the Workplace: Aesthetic Expression and Accommodation', *Clothing and Textiles Research Journal* 30(4): 285–299.
Smith, T.V. 2006. *Getting There: Punk Rock Tour Diaries.* Vol. 1. London: Arima Publishing.

Snyder, F.G. 1985. '"Folk Law" and Historical Transitions: Some Conceptual Issues', in A. Allott and G.R. Woodman (eds), *People's Law and State Law: The Bellagio Papers*. Dordrecht: Foris Publishing, pp. 263–274.

Sobe, J. 2008. 'Born in GDR', in I.D.A. Papier (ed.), *Keine Zukunft war gestern: Punk in Deutschland*. Berlin: Archiv der Jugendkulturen Verlag KG, pp. 213–24.

Solga, H. 2006. 'The Rise of Meritocracy? Class Mobility in East Germany before and after 1989', in M. Diewald, A. Goedicke and K.U. Mayer (eds), *After the Fall of the Wall: Life Courses in the Transformation of East Germany*. Stanford: Stanford University Press, pp. 140–69.

Ssorin-Chaikov, N. 2000. 'Bear Skins and Macaroni: The Social Life of Things at the Margins of a Siberian State Collective', in P. Seabright (ed.), *The Vanishing Rouble: Barter Networks and Non-monetary Transactions in Post-Soviet Societies*. Cambridge: Cambridge University Press, pp. 345–61.

Standing, G. 2014. *A Precariat Charter: From Denizens to Citizens*. New York: Bloomsbury.

Stanley-Niaah, S. 2004. 'Kingstons's Dancehall: A Story of Space and Celebration', *Space and Culture* 7(1): 102–118.

Steel, E., and F. McNasty. 1997. 'Red London: Keine Kohle im Revier', *Skin Up* 43: 14–17.

Stratton, J. 2007. 'Jews, Punk and Holocaust: From Velvet Underground to the Ramones – the Jewish-American Story', *Popular Music* 24(1): 79–105.

Street, J. 2012. *Music and Politics*. Cambridge: Polity Press.

Swaner, R., and E. White. 2010. 'Drifting between Worlds: Deliquency and Positive Engagement among Red Hook Youth'. Center for Court Innovation. A Project of the Fund for the City of New York.

Tagg, P. 2011. 'Caught on the Back Foot: Epistemic Inertia and Visible Music', *IASPM Journal* 2(1–2): 3–18.

Taylor, T.D. 2007. 'The Changing Shape of the Culture Industry; or, How Did Electronica Music Get into Television Commercials?', *Television and New Media* 8(3): 235–58.

Thompson, E.P. 1964. *The Making of English Working Class*. London: Victor Gollancz.

Thompson, S. 2004. *Punk Productions: Unfinished Business*. New York: State University of New York Press.

Thornton, S. 1996. *Club Cultures: Music, Media, and Subcultural Capital*. Cambridge: Polity Press.

Todd, S. 2015. *The People: The Rise and Fall of the Working Class*. London: John Murray.

Tolman, D. 1996. 'Adolescent Girls' Sexuality: Debunking the Myth of the Urban Girl', in B.J.R. Leadbeater and N. Way (eds), *Urban Girls: Resisting Stereotypes, Creating Identities*. New York: New York University Press, pp. 255–72.

Toop, D. 1992. *Rap Attack: African Jive bis Global Hiphop*. Munich: Wilhelm Heyne Verlag.

Toren, C. 1997. 'The Drinker as Chief or Rebel: Kava and Alcohol in Fiji', in M. McDonald (ed.), *Gender, Drink and Drugs*. Oxford: Berg, pp. 153–74.

Torrez, E. 2012. 'Punk Pedagogy: Education for Liberation and Love', in Z. Furness (ed.), *Punkademics: The Basement Show in the Ivory Tower*. New York: Minor Compositions, pp. 131–142.

Traber, D.S. 2001. 'White Minority": Punk and the Contradictions of Self-Marginalization', *Cultural Critique* 48: 30–64.

———. 2013. 'Pick It Up! Pick It Up!: The Transnational Localism of Ska', *Popular Music and Society* 36(1): 1–18

Trell, E.-M., and B. von Hoven. 2014. '"It's a Place Where All Friends Meet": Shared Places, Youth Friendships and Negotiation of Masculinities in Rural Estonia', in A. Gorman-Murray and P. Hopkins (eds), *Masculinities and Place*. Farnham: Ashgate, pp. 317–36.

Tsipursky, G. 2012. 'Having Fun in the Thaw: Youth Initiative Clubs in the Post-Stalin Years', *The Carl Beck Papers in Russian and East European Studies* 2201: 1–45.

Tsitsos, W. 1999. 'Rules of Rebellion: Slamdancing, Moshing, and the American Alternative Scene', *Popular Music* 18(3): 397–414.

Tucker, B.L. 2008. 'Punk and the Political: The Role of Practices in Subcultural Lives'. Master's thesis, Ohio University, Athens, OH.

Tucker, H. 2002. *Living with Tourism: Negotiating Identities in a Turkish Village*. London: Routledge.

Turner, J., and G. Bushell. 2010. *Cockney Reject*. London: John Blake.

Vanderbeck, R.M., and C.M. Dunkley. 2003. 'Young People's Narratives of Rural-Urban Difference', *Children's Geographies* 1(2): 241–259.

Vaudhyanathan, S. 2001. *Copyrights and Copywrongs: The Rise of Inellectual Property and How It Threatens Creativity*. New York: New York University Press.

Ventsel, A. 2004. 'Sakha Pop Music and Ethnicity', in E. Kasten (ed.), *Properties of Culture – Culture as Property: Pathways to Reform in Post-Soviet Siberia*. Berlin: Dietrich Reimer Verlag, pp. 67–86.

———. 2006. 'Sakha Pop Music: A Celebration of Consuming', *Anthropology of East Europe Review* 24(2): 68–86.

———. 2009. 'Sakha Music Business: Mission, Contracts, and Social Relations in the Developing Post-socialist Market Economy', *Sibirica* 8(1): 1–23.

———. 2010. '"Our Beer Is Better Than Theirs": Sub-cultural Comics as a Joking Relationship with Identity', *Folklore: Electronic Journal of Folklore* 46: 143–60.

———. 2012. 'This Is Not My Country, My Country Is the GDR: East German Punk and Socio-economic Processes after German Reunification', *Punk & Post Punk* 1(3): 343–59.

———. 2014. '"That Old School Lonsdale": Authenticity and Clothes in Streetpunk and Skinhead Culture', in R. Cobb (ed.), *Genuine Copies: The Paradox of Authenticity in a Globalized World*. New York: Palgrave Macmillan, pp. 261–76.

Ventsel, A., and L. Araste. 2015. 'They Have No Right to Wear Those Clothes: The Ambivalence of the Dress Code of German Skinheads and Estonian Metal Heads', *Fashion, Style & Popular Culture* 2(2): 257–72.

Verdery, K. 1993. 'Ethnic Relations, Economies of Shortage, and the Transition in Eastern Europe', in C.M. Hann (ed.), *Socialism: Ideals, Ideologies, and Local Practice*. London: Routledge, pp. 172–187.

Virchow, F. 2007. 'Performance, Emotion, and Ideology: On the Creation of "Collectives of Emotion" and Worldview in the Contemporary German Far Right', *Journal of Contemporary Ethnography* 36(2): 147–164.

Von Benda-Beckman, F., and K. von. Benda-Beckman. 2001. 'State, Religion and Legal Pluralism: Changing Constellations in West Sumatra (Minangkabau) and Comparative Issues', *Max Planck Institute for Social Anthropology. Working Papers*, no. 19.

Wade, P. 1999. 'Working Culture: Making Cultural Identities in Cali, Colombia', *Current Anthropology* 40(4): 449–70.

Walker, R., et al. 2013. 'Poverty in Global Perspective: Is Shame a Common Denominator?', *Journal of Social Policy* 42(3): 215–233.

Wallace, C., and S. Kovatcheva. 1998. *Youth in Society: The Construction and Deconstruction of Youth in East and West Europe.* London: Macmillan.
Wallach, J., H.M. Berger and P.D. Greene (eds). 2011. *Metal Rules the Globe: Heavy Metal Music around the World.* Durham, NC: Duke University Press.
Ward, E., G. Stokes and K. Tucker. 1986. *Rock of Ages: The Rolling Stones History of Rock and Roll.* Bungay: Rolling Stone Press.
Ward, J.J. 1996. '"This Is Germany! It's 1933!" Appropriations and Constructions of "Fascism" in New York Punk/Hardcore in the 1980s', *Journal of Popular Culture* 30(3): 155–84.
Watson, G. 2001. *Skins.* Chicago, Illinois: Olmstead Press.
———. 2008. *Skins & Punks: Lost Archives 1978–1985.* New York: Vice Books.
Wasserman, S., and K. Faust. 1994. *Social Network Analysis: Methods and Applications.* New York: Cambridge University Press.
West, C., and D.H. Zimmerman. 1987. 'Doing Gender', *Gender and Society* 1(2): 125–51.
Westhusen, M.M. 2005a. *Zonenpunk. Punk in Halle (Saale) in den 80er Jahren.* Halle: Verein für erlebte Geschichte.
———. 2005b. 'Zwischen Händel und Chemie. Punk in Halle, Eisleben und Dessau', in R. Galenza and H. Havemeister (eds), *Wir wollen immer artig sein ...:Punk, New Wave, HipHop, Independent-Szene in der DDR 1980–1990.* Berlin: Schwarzkopf & Schwarzkopf, pp. 334–47.
Whyte, W.F. 1998. *Street Corner Society: The Social Structure of an Italian Slum.* Chicago: University of Chicago Press.
Wilkie, L.A. 2010. *The Lost Boys of Zeta Psi: A Historical Archaeology of Masculinity at a University Fraternity.* Berkeley: University of California Press.
Wilkins, A.C. 2004. '"So Full of Myself as a Chick": Goth Women, Sexual Independence, and Gender Egalitarianism', *Gender & Society* 18(3): 328–49.
Williams, J.P. 2006. 'Authentic Identities: Straightedge Subculture, Music, and the Internet', *Journal of Contemporary Ethnography* 35(2): 173–200.
———. 2011a. 'Structuring Knowledge of Subcultural Folk Devils through News Coverage: Social Cognition, Semiotics, and Political Economy', *Studies of Transition States and Societies* 3(2): 3–13.
———. 2011b. *Subcultural Theory: Traditions and Concepts.* Cambridge: Polity Press.
Willis, P. 1990. *Common Culture: Symbolic Work at Play in Everyday Cultures of the Young.* Milton Keynes: Open University Press.
———. 2000. *Learning to Labour: How Working Class Kids Get Working Class Jobs.* Aldershot: Ashgate.
Willis, S. 1993. 'Hardcore: Subculture American Style', *Critical Inquiry* 19(2): 365–83.
Willisch, A., and A. Eckert. 2012. 'Fahhrad, Rucksack, Nebenjob. Selbsthilfe in prekären Alltag', in A. Willisch (ed.), *Wittenberge ist überall. Überleben in schrumpfenden Regionen.* Berlin: Ch. Links Verlag, pp. 151–194.
Wolf-Meyer, M. 2006. 'The Politics of Materiality, or "The Left Is Always Late"', *PoLAR* 29(2): 254–75.
Woodburn, J. 1982. 'Egalitarian Societies', *Man, New Series* 17(3): 431–51.
———. 1998. '"Sharing Is Not a Form of Exchange": An Analysis of Property-Sharing in Immediate-Return Hunter-Gatherer Societies', in C.M. Hann (ed.), *Property Relations: Renewing Anthropological Traditions.* Cambridge: Cambridge University Press, pp. 48–63.

Worley, M. 2012. 'Shot by Both Sides: Punk, Politics and the End of "Consensus"', *Contemporary British History* 26(3): 333–54.

———. 2013. 'Oi!, Oi!, Oi!: Class, Locality and British Punk', *Twentieth Century British History* 24(2): 606–36.

———. 2014. '"Hey Little Rich Boy, Take a Good Look at Me": Punk, Class and British Oi!', *Punk & Post Punk* 3(1): 5–20.

———. 2017. *No Future: Punk, Politics and British Youth Culture 1976–1984.* Cambridge: Cambridge University Press.

Worley, M., et al. 2014. 'Introduction: From Protests to Resistance', in T.S. Network (ed.), *Fight Back: Punk, Politics and Resistance.* Manchester: Manchester University Press, pp. 1–10.

Yablonsky, L. 1962. *The Violent Gang.* New York: Macmillan.

Yong, K., and L. Craig. 1997. 'Beyond White Pride: Identity, Meaning and Contradiction in the Canadian Skinhead Subculture', *CRSA/RCSA* 34(2): 176–206.

Young, R. 2013. 'Can Neds (or Chavs) Be Non-delinquent, Educated or Even Middle Class? Contrasting Empirical Findings with Cultural Stereotypes', *Sociology* 10(6): 1140–60.

Yurchak, A. 1999. 'Gagarin and the Rave Kids: Transforming Power, Identity, and Aesthetics in the Post-Soviet Nightlife', in A.M. Barker (ed.), *Consuming Russia: Popular Culture, Sex, and Society Since Gorbachev.* Durham, NC: Duke University Press, pp. 77–109.

———. 2006. *Everything Was Forever, until It Was No More: The Last Soviet Generation.* Princeton: Princeton University Press.

Ziker, J.P. 2002. *Peoples of the Tundra: Northern Siberians in the Post-communist Transition.* Prospect Heights, IL: Waveland Press.

Zips, W., and H. Kämpfer. 2001. *Nation X: Schwarzer Nationalismus, Black Exodus und Hip-Hop.* Wien: Promedia.

INDEX

www.ingramcontent.com/pod-product-compliance
Lightning Source LLC
LaVergne TN
LVHW050058140826
845500LV00029B/279